HERO *of* RHINE
THE

The Karl Timmermann Story

HERO *of* THE RHINE

The Karl Timmermann Story

By Ken Hechler

Ken Hechler

Pictorial Histories Publishing Company, Inc.
Missoula, Montana

Library of Congress
Control Number 2004094786

ISBN 1-57510-110-6

First Printing July 2004

COVER DESIGN
MiraGraphics, Charleston, WV

TYPOGRAPHY & BOOK DESIGN
Arrow Graphics, Missoula, MT

Photos from the Timmermann family
or Ken Hechler unless stated otherwise.

PUBLISHED BY
Pictorial Histories Publishing Company, Inc.
713 South Third Street West, Missoula, MT 59801
PHONE (406) 549-8488, FAX (406) 728-9280
phpc@montana.com
WEBSITE pictorialhistoriespublishing.com

179-3300

CONTENTS

Acknowledgments

THE TIMMERMANN FAMILY and the Weisbecker family in Germany both inspired and helped me on this book. Karl Timmermann gave me the military details of his exploit in two interviews in the European Theater of Operations. Karl's father and especially his mother spent endless hours sharing all they knew about Karl when I visited them in West Point, Nebraska.

Karl's wonderful daughter, Gaye Estey, made available all of Karl's priceless letters. Karl's widow, La Vera Meyer Timmermann, shared with me the full details of his personal life. Jack Hansen, the loyal husband of La Vera in recent years, has been unfailingly helpful in the preparation of this book.

Karl's sister Mary down through the years has been the number one advocate that a book about Karl should be written. Karl's brother Fritz and his widow Mary have supplied very helpful information.

Countless residents of West Point, Nebraska, have helped and to name them all would fill another book. But I must single out Robert Wostoupal, Cuming County's able Veterans Service Officer, as the prime mover in organizing the outstanding 1995 tribute to Karl Timmermann which finally recognized the full significance of his heroism. Thanks also to Alex Meyer of Scribner, Nebraska. Gerhard Willms, Karl's closest boyhood friend, shared many of Karl's early escapades.

To all the members of the 27th Armored Infantry Battalion and the rest of the 9th Armored Division I am eternally grateful.

Betty Paolini did a superb job of keyboarding the manuscript. And Barbara Stanley designed a first-rate cover.

Kitty Herrin of Arrow Graphics and Stan Cohen of Pictorial Histories Publishing Co., both of Missoula, Montana, are great people to have on your side in putting the finishing touches on publication.

ONE

Path to Glory: The European Theater of Operations

CHUCK YEAGER was once asked his definition of "The Right Stuff." He answered: "Very simple, it's being at the right place at the right time."

When 2nd Lt. Karl H. Timmermann hit the sack on Tuesday night, March 6, 1945, in the German City of Stadt Mechenheim, he did not dream that in less than twenty-four hours he would suddenly become an international hero. That afternoon, still another company commander of Company A, 27th Armored Infantry Battalion, Capt. Frederick Kriner, had been wounded in action, and Karl was immediately tapped to take his place.

Karl's life is stranger than fiction. He had actually been born in Germany. His father, a Nebraska native, had joined the American occupation army after World War I, then deserted to marry a German fraulein in a suburb of Frankfurt. Millions of German citizens were starving and out of work in the early 1920's, so you can imagine the more serious straits suffered at that time by an American army deserter and his new bride, burdened by an unexpected child. How they ever managed to get back to Nebraska will be explained later.

Throughout a stormy childhood, Karl always harbored the idea that he wanted to do something to clear the Timmermann name. All through school, he took a special interest in History and Latin, and studied the military exploits of Julius Caesar in his Commentaries. He confounded his classmates by learning the nomenclature of military weapons and identification of combat aircraft.

Isolationist Nebraska thought it was peculiar that in the summer between his junior and senior year in high school, he hitchhiked 75 miles from his home in West Point, Neb., to Fort Crook in Omaha to enlist in the Citizens' Military Training Corps. On his 18th birthday in 1940, just after graduating from high school, he went back to Fort Crook to enlist in the regular army. After two years he successfully completed the rigorous Infantry Officer Candidate School at Fort Benning, Ga., to receive his gold bars on February 16, 1943.

Two days after being commissioned, while on furlough in West Point, Karl fell madly in love with La Vera Meyer, a young schoolteacher who had graduated from West Point High School while Karl was attending Guardian Angels, the Catholic high school in West Point. It seemed an unlikely pairing, with La Vera a confirmed Missouri Synod Lutheran and the Catholic Church taking a decidedly dim view toward Karl's new-found love. But a whirlwind courtship conducted primarily through increasingly tender letters rocketing back and forth between West Point and Fort Riley, Ks., where Karl was undergoing combat training, resulted in a May 25 wedding. When the Catholic Church adamantly refused to sanction the wedding, they hurried to Omaha to exchange their vows in a private ceremony.

From Fort Riley, Karl was sent to the Desert Training Center in California in the closing months of 1943, and then he underwent additional combat training and maneuvers at Camp Polk, La. Everybody sensed that they would soon go overseas when their next station was Camp Kilmer, N.J. For 12 days Karl and the other officers and men of the 9th Armored Division spent their final days stateside boning up on ship-boarding techniques, taking physical exams and filling out last wills and testaments.

Pier 82 of the New York Port of Embarkation was a beehive of activity early in the morning of August 20, 1944, as 25,000 troops boarded the Liner *Queen Mary* for its 17th ocean crossing to the European Theater of Operations. In peacetime, the Queen could streak across the pond in five days or less. With Admiral Doenitz's U-boats out in force, it not only took eight days of zigzagging, but also a detour via the Azores before finally landing at Guoroch, Scotland, in the Firth of Clyde on August 27.

Karl was under the weather almost every day of the crossing. On August 25 he wrote his wife: "I was unable to write during the last few days because I was sea-sick and plus that I had a terrible cold. I feel a little better this morning."

After midnight on August 27–28, most of the 9th Armored toting their duffel bags, boarded crowded trains for the trip through Scotland and the northeastern coastline of England to the tiny Town of Tidworth near Andover and Salisbury.

Karl was still feeling the effects of the ocean trip, so was not impressed with Scottish Red Cross girls who provided bag lunches for their American visitors. Soon he was able to report: "I feel pretty fair this morning; my stomach stopped taking flip-flops, but I still have a cold."

Gradually, he returned to normal and wrote La Vera: "I ate my three regular meals today; breakfast was the only one that came up."

But on August 31, Karl wrote to his wife: "La Vera, I feel sick again tonight. I haven't felt well since I got on the boat."

During September the 27th Armored Infantry Battalion and the rest of the 9th Armored Division made their final preparations before crossing the channel to the combat zone in France. New half-tracks (that lumbering, squeaky vehicle with tires in the front and tank tracks in the rear)—the regular method of transporting infantry cross-country—were added to the battalion. Karl's platoon and the rest of the division trained intensively on tactics, firing practice, tank-infantry maneuvers, and forced marches.

The late fall weather in England was unusually cold and clammy, so on September 27, he wrote La Vera: "I put on my wool underwear today to keep my legs warm. They look like trapeze pants."

[Lt. Lyman H. Smith, who commanded Headquarters Company of the 27th Armored Infantry Battalion, wrote to me: "I believe I knew Timmermann as well as anyone in the battalion. He talked to Carl Edwards and myself a great deal. He was very moody."]

There was a reason why Karl was "moody."

"It's really hard for me to realize that we're going to be parents. La Vera, I'm really happy and I know you are too over the fact that we're going to have a baby."

Karl wrote hundreds of love letters to La Vera, sometimes managing to pen two or three a day. In every letter was not only reiterated his deep and lasting love, but his awe at the fact he was to become a father.

"La Vera, it doesn't seem real that we're about to be parents. It's like a dream, and I do day dream of you and our baby all day long."

La Vera peppered Karl with questions about his unit, his location, his living conditions, his fellow-soldiers, and everything she could persuade him to write home about. Observing the requirements and censorship regulations (even though he censored his own mail, which officers were authorized to do, occasionally his letters were opened at the base censorship office), Karl wrote: "I can't tell you what Army I'm in, nor the sector of Europe. I guess I'll have to tell you after the war."

THE 27TH ARMORED INFANTRY Battalion was made a part of the 9th Army in the last part of September and moved to the south coast of England on September 28 to Weymouth to get ready to cross the English Channel. The very next day they boarded an LST (landing ship, tank) and to Karl's discomfort it took until October 1 before they could debark on Utah Beach on the coast of France.

"La Vera, I'm aboard ship, but that's all I can say about that."

Finally, after a stormy crossing, Karl was able to report:

1st Oct. '44

8:00 p.m.

My darling La Vera:

I'm in France now.

Until October 14, this battalion bivouacked near Saint Marie-De Mont, France. Karl explained that they lived in makeshift quonset huts: "The building that we live in looks like a corrugated barrel cut in half and plugged up at both ends."

Karl's battalion mounted up half-tracks for a six-day journey across France to the vicinity of Huldingen, Luxembourg. En route they passed through St. Lo, Paris and bivouacked on the World War I battlefield of Verdun. At Huldingen, the battalion was reassigned from the 9th Army to the 1st Army and went into combat just west of Prum, Germany, relieving the 3rd Battalion of the 9th Infantry Regiment, 2nd Infantry Division.

It was the baptism of fire for Karl and the battalion in the Siegfried Line, starting October 26. The battalion suffered three men killed in action, six wounded and three captured as prisoners. The gooey mud and barren trees were dismal, and sending out patrols met many hazards from the German anti-personnel mine fields.

On November 8, Karl's battalion was sent back to Belgium after two weeks at the front. He apologized to La Vera for not being able to write regularly.

While at the front in the Siegfried Line, Karl wrote:

30th Oct. 1944

6:15 pm

My Darling,

It was a hard day and I'm glad it's over.

I'm still in Germany and life is getting more rugged every day, plus that winter is coming.

Somewhere in Belgium
11th Nov. '44
6:45 p.m.

My Darling La Vera,

I'm sorry for not writing in the last few days, but really, I was unable to.

Three days later he was able to tell her: "I'm back in a rest area now. I was up in the 'Siegfried Line' and what is called the 'front line.' I wish that this awful nightmare were over."

Still uppermost in Karl's mind was the health of his wife, who wrote him how sick she was during her pregnancy. In every letter Karl speculated on when the baby would be born and what they should name their child. Karl hoped it would be a boy, and had even selected the name: James Karl. With increasing frequency, he asked about how "Jimmy" was doing.

"How's our little boy getting along? I hope that he's behaving himself? Of course, our baby will be a boy. But, if it is a girl, we won't be disappointed, will we, La Vera?"

Karl finally got around to acknowledging that he might become the father of a baby girl. Since he was writing long before Jessica Lynch was captured and her roommate Native American Pfc. Lori Piestewa became the first woman to die in combat in the 2003 war in Iraq, Karl could rationalize:

"How's our little boy getting along? I hope that it's a girl so that it won't ever had to fight any wars. And if it is a girl, any name you pick will be O.K. with me."

On Thanksgiving Day, 1944, Karl's unit was lucky enough to be in position to enjoy a hot turkey dinner, a welcome change from the K-rations "enjoyed" while at the front. Karl used the opportunity to travel to Belgium to have several long visits with his younger brother Fritz, who was stationed with the 148th Engineer Combat Battalion. Karl and Fritz were photographed together much to the delight of the Timmermann family.

During the first half of December, the American army took a big risk by manning an 80-mile front in the Ardennes with the green 106th Infantry Division recently arrived from the states, plus the exhausted and depleted 28th and 4th Infantry Divisions. This risk was compounded by one of the greatest mistakes ever recorded by American Military Intelligence—the predictions that the German army was on its last legs and incapable of mounting an attack. Adolph Hitler had other ideas. Scraping together an elite force with massive support from artillery and armor, the Nazis swarmed into the

Karl met his brother Fritz in Belgium in 1944.

thinly held American lines on December 16, 1944, the start of the murderous Battle of the Bulge. German meteorologists had correctly predicted that fog and low-hanging clouds would prevent the American Air Corps from getting off the ground for many days after the initial attack.

The 9th Armored Division was split into three combat commands and dispatched as an emergency fire brigade to try and plug the loopholes in the line. Combat Command B, which included Karl's battalion, was sent to the vicinity of St. Vith where twelve members of Karl's Company A were captured and murdered by the Germans.

Karl knew that La Vera would be hearing and reading the news of the German assault. He wrote to her: "La Vera, remember the shows which we saw about the Germans in Norway, etc.? Remember all the cruel things which they did? Well, you can believe them, because they're the truth, and the movies didn't put it strong enough. They've really committed some terrible crimes. People in the U.S. don't know the half of it."

UNLIKE THANKSGIVING, Christmas was a terrible time for Karl, weary after continuously being under artillery fire and desperately trying to retreat before being over-run by the murderous enemy. Not until January 9, 1945, was he able to reassure La Vera: "I'm no longer on the 'front'. I hope that I never have to go back. I was on the 'front' on Christmas Day, and what a Christmas!"

Only now could Karl philosophize about war in a poignant letter to his wife: "La Vera, there's no glory in war. Maybe those, who have never been in battle, find that certain glory and glamour that doesn't exist. Perhaps they get it from the movies or comic strips. I hope that the war is over soon so that we can be together and live as human beings."

IN HER LETTERS to Karl, La Vera bared her apprehension about his safety, and with good reason. On December 22, 1944, Karl was wounded by shrapnel in his right arm, the scar of which he would carry the rest of his life.

He tried to be nonchalant about it, and almost casually wrote to La Vera: "I got the Purple Heart today. I'll enclose the ribbon in this letter and I'll send the medal later."

Quite naturally, La Vera pressed him for details, to which he answered matter-of-factly: "The Purple Heart is only given for wounds received in battle."

Finally, La Vera was so upset at his non-answer that she laid it on the line that Karl deserved to give her an explicit description. Not until April 1945 did Karl finally "fess-up" with this explanation: "I got the Purple Heart

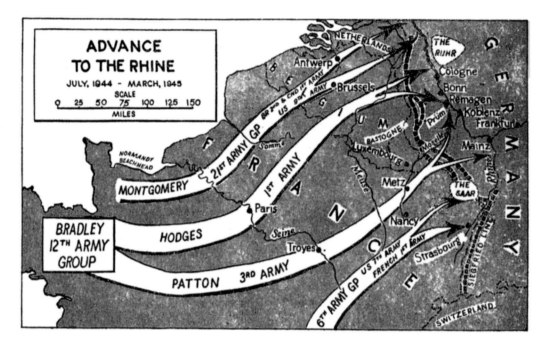

because of slight wounds which were healed in a few days. The only reason why I got the Purple Heart for that was I was in the Bn. Aid station to get dressed."

The 9th Armored Division was split into so many sectors from St. Vith to Luxembourg that to the Germans it became known as the "Phantom Division" since it was everywhere. On several occasions, the Germans contended that the 9th Armored had been "destroyed," leading the division to remove division markings from its vehicles to further confuse the enemy.

In the early months of 1945, determined counter-attacks by allied infantry, armor and artillery, supported by air power as the fog lifted, resulted in a flattening of the bulge created by the temporarily successful German breakthrough in the Ardennes.

Brought back in reserve to be re-equipped after their combat in the Battle of the Bulge, Karl reported to La Vera his brief change of station:

> 16th Jan. '45
> 6:30 p.m.
> France

My Darling La Vera,

Well now I'm in Patton's 3rd Army. I was in the 1st. At present I'm in the part of France which is called Lorraine.

A strong family man, Karl now had a chance to concentrate to a greater extent on his loved ones back home. First and foremost was La Vera, who received a steady stream of love letters, each one including paeans of praise and affection along the following lines: "I feel terrible tonight; I feel like crying. La Vera, I love you so very much. I love you more than I'll ever be able to say. I'll love you forever and ever. You're the sweetest and finest lady on earth. You're just perfect, wonderfully beautiful. La Vera, no man could ever love a woman more than I love you."

Reflecting back on his May 25, 1943, wedding day, Karl penned this note to La Vera:

> Here's a poem written by me:
>
> *Today, you're in my heart*
> *Always, forever and a day;*
> *We're never really apart;*
> *Because of that blessed day in May.*
>
> How's that?

KARL'S VIVACIOUS AND enterprising 17-year-old sister Mary (whom everybody called "Molly") took a job driving a street car in downtown Omaha. One day she had an accident, and afraid of being disciplined or fired she ambled across town to the Army Recruiting Office to sign up for the W.A.C.'s. She fibbed about her age and was immediately shipped to Fort Des Moines, Iowa, for basic training.

Ever since being stationed at Fort Riley in 1943, Karl had taken a dim view of the W.A.C.'s. When La Vera had asked him before their marriage about any pretty women at Fort Riley, Karl gave her an exaggerated, sexist answer of how much he disliked the W.A.C.s. He even portrayed them as tender traps for future husbands, including those who had been discharged for making sexual advances in public. When he wrote La Vera in 1943:

"There are W.A.C.'s here in Ft. Riley now. They are sure a bunch of silly looking bags. They are hated by nearly every one."

So when he heard about his sister, he exploded to La Vera:

"So Molly joined the W.A.C.s. She's crazier than what I thought she was."

KARL'S YOUNGER BROTHER, obstreperous Rudy, was the wild card of the Timmermann family. Their father's razor strap didn't straighten him out,

Left: Karl's sister "Molly" as a street car pilot in Omaha. Right: as a private in WAC's at Fort Des Moines, Iowa.

and he served a spell at Father Flanagan's Boys Town. Rudy matured at Boys Town and later joined the army as a paratrooper. Karl kept in touch with him by sending him stamps and paper money from the countries where he was stationed.

As February wore on, Karl was able to report to La Vera:

> 24th February '45
> 9:45 p.m.
> Belgium

Hello, My Darling,

I saw Fritz again today. His company and mine are only six miles apart at present. He was here with me from nine o'clock this morning until just a little while ago. I just came back from driving him home. I might be able to drive over and see him tomorrow. Fritz has gained a little weight. He says I'm getting fat (but it isn't true).

Karl and his youngest brother, Rudy.

Happy, carefree days were now over, as the Fighting 27th was ordered to cross the Roer River in the Rhineland at Duren, Germany and assemble near Sollar, Germany. Karl's outfit joined up with the 14th Tank Battalion as a task force to attack eastward toward the Rhine River some forty miles away.

The Germans had flooded the dams on the Roer and the going was rough in the high water and mud. The first of Company A's commanders to be wounded and evacuated was Lt. Jay Swisher, a popular South Dakotan. General Omar Bradley, at that time commanding the Twelfth Army Group, wrote after the war about the advance from the Roer to the Rhine: "If I were asked what campaign in the war brought me the greatest professional pride, I would point unhesitatingly to this one."

Such an attitude brought little comfort to Karl, leading the platoon of Company A as the casualties in killed and wounded mounted every day. Heavy rains and melting snow churned the roads into sticky, soupy messes. Gen. William M. Hoge, heading Combat Command B of the 9th Armored Division, spurred the sleepless troops relentlessly forward in a series of night attacks. When Karl and his outfit reached Stadt Mechenheim late in the afternoon of March 6, he and his men were thoroughly exhausted and hungry.

As the newly designated Company Commander of Company A after the wounding of Capt. Kriner, Karl had little time to reflect that March 6 was La Vera's birthday—a date which he had predicted he and La Vera would become parents. Little did he know that the blessed event had already occurred on February 28!

[As an Army combat historian in Europe during World War II, I had an opportunity and responsibility to interview Karl on two occasions during March and April, 1945. Most of the account of his heroic achievement on March 7 is drawn from these and other personal interviews with his company, commanding officers and official Army records.]

On the morning of March 7, 1945, Karl was shaken awake before 6:00 A.M. He didn't mind the early hour because he had enjoyed five hours of his first sound sleep in more than a week of night attacks since crossing the Roer River. He also felt exhilarated by the prospect of serving his first full day as A Company Commander. "Company Commanders are usually Captains," he thought to himself as he viewed his gold Second Lieutenant bars.

The welcome smell of hot cakes lured Karl over to get a stack for his mess kit, but a message center runner interrupted his first hot breakfast in the month of March.

"Better get up to Task Force Headquarters, sir. The old man needs you for a meeting and he's getting restless."

Lt. Col. Leonard Engeman of Redwood Falls, Minn., scarcely looked like an "old man," but that was army lingo for high-ranking officers. Dynamic, crisp in his orders, and imaginative on the field of battle, Col. Engeman was an entirely different personality from his opposite number, Major Murray Deevers of Hagarville, Ar., the C.O. of the 27th Armored Infantry Battalion. Deevers was very laid back, and had only received his command when

Lieutenant Colonel Leonard Engeman, commander of the 14th Tank Battalion, with his Sherman tank. PERSONAL PHOTOGRAPH OF COL. ENGEMAN

Lt. Col. George Seeley had to be evacuated due to a heart attack during the Battle of the Bulge.

At the meeting, Col. Engeman singled out Timmermann and his Company A to move out at 7:00 A.M. as the advance guard for the task force. "Put your doughs on half-tracks and I'll give you a platoon of General Pershing tanks," Engeman ordered Karl. "Don't get bottled up in towns. And if there's any stopping, just remember I'll be on your neck."

Engeman was mindful that CCB Commander Brig. Gen. William M. Hoge, as always, would be chewing him out if his task force didn't push forward regardless of the enemy opposition. Engeman mentioned that one objective was to get to the Rhine River ten miles away. He said nothing about a bridge at Remagen. He did mention that in the big picture the major strategy was to form the northern pincer of a giant trap when the combat command met General Patton's 3rd Army and the 4th Armored Division forming the southern pincer.

Karl and the others saluted and returned to brief their troops on the mission. He took stock of his assets and liabilities. The rough fighting in the past week had seriously depleted his company. There was only one platoon among

Brigadier General William M. Hoge, Combat Command B, 9th Armored Division.
U.S. ARMY SIGNAL CORPS, NATIONAL ARCHIVES

the riflemen commanded by an officer—2nd Lt. Emmet "Jim" Burrows of Jersey City. Karl's old first platoon was now commanded by Staff Sergeant Michael Chinchar of Rochelle Park, N.J. Dartmouth-trained, Lt. Charles McDowell of Manchester, N.H., was wounded on March 4, depriving the third platoon of an officer. Lt. McDowell's place as platoon leader was filled by Sgt. Joseph DeLisio of Bronx, N.Y. The rifle platoons at full strength constituted about 50 men, but by March 7 the first platoon was down to 20, the second platoon 15, and the third platoon 30 men. Timmermann took heart in the fact that all but

Sgt. Michael Chinchar, Co. A, 27th Armored Infantry Bn.

a few of the surviving riflemen in his company had trained together since Fort Riley in 1943, and all of them were seasoned and dependable soldiers. He also had confidence in the tankers of the 14th Tank Battalion accompanying him. Finally, he was pleased to recall that his anti-tank platoon was commanded by an able officer, Lt. David Gardner.

Although Col. Engeman had ordered a 7:00 A.M. jump-off, Karl was frustrated to discover that the Air Corps had done such a thorough job of bombing Stadt Mechenheim that the rubble was piled ten feet high. It took until 10:00 A.M. before bulldozers could clear a path and the tanks and half-tracks could hit the road eastward toward the Rhine.

Karl went back to brief his platoon leaders. "Jim," he advised Burrows, "Your platoon will be the point today. Pvt. Giles and his half-track out front. Use your field glasses constantly to spot any strong points up ahead. They tell us the fighting will be easier than last week, but you never know so be prepared. They want us to bypass towns and let those behind us clean up. Now this pile of bricks and mortar you see all around you might hold us up awhile, but get ready to move."

Col. Engeman was angered by the delay. "What the hell's goin' on here? Why don't you get movin'?" Several men silently pointed to the rubble which was an impossible road-block.

Timmermann filled the waiting time by repeating S.O.P. instructions: "Check your ammo and other supplies, test the head space on your machine guns," he advised.

Many of the company clustered around their new C.O. and began the usual banter to ease the tension. Having heard Karl talk in German to some of the captured enemy, one G.I. ventured: "What are they saying about us, Lieutenant?"

Karl put on his most serious face: "They want to know if you ever shave. As a matter of fact, they say you're the dirtiest, scraggliest bunch of soldiers they've ever seen. They wonder how you got this far."

A chorus of Bronx Cheers greeted the response, until Timmermann slapped the hood of his jeep with a horse laugh and said: "Just kidding."

Just before they gave the "all clear" signal that the roads were O.K. for vehicles, he explained: "Most of the Germans wish the war was over and want to give up. But there are S.S. fanatics in every outfit, ready to tattle on anybody who won't fight to the finish."

[John Schafer of Beacon, N.Y., recently wrote to me: "I was an armorer in Company A. We rode in the last half-track in the company. Whenever prisoners were captured, they were brought to our half-track for holding. On one occasion Timmermann had three S.S. prisoners of war which he left at our half-track. He asked us if we knew how to handle S.S. POW's. He said "First tell them to bend over and touch their toes. Then kick them in the ass. From then on they will obey your orders."

Schafer added: "The reason for this treatment was that even after captured S.S. elite troops were arrogant and non-compliant."]

The company got off to a slow start when Alex Giles thought he saw an enemy tank which on closer inspection turned out to be a burned-out German vehicle. The infantrymen dismounted and when Burrows found no enemy, he suggested: "I predict a quick reaction to this, so hold on to your helmets."

Sure enough, the men in the leading half-tracks heard the roar of Timmermann's jeep rushing forward to find out what was holding up the parade. Giles turned to his buddies and proclaimed: "Let's give Tim a race." Timmermann caught up with the column, let out a loud laugh, and with the wave of his arm toward the east yelled "And keep goin'!"

Those involved in this race with Timmermann looked back and discovered they had outrun the rest of the platoon, the next vehicle of which seemed like a half-mile behind. In the fairly open country, with occasional patches of woods and rolling hills, the silence was so eerie that the leading elements feared a German ambush.

Suddenly as they approached Fritzdorf the silence was interrupted by a road block at the entrance to the town, and firing started from windows of a house overlooking the road block. Now it was a team effort by Timmermann's men as Herman Michael, Forrest Miner, Charles Penrod and Ralph Munch set off a reverberating chatter with their .50 caliber machine guns. White flags went up and prisoners began to surrender. As the column moved on toward Overich and Niederich, Karl moved to the front of the attacking troops. His presence brought renewed confidence to his men, demonstrating that he was not only a commander but also a leader. Toward noon, Burrows became concerned about the presence of many overhead telephone wires and cautioned: "There just isn't enough noise around here, Tim. I'll bet they're planning a trap. Don't you think we ought to do something about all those wires?" Timmermann resisted, and Burrows persisted. "I tell you we've just got to do something about those wires before we go any further."

[In my book, *The Bridge At Remagen*, I related that "Timmermann slapped Burrows playfully between the shoulders and laughed his big, friendly laugh. He reached into his jeep for his carbine and said 'I'll fix yer damn wires for you.' Timmermann took a couple of pot shots at the wires. Miraculously, one of them came down. Timmermann hopped into his jeep, firing wildly as he took off in front of the column. He gave a whoop as another wire came down.

After a few minutes when the fun was over, he drove back and repeated the command: 'Now let's get pushing.'

When Burrows read the above description, 12 years after the incident, he wrote to me: "Honest, Ken, I could feel Timmerman's 'slap on the back.' So many times he had done so, in his playful, 'bear-like' manner. We were so close in those days. An intimacy bound by the responsibility of other men's lives, cannot be compared to ordinary friendship."]

AT LEIMERSDORF AND Birresdorf there were only white flags flapping in the wind, and the streets were deserted. As Timmermann's company approached the outskirts of the town of Remagen, the Allmang family at their former tavern named the Waldschlossen rounded up the youngsters and headed for the cellar. Frau Allmang, looking out a window, saw Burrows' half-track rumble past. She said to her frightened family: "This is no way to greet our liberators," and fetched a white tablecloth from the kitchen to wave vigorously at the attacking troops.

Karl stopped his jeep and addressed Frau Allmang in German: "Any soldiers here? Any guns? Any ammunition?" The children emerged tentatively from the cellar and they all chorused: "Nein, Nein, Nein." Observing that the children were hungry and pock-marked with sores of a strange disease, Karl said gently: "I'll send you some food and medicine this afternoon."

Carmine Sabia and his reliable half-track were proceeding through some pine woods when he became obsessed with the deathly silence and was impelled to fire his machine gun toward nothing in particular. When he approached a small clearing, Sabia saw the crest of a mountain looming over the trees. He did not realize at the time, but the mountain was actually on the east side of the Rhine River.

Penrod and Munch inched forward as the road at the edge of the woods turned sharply to the right. Suddenly they saw below them something which caused them to wave violently to Lt. Burrows. Burrows rushed forward and summoned Lt. Timmermann to take a look at the startling view down below and to the right.

"Hey, Tim, take a look at that!" Burrows breathlessly exclaimed.

Karl was flabbergasted. He saw the blue waters of a river and down to the right was a bridge still standing. All he could say was "Dammit, that's the Rhine! I didn't think it was that close." The sun had scorched its way through the clouds and drizzle, and suddenly it became hot.

They paused and immediately wondered how to get artillery down on the German soldiers and vehicles crossing the bridge below. They called up the forward observer of the 400th Armored Field Artillery Battalion, and after a few minutes got a message back refusing to fire because friendly troops were too close.

Within a short time, Major Deevers, the battalion commander, arrived to look at the breathtaking sight below. Soon Major Ben Cothran, S-3 of Combat Command B was on the scene. Lt. Lyman Smith, C.O. of Headquarters Company of the 27th, reported overhearing a puzzling exchange between Deevers and Cothran. Deevers and his S-3 (operations officer) Major Don Russell according to Lt. Smith "were standing behind a large pine tree on the left side of the road. Deevers often repeated himself and that day was no exception. What with lack of sleep, a little wine and the impact of the situation he said several times 'What'll we do?' Cothran looked at him and laughed and said 'I don't know. I'm a lover, not a fighter.' Cothran obviously realized this was a decision which had to be made by his boss, General Hoge."

General Hoge, who liked to be up front with the main effort, was with the 52nd Armored Infantry Battalion which had been charged with the primary mission of seizing the bridge across the Ahr River, which flows into the Rhine to the south of Remagen. Unable to reach the General by radio, Cothran took after him with his jeep and they both arrived in record time. They found Col. Engeman already assessing the situation atop the hill.

Engeman also tried without success to get artillery onto the bridge, again receiving the negative answer that there were too many friendly troops in the area. He then ordered Deevers to send infantry to clean out the town of Remagen. Timmermann and Lt. William E. McMaster, commanders of companies A and C, made a reconnaissance 500 yards down along a narrow footpath into the town. Karl laughed as he saw a sign at the entrance to Remagen which when translated read: "Citizens and Friends. Preserve the Parks."

With Timmermann in the lead, Lt. Jack Liedike's B Company followed, its mission to clear the southeastern part of the town while protecting the right flank of the attack. Lt. McMaster's C Company was assigned to clear the northwestern part and protect the left flank.

Karl assigned his platoon leaders three different missions. He sent Lt. Burrows to take the main road through the center of Remagen, hugging the buildings because of snipers. Karl then ordered DeLisio's third platoon to fan out along the river road on the left flank, crouching low along the river because the Germans could observe clearly from the east bank. Chinchar's first platoon was ordered through town on the right flank before heading for the bridge.

Burrows' platoon had its biggest scuffle in the main square near the city hall, where an automatic weapon slowed the advance. Two of Lt. John Grimball's General Pershing tanks rumbled up and fired their powerful .90 millimeter guns to silence the opposition. While Chinchar was taking his first platoon through town, Polish and Russian displaced persons helped them identify where the enemy was located.

Irrepressible Joe DeLisio's third platoon had a totally fearless leader who led them through Remagen with the cry "c'mon, you guys, just another town!"

An excited member of his platoon rushed up to DeLisio and yelled: "Joe, Sergeant Foster wants you on the double. He's got a German General!"

DeLisio ambled down the street to where Foster had the muzzle of his M-1 pressed against the stomach of a very gaudily attired elderly German with an elaborately braided blouse and trousers and enough "scrambled eggs" for several admirals on his hat.

"Here's yer General, Joe" Foster announced triumphantly. "Now we'll find out the straight dope about the bridge."

"Lower your gun, Foster. Lemme talk with him." DeLisio began. After a few questions in halting German, DeLisio pronounced:

"General, my ass. You know what this guy is? He's the chief station agent for the railroad! Now scatter out, you guys and let's check these houses."

As Chinchar was moving his men through Remagen, Art Massie suddenly fired a shot which Chinchar thought was right over his head. "I got him—I think I got him," said Massie. "A German. He was going to shoot you," Massie explained.

According to Chinchar's recorded account, "We went to where he'd fallen and he was moaning from a wound in his groin. I put my gun against his temple and said, 'I'll put him out of his misery.' Massie said, 'Mike, please don't. I'll get the medics and take him back.' I said 'Okay.'" Chinchar added: "I'm glad he did that. I'm glad he stopped me."

Timmermann successfully led his men to the approaches to the railroad bridge, named the "Ludendorff Bridge" after Germany's World War I commander, Gen. Erich Ludendorff. The German defenders, led by Captains Willi Bratge (infantry) and Karl Friesenhahn (engineer) had a carefully worked-out plan to blow up the bridge. First they planned to blow a deep crater on the approach, to prevent tanks and any other vehicles from crossing. Subsequently, they would activate the main charge to dump the structure into the Rhine below.

Hitler had ordered all the Rhine bridges destroyed as the allies approached. At the same time, he had issued a peremptory order threatening execution if any bridge was blown too soon. The bridge defenders were handicapped by the fact that when the French had occupied the Remagen area after World War I they had methodically filled the demolition chambers in the piers with cement, thus preventing the most logical way to destroy the structure. The demolition plan was further complicated by the late arrival of the TNT, which to the distress of the defenders was "donerit"—a somewhat less powerful form of civilian explosive.

Of course, Timmermann's men knew nothing of these enemy problems. Neither side expected that the Americans would have any interest in a bridge where the road net was so poor, and where the eastern side of the Rhine with its forests and mountains was the worst place for tanks to operate.

In the early afternoon of March 7, a totally unrelated development electrified the high command on the American side. South of Remagen where the main effort of Combat Command B was to capture the crossing of the Ahr River, a German prisoner alleged that the Ludendorff Bridge would be blown up promptly at 4:00 P.M. This information was completely false. The German defenders, Bratge and Friesenhahn both testified that there was never any such plan, and that the bridge was to be blown when the Americans appeared ready to cross. But this "intelligence" was believed on the American side, especially by Combat Commander General Hoge, as he looked through his field glasses at the bridge and the scene below.

Gen. Hoge, a West Point graduate, had in his hand his explicit, repeated orders to turn south at the Rhine to form the trap with General Patton. To cross the bridge would directly violate these orders, with the further threat that if the Germans blew the bridge with many deaths as a result of his action, a court martial would certainly result. Nevertheless, Hoge was spurred into immediate action by the belief that the bridge would be destroyed at 4:00 P.M.

Like General Patton, Hoge believed that quick and aggressive attacks were the surest way to reduce casualties, because speedy movement overcame enemy efforts to dig in. Furthermore, surprise in speed kept an enemy off guard. To achieve speed, he expected his orders to be followed right away. At Remagen, he had a chance to prove his theory by speedy action to cross the bridge.

Receiving the order from task force commander Engeman, Battalion Commander Deevers asked Timmermann: "Do you think you can get your company across that bridge?"

Timmermann answered: "Well, we can try, sir." Then he demanded: "What if it blows up in my face?"

The Ludendorff Bridge was a railroad bridge, which was planked to allow vehicular traffic.

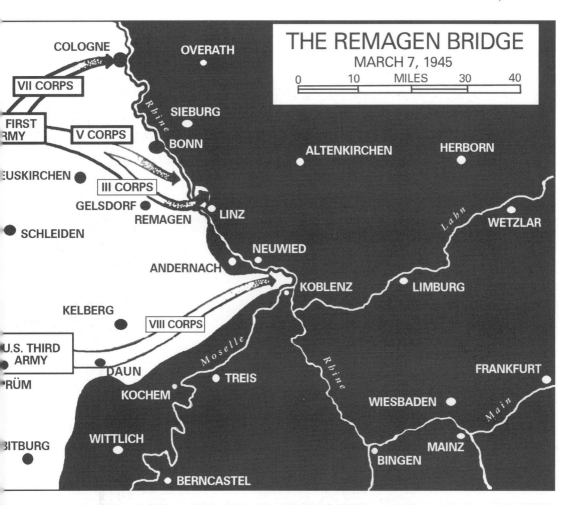

THE REMAGEN BRIDGE
MARCH 7, 1945

COLOGNE

OVERATH

VII CORPS

SIEBURG

FIRST ARMY

V CORPS

BONN

ALTENKIRCHEN

HERBORN

EUSKIRCHEN

III CORPS

GELSDORF

REMAGEN   LINZ

SCHLEIDEN

Lahn

WETZLAR

NEUWIED

ANDERNACH

KOBLENZ   LIMBURG

KELBERG

VIII CORPS

Moselle

U.S. THIRD ARMY

DAUN   TREIS

FRANKFURT

RÜM

KOCHEM

Rhine

WIESBADEN

Main

BITBURG

WITTLICH

MAINZ

BINGEN

BERNCASTEL

0   10   MILES   30   40

Deevers walked away without answering.

Headquarters Company C.O. Lyman Smith was close by and heard the exchange. According to Lt. Smith's account, "I remember walking out with Timmermann and lying down on the slope of the road. Timmermann said to me: 'What'll I do if the bridge blows up when I am on it?' I said foolishly to him: 'Then you've had it.'"

As if tired of the question, when some of his company crowded around and made the same query, Karl answered bluntly and with a slight stutter: "S-S-Swim."

Now he acted, crisply ordering his platoon leaders without hesitation: "O.K., Jim, Mike and Joe, we'll cross the bridge—order of march, first platoon, third platoon and then second platoon." He explained to Burrows that he wanted an officer-led platoon to push from the rear. As for himself, Timmermann planned to be near the front.

Chinchar, the platoon leader of the first platoon, assessed the situation. Just then came the roar of a tremendous explosion as the Germans blew a 30-foot crater in the bridge approach, according to their plan. Company C's C.O., Lt. McMaster, came up and said to Chinchar: "I'll place a machine gun over to the side to cover your attack." Chinchar answered: "Let me run over and see where you mean."

Timmermann meanwhile was busy reassuring the rest of the company about their vital mission. Up on top of the hill, Gen. Hoge was peering through his field glasses, expecting to see the first infantry start to cross the bridge. When nothing happened for several minutes, Hoge cut loose to demand why his order was not being carried out. According to his operations officer Major Cothran, Hoge "stormed and he shouted and he stormed and he shouted."

Hoge vented his wrath on Col. Engeman, to which Engeman bristled "I'm doing everything possible." The chewing out stung Engeman who jumped in a jeep to find out what was causing the hold-up. On his way down through Remagen, Engeman cut open his 508 radio and called Lt. Grimball: "Get to that bridge." Grimball's rich South Carolina accent clearly pierced the radio: "Suh, I am at the bridge!"

Now occurred an angry confrontation between two courageous and principled men who deeply respected each other, according to Ralph Shackelford, who was there: "Col. Engeman got loud with Lt. Timmermann to get men started across the bridge. Then Lt. Timmermann got louder with us." Lt. Lyman Smith, in the understatement of the war, reflected "It was not very pleasant." Timmermann and Chinchar, in the heat of combat, were suddenly confronted with circumstances beyond their control.

Not realizing that Chinchar had been sprinting full speed to set up the location of the machine gun to cover the crossing, Timmermann, who had already given the order to cross, was smarting from the chewing out administered by Col. Engeman. Chinchar was also panting and winded from chasing and capturing a German prisoner on the way. Timmermann barked: "Sgt. Chinchar, where the hell have you been? Get across that bridge!" Chinchar later said: "I got angry by the way he said that, and answered: "Let me catch my breath." Timmermann threatened: "I'll court martial you." Chinchar shot back: "Good, here's my gun."

At this point Sabia, Tony Samele and Craig clustered around the two and pleaded: "Calm down, calm down, you're both over-excited." Timmermann took a moment, turned around three or four times, and lowered his voice: "All right, now we're goin' to cross this bridge before — — —."

The words had scarcely left Karl's mouth when he was interrupted by a deafening rumble and roar, accompanied by flying timbers and steel as the bridge seemed to lift up from its foundations and then be obscured by dust, debris and thick black smoke.

Inside the railroad tunnel on the east side of the bridge, Capt. Karl Friesenhahn tried to activate the main charge to blow up the bridge, but apparently a lucky artillery or tank shell had disrupted the circuit. A Sgt. Faust then volunteered to crawl out and set off an emergency charge which seemed, at first, to destroy the bridge.

Chinchar was knocked off his feet by the concussion, his face was buried in the mud by the blast, as was Craig. Sabia was lifted off his feet, and shook his head dazedly. Berry started laughing uncontrollably as the trio staggered around spitting out mud and trying to regain their equilibrium.

Timmermann spoke up with a three word introduction some of the men hadn't heard since combat training in the states: "As you were, we can't cross that bridge because it's just been blown."

Chinchar's moment of disobedience had saved his life. Had he not been out of breath and started to cross when first ordered, he would have been blown up. He later confirmed this by stating: "That little argument saved my life and the lives of the guys who would've been with me on the bridge when it blew up."

Meanwhile Col. Engeman had ordered Company B of the 9th Armored Engineer Battalion to check the bridge for further explosives. Whenever a dangerous mission was given to the armored engineers, it was usually assigned to Lt. Hugh Mott of Nashville, Tn., the second platoon leader. Mott chose his two reliable assistants, Sgts. Eugene Dorland of Manhattan, Ks., and John Reynolds of Lincolnton, N.C., to crawl out under the bridge to destroy the remaining explosives. Risking their lives the intrepid engineers worked feverishly with wire cutters and other tools to rip out wires, and dump 500 pounds of TNT into the Rhine below.

[Alex Semryck of Rawlins, Wy., described the way the Mott-Dorland-Reynolds team operated: "Your portrayals of Mott, Reynolds, and Dorland brought back vivid memories of them and the many other fine men of B Co., 9th Armd Engr Bn. Military leadership among civilian-soldiers and what evokes it is hard to explain. I concluded that the best and most effective that I had witnessed could be described only as the quiet type. These three men had that type of leadership. Their stroll on the bridge on March 7 was only one of many that they took together. They always started with Mott's lazily asking Reynolds, Dorland, or both to 'take a little walk' with him. Whether they were investigating fire, mines, crossings, or just a traffic jam the second platoon knew that these three pedestrians would come back with the right information and usually a tough mission."]

GENERAL SHERMAN TANKS, lined up atop the hill above Remagen blasted enemy defenders across the Rhine. When a barge in the river began harassing the attackers, Timmermann ran back to yell at one of the tankers: "How about putting something on that barge?"

The tanker found the range and a perfectly targeted .75 millimeter shell resulted in a white flag fluttering.

"That's one thing they never taught us at Fort Knox," the member of the tank crew related in reviewing his naval exploit.

Timmermann jumped onto the bridge and started to wave his arm overhead in the traditional "Follow me" gesture.

A chattering of machine gun fire from one of the two towers on the far end of the bridge made him duck. Jack Berry ran up to Grimball's General Pershing tank, pointed at the source and Grimball fired a .90 millimeter round which temporarily silenced the machine gun.

Now it was time for a leader to lead the way. Timmermann shouted: "Dammit, what's holding up the show? Git goin'!"

Big Tony Samele from the Bronx turned to Chinchar, his platoon leader: "C'mon, Mike, we'll just walk it across." Chinchar wasn't about to walk in that dangerous situation. So he ran. Hurtling forward along the left catwalk on the bridge, since the right side had been torn up by the German demolition, Chinchar doesn't even remember his feet touching the boards. "I must have flown across," he related later.

But Chinchar's first platoon soon got pinned down by fire from the towers on the far end, and from the railroad tunnel. Timmermann called to Joe DeLisio's third platoon to move up to uncork the attack: "Joe, get your platoon up there and get these men off their tail," Karl yelled.

On the west bank, Battalion Commander Deevers encouraged the rest of his troops: "I'll see you on the other side and we'll all have a chicken dinner."

"Chicken dinner, my ass. I'm all chicken right now," one of the men shot back.

As DeLisio, the totally fearless sergeant from the Bronx began bobbing and weaving across the bridge, one of the motionless figures hugging the bridge flooring mumbled: "There goes a guy with more guts than sense."

Forrest Miner came up behind another soldier who wasn't moving and yelled, "What's holding you guys up?"

"Don't you hear that machine gun fire?"

Miner lied: "Fer cryin' out loud. That's our own machine gun fire coming from behind us." The man looked incredulous and then hobbled to his feet with a blank expression on his face.

Above all the noise came Timmermann's constant "Git goin', Git goin'!" The company commander was everywhere, spurring, encouraging and leading his men. DeLisio and Chinchar were doing the same as platoon leaders.

DeLisio worked his way up to where one of the attackers was not moving and shouted, "What's the trouble?"

"Trouble, Chrissakes can't you see all that sniper fire?"

"Why worry about a couple of snipers?" DeLisio laughed.

"If this bridge blows up, we've got a whole battalion on it. Let's get off. C'mon guys!"

DeLisio, of course, was exaggerating—there wasn't a whole battalion on the bridge, only part of A Company, but the psychology worked.

He helped to uncork the attack. Other men with "more guts than sense" started to weave and bob behind him.

Sabia started to run, but the bridge turned into an endless treadmill. His leaden feet got heavier and heavier, and he felt as if he had been running for hours and getting nowhere.

Ayres, his grenades and canteen bobbing up and down, suddenly wished he had not consumed so much wine in Remagen, and he vomited on the bridge. Through a blown-out hole in the bridge flooring he saw the swift current below.

"If I fall," he asked himself, "will this pack drag me under?"

Across the river, a German train steamed into view, chugging south.

Col. Engeman, back in Remagen with his tanks, spotted the train and joyfully exclaimed: "Hallelujah! I've always wanted to fire a tank at a locomotive." Four or five tanks opened up. The firebox of the railroad engine exploded. German troops started pouring out of the train, and set up positions to fire at their tormenters on the bridge and in Remagen.

DeLisio waved back for his support squad, led by Joe Petrencsik and Alex Drabik. Then he edged forward. Heavy fire started to come down on the bridge—20 millimeter shells from German anti-aircraft guns. Petrencsik with a sudden hunch yelled: "Duck!" DeLisio crouched, and something swooshed over his head and took a piece out of one of the stone towers.

In the middle of the bridge, Mott, Dorland and Reynolds found four packages of TNT weighing 20 to 30 pounds each, tied to I-beams underneath the decking of the bridge. They climbed down and worked their wire cutters hot until the charges splashed into the Rhine. Above them they heard the

The railroad tunnel on east end of bridge was a strong German defensive point.

heavy tramp of the infantrymen and the hoarse cry of Timmermann which everybody had now taken up: "Git goin'."

Back on the bridge, Dorland started to hack away at a heavy cable.

"Why don't you shoot it in two with your carbine?" Berry asked.

Dorland put the muzzle up against the cable, and blasted it apart.

By this time DeLisio had traveled two-thirds of the way across the bridge. The little sergeant had a theory that if you advanced fast enough you wouldn't get hit, so instead of hugging the bridge when the Germans fired on him from the towers, he simply ran on until he got behind the towers on the German side of the bridge. DeLisio chortled to himself at his good luck, until he looked back and saw that the German fire from the towers was still pinning down the men who were supposed to be following him.

Somebody yelled: "Who's gonna clean out that tower?"

DeLisio took the question as a challenge, and ran back to the tower. Just as he started into the door, a stray bullet went into the stone wall and ricocheted off. Sabia came up and yelled: "You're hit, Joe."

"You're crazy, Sabia. I don't feel nothin' at all."

Sabia insisted: "I saw that bullet, I tell ya I seen it go right through ya."

DeLisio ran his hands quickly around his field jacket, and finding no blood he brushed Sabia away and went on up into the tower.

Chinchar, Samele, and Massie then went up into the left tower. Everybody else moved forward. Many of them recalled what Nelson Wegener, DeLisio's old platoon sergeant, used to say after nearly every battle: "Guinea, you're one of the luckiest men alive. I dunno how you do it, but you always seem to get out of the toughest scrapes."

DeLisio started running up the circular staircase. There were three floors in the tower, and he couldn't take anything for granted. He heard machine gun fire above him, and then it suddenly stopped. Had the Germans heard him coming, and was he heading into a trap?

He slapped open a steel door with the heel of his hand and burst in on three German soldiers. They were bending over a machine gun, as though it were jammed. There was an agonizing second as the three men jerked their heads around. DeLisio pumped out a couple of shots with his carbine, firing from the hip.

"Hande hoch!" he yelled.

The three Germans wheeled around with their hands in the air. DeLisio motioned them to one side with his carbine, and seizing the gun they had been using he hurled it out of the window. Men starting across the bridge saw the gun plummet from the tower and began to move with more confidence.

In his pidgin German and his sign language, DeLisio tried to find out if there were any more soldiers left in the tower. His captives assured him that there weren't. But DeLisio was skeptical and he motioned for them to precede him up the stairs.

On the top floor of the tower, DeLisio pushed the three Germans into a room, where he found a German lieutenant and his orderly. The lieutenant dived for the corner of the room, but DeLisio stopped him with a couple of shots. He took away the lieutenant's Walther pistol. Then he marched all five prisoners down the stairs and told them to proceed unescorted over the bridge to Remagen. They were the first in a long parade of German prisoners taken near the bridge.

Over in the left tower, Chinchar, Samele and Massie also tossed a German machine gun out the window and captured one cowering soldier. The flushing of the towers cost all of those involved the honor of being the first across the Rhine.

Alex Drabik, one of DeLisio's assistant squad leaders, had not seen him go into the tower and started looking for his platoon leader. He asked several people on the bridge, but nobody seemed to know. He made up his mind that there was only one thing to do.

"Let's go!" he shouted. "DeLisio must be over there on the other side all alone."

Drabik took off for the east bank, weaving and bobbing. Just before he got across the bridge he jounced so much that he lost his helmet. He did not stop to pick it up but kept running at top speed until he became the first soldier actually to cross the bridge itself.

Technically Chinchar touched the east bank before anyone else, inasmuch as the tower he cleaned out was actually located beyond the river's edge and unlike DeLisio he climbed down to the east bank from the tower at one point. Drabik received credit for being the first man to cross the bridge.

The Ludendorff Bridge was severely damaged when Timmermann's men made their historic crossing on March 7. For weeks prior to the crossing, American bombers had scored enough hits to require extensive repair work by the Germans. Some of the damage was severe enough to require closing the bridge for several days. American artillery further weakened the bridge. Finally, the abortive attempt by the Germans to demolish the structure on March 7 tore gaping holes in the bridge and seriously weakened the girders and superstructure.

[Following the publication of *The Bridge At Remagen*, I received a letter from an Air Corps bomber pilot who insisted I had failed to give the Air Corps enough

T/Sgt. Michael Chinchar is awarded the Distinguished Service Cross by Maj. Gen. John W. Leonard; Timmermann is at Chinchar's right. U.S. ARMY SIGNAL CORPS, NATIONAL ARCHIVES

9th Armored Division Commanding General, John W. Leonard, awards the Distinguished Service Cross to Lt. Karl Timmermann. U.S. ARMY SIGNAL CORPS, NATIONAL ARCHIVES

American engineers repairing Remagen Bridge. U.S. ARMY SIGNAL CORPS, NATIONAL ARCHIVES

credit in my book. He wrote: "We tried to destroy the bridge several times before it was captured, and if we had succeeded you never would have had a story."]

The night of March 7 was rainy and pitch black. But Timmermann's men on the east side of the Rhine were vulnerable to enemy counterattack unless they were supported by tanks. It was a precarious mission for the 35 ton General Sherman tanks of Company A of the 14th Tank Battalion to pick their way slowly across the damaged railroad bridge. Capt. George Soumas, Lt. Windsor Miller and Sgt. William Goodson received Distinguished Service Crosses for braving the elements and guided by white tapes to cross the shaky bridge and support the bridgehead east of the Rhine.

Even after their victorious crossing, it was no picnic for Timmermann's men, battered by determined counterattacks as the Germans rushed troops, tanks and artillery in desperate efforts to wipe out the bridgehead. Fortunately for Timmermann and his force, the Americans rushed 8,000 troops across in the first 24 hours.

Karl had his hands full and was forced to suspend his daily letters to La Vera. Finally on March 12, by which date his daughter was nearly two weeks old and he didn't even know she had been born, he penned this hurried note:

March 12, 1945
6:30 p.m.

La Vera, my Darling I'm sorry that I haven't written in the last 2 weeks but it really was impossible to write.

All of the infantrymen who crossed the Ludendorff Bridge under fire were sure that it seemed almost a mile before they could reach the east bank. Not so Karl Timmermann, who probably spent more time on the bridge on March 7 since he was directing the attack.

Shortly after his heroic feat, Karl wrote to La Vera: "Before seeing the Rhine, I expected to see a river like the Mississippi or Colorado. I thought that it would be a great wide river. To me the Rhine looks like the Missouri River."

Just before the Rhine reaches Remagen it narrows into a gorge, with the 600-foot high Erpeler Ley on the east side of the river helping to form the gorge.

Not long after Lt. Timmermann's men stormed across the Ludendorff Bridge on the afternoon of March 7, 1945, Sgt. Richard Ballou of Camden, New York, was sent forward with his .30 caliber water-cooled machine gun section to support the riflemen of Company A who were on the east side of the Rhine. Sgt. Ballou had not yet been informed about Lt. Timmermann being made company commander the night before. So it was quite natural that when he made his way up the stairs of the right tower on the east side of the bridge and addressed Timmermann, he asked: "Lieutenant, I'm looking for the company commander of Company A."

Karl answered simply: "I'm it." He had set up his company C.P. in the tower.

Sgt. Ballou asked where he could best place his machine guns. Lt. Timmermann answered: "Our infantry could get a counter-attack on the other side of the bridge. Send your men to the left toward the town of Erpel once you cross to the east side of the Rhine. Put half of them on the upper level and the other half down below."

Sgt. Ballou's machine guns were the first heavy weapons to make their way across the bridge. After dark on the 7th, the Sherman tanks of Company A of the 14th Tank Battalion came across the shaky railroad bridge.

It is difficult to imagine all the thoughts which rushed through Karl's mind as he made his mark in history. Before March 7, every letter he wrote to his wife showed that his top priority was his eager anticipation of parenthood. Psychologically, it certainly appeared that he was determined to build a record in the army to clear the family name of Timmermann. Yet in the heat of battle it is doubtful if this could have been uppermost in his mind as he confronted the imperative of the responsibility of the moment.

Reactions to Karl Timmermann by enlisted men who served with him were 100 percent favorable. Among officers and those higher up, the reaction was somewhat mixed. Two Company A Lts., Jay Swisher and Charles McDowell, had doubts about his courage, although Swisher characterized him as "An enlisted man's officer." Lt. McDowell recalled an incident on the attack from the Roer to the Rhine when he stated that on March 2, 1945, Karl flat out refused to join an attack on the grounds that he was completely exhausted without sleep. Later Lt. McDowell alleged that Karl flaunted and taunted people with the question, "Which bridge did you cross?"

A sampling of the reaction of enlisted men in Karl's company follows:

Helmer Larson wrote: "He was as very good officer as I went thru battles with him, & also soldiered with him in the states."

Another member of Karl's unit gave this assessment:

Lieutenant Timmermann was a good enlisted man's officer. He wasn't treated the best in West Point, Nebraska, where he grew up. This was due to his dad's record of WWI, and his mother was German. He didn't get along with the other officers too well. The other officers were usually from well-to-do families.

He always kidded that the reason he joined the Army was the garbage can lids were frozen down in wintertime. He always said he was from the wrong side of the tracks. He wasn't a yes man at officer's meetings. He spoke what he thought.

I don't think he was treated right when he was relieved of A Company command.

Ralph Shackelford, Co. A, 27th Armored Infantry Bn.

Thanks, Ralph Shackelford, Platte City, MO

For Elmer Lindsey: "He was a wonderful officer and everyone liked the way he did things. He didn't hint around about it."

On behalf of her husband Carl Parnell, Mrs. Parnell had this to say: "Carl says Lt. Karl Timmermann was one of the finest examples of the American soldier. There wasn't a man that knew him that didn't like and respect him."

John L. Craig added: "Over time I developed a great respect for Lt. Timmermann. He was well liked by his men and a great leader. When we reached Germany, his ability to speak German enabled him to easily communicate with civilians and captured German soldiers. In combat, he was always up front with his men. I often worked with him as his runner. Even during the Bulge, he was a leader you could trust and would follow."

Alex Semryck of the 9th Armored Engineer Battalion concluded: "Perhaps your analysis of the man mingles with my vague memories of him, but the impression that emerges is that of a marked man, unhappy and determined almost to the point of grimness. Beyond relaying orders to our platoons, an exchange of nods was the only contact we had when our engineer company was virtually integrated into the 27th during the Bulge. He was not a man you would seek out for small talk during a break. But there was something extraordinary about him that all of us recognized. Your tantalizing mention of a book about him has whetted my curiosity and I will be awaiting its publication eagerly."

Pvt. Alex Giles, who was a driver for Lt. Timmermann and also drove the lead half-track in the March 7 assault on Remagen, had this to write about Karl: "Lt. Karl Timmermann was well thought of by members of the 27th AIB, Company A. He appeared comfortable with the officers of the company as well as with the enlisted men. His actions always conveyed concern for his men, showing impartiality to all his men and at the same time always displaying awareness of their safety."

When the 9th Armored Division commanding general, Maj. Gen. John W. Leonard, applied for a presidential citation for the capture of the Ludendorff bridge, General Leonard included the phrase "Seizure of the bridge had been effected without orders." When the recommendation got up to III Corps, the Corps issued a strongly phrased endorsement and ordered the quoted phrase be removed. The 9th Armored Division subsequently withdrew the offending phrase "without orders."

Alexander Giles, Co. A, 27th Armored Infantry Bn.

Back home in West Point, Neb., the *Omaha World-Herald* telephoned Karl's mother who was a waitress at the Golden Rod Café. The reporter insistently and in a loud voice proclaimed: "Karl Timmermann was the first officer of an invading army to cross the Rhine River since Napoleon."

Karl's mother answered simply: "Napoleon I don't care about. How is my Karl?"

Karl's mother

The Significance of Remagen Bridge

THE CAPTURE OF THE Ludendorff Bridge materially hastened the ending of the war. After the war, General Eisenhower had this to say about the significance of the seizure of Remagen Bridge: "Broad success in war is usually foreseen by days or weeks, with the result that when it actually arrives higher commanders and staffs have discounted it and are immersed in plans for the future. This was completely unforeseen. We were across the Rhine, on a permanent bridge; the traditional defensive barrier to the heart of Germany was pierced. The final defeat of the enemy, which we had long calculated would be accomplished in the spring and summer campaigning of 1945, was suddenly now, in our minds, just around the corner." General Eisenhower's Chief of Staff, Lieutenant General Walter Bedell Smith, termed the Remagen Bridge "worth its weight in gold."

President Franklin D. Roosevelt, with only six weeks to live, shared the elation of the field commanders over the significance of Remagen. The victorious Army Chief of Staff, General George C. Marshall, had this appraisal to make:

> The prompt seizure and exploitation of the crossing demonstrated American initiative and adaptability at its best, from the daring action of the platoon leader to the Army commander who quickly directed all his moving columns. . . . The bridgehead provided a serious threat to the heart of Germany, a diversion of incalculable value. It became a springboard for the final offensive to come.

War correspondents on the scene added their eyewitness accounts on the significance of seeing American troops on the east bank of the Rhine. The

WORLD-HERALD

NEBRASKA, FRIDAY, MARCH 9, 1945.—TWENTY-EIGHT PAGES.

Nebraskan Heads First Unit Across

Split-Second Decision Precedes Operation; Opposition Is Light

Front dispatches Thursday night reported that First Lieut. Karl Timmermann of West Point, Neb., commanded the first American company to cross the Rhine River.

C. R. Cunningham, United Press correspondent who crossed the river with the Americans, said the full story of the crossing cannot be told, "but we came to a spot where the Germans were asleep."

"It was not the mission of the infantry company involved to cross the Rhine, but it was a moment for split-second decision, one of those that change the course of wars," he reported.

"A second lieutenant named Burroughs and First Lieut. Karl Timmermann, West Point, Neb., were there. They found the Rhine could be crossed. The word went up from company to battalion headquarters.

Casualties Light

"Lieut. Col. Leonard Engemann of Minnesota made the necessary decision—go across—without a moment's hesitation.

"Ten or 15 minutes later the first company was firmly across the Rhine, and on the other side the First Army men were throwing everything."

Lieutenant Timmermann said there was no opposition to the crossing except from snipers and a few 20-mm. guns. Near the end of their crossing the raiders ran into heavy machine gun fire, but casualties were light.

American troops have crossed the Rhine south of Cologne (arrow with American flag) and may be in a position to sweep north (open arrow) and cut off the German Ruhr industrial area. Small arrows indicate Allied drives southwest of Mayen, northward along the Rhine toward Remagen, into Bonn and Bad Godesberg and toward Xanten.—AP Wirephoto.

Associated Press cabled on March 8: "The swift, sensational crossing was the biggest military triumph since Napoleon's conquering legions crossed the Rhine early in the last century." Hal Boyle wrote from the front that "with the exception of the great tank battle at El Alamein, probably no tank engagement in World War II will be remembered longer than the dashing coup which first put the American army across the Rhine at Remagen." He added that the crossing of the Rhine by the men "who knew there was a strong likelihood the dynamite-laden bridge would blow up under them at any moment has saved the American nation 5,000 dead and 10,000 wounded."

"It was a moment for history," stated *Time* magazine.

All around the country, local civic and patriotic organizations honored the men who had wrought the miracle of Remagen. The feeling toward the Remagen heroes was perhaps best expressed in an editorial in the March 10, 1945, *New York Sun*, which concluded with these words:

> Great shifts in history often do hang upon the developments of minutes. Americans know, and the enemy has learned, that given the least opportunity, American soldiers are quick to seize any break and exploit it to the fullest. The men who, in the face of scattered fire and the great threat of the bridge blowing up under them, raced across and cut the wires have materially shortened a struggle in which every minute means lost lives. To all who utilized that ten minutes so advantageously goes the deepest gratitude this country can bestow.

THE GERMANS HAD AN ANGRY reaction. In his conference with Field Marshal Kesselring two days after the capture of the Ludendorff Bridge, Hitler told him bluntly that the really vulnerable spot on the western front was Remagen, and that it was urgent to "restore" the situation there. Hitler took a personal hand in hurrying all available troops to reduce the Remagen bridgehead. The 11th Panzer Division wheeled southward from the Ruhr. The Panzer Lehr and 9th Panzer divisions followed, swallowing many gallons of precious, high-priority gasoline. Many other divisions and scraps of divisions joined in the frantic German fight to contain the bridgehead.

Field Marshal Model's Chief of Staff, Major General Carl Wagener, summed up the German view as follows: "The Remagen affair caused a great stir in the German Supreme Command. Remagen should have been considered a basis for termination of the war. Remagen created a dangerous and unpleasant abscess within the last German defenses, and it provided an ideal springboard for the coming offensive east of the Rhine. The Remagen bridgehead made the other crossings of the Rhine a much easier task for the enemy. Furthermore, it tired German forces which should have been resting to withstand the next major assault."

The Remagen bridgehead was vital in helping to form the southern and eastern pincers for the Allied troops that surrounded and trapped 300,000 German soldiers in the Ruhr.

As sorely needed German troops were thrown against the Remagen bridge-head, the resulting disorganization and weakening of defenses made it much easier for other American Rhine crossings to be made to the north and south of Remagen. Just as the loss of the bridge was a blow to German morale, so did it provide a strong boost to American and Allied morale. Not only did it make the end of the war seem close at hand, but it also emboldened the combat troops when they were confronted with chances to exploit opportunities. It underlined the fact that the German army's soft spots could be found through aggressive attacks, thereby spurring American forces to apply greater pressure.

In the summer of 1945, I had the opportunity to interview Field Marshal Kesselring in the prisoner of war enclosure at Mondorf, Luxembourg, where Goering and the top Nazi officers and diplomats were interned. In interviewing those with whom I sharply disagree, I frequently stretch the truth if I presume it might make the subject more cooperative. In this instance, when

Karl (standing, second from right) poses with other DSC winners in front of the famous sign placed on the Ludendorff Bridge. U.S. ARMY SIGNAL CORPS, NATIONAL ARCHIVES

talking about Remagen, I casually remarked that "Captain Willi Bratge, commanding the German defenders of the bridge, was sort of a 'dummkopf!'

Kesselring's reaction was immediate and violent. His face turned red, and he literally roared: "He vass no dummkopf. He vass a CRIMINAL!" He spat out the characterization vehemently while pounding the table.

AN AMERICAN PARATROOPER with the 17th Airborne Division goes so far as to contend that Karl Timmermann saved his life. John F. Magill and his unit jumped behind enemy lines east of the Rhine River on March 24, 1945—17 days after Timmermann's heroic leadership at Remagen. According to Magill, the 17th Airborne suffered heavy casualties, but he points out that after March 7 huge numbers of the German defenders had been rushed to try and eliminate the Remagen bridgehead.

Captain Karl Friesenhahn, the little German engineer who was in charge of the company at Remagen in 1945, at my request returned to Remagen in 1954. I saw him gaze over the ruins of the bridge, and he quietly asked what awards the American Army had given to Lieutenant Timmermann, Sergeant Drabik, Lieutenant Mott and the other first Americans who had crossed. When I told him that they had received Distinguished Service Crosses, Captain Friesenhahn replied with some feeling: "They deserved them—and then some. They saw us trying to blow that bridge, and by all odds it should have been blown up while they were crossing it. In my mind, they were the greatest heroes of the whole war."

TWO

Roots and Escape from Germany

Both of Karl's grandfathers and one of his grandmothers were born in Germany. Arnold Timmermann was born in the little town of Twistringen, Germany, in August 1846 near the northern German city of Hanover. He married Anna Wortman of Ohio, the only one of Karl's American-born grandparents, after his arrival in this country in 1871. Anna Wortman's parents came to this country from Westphalia in Germany. Karl's father insisted she was half-Native American and born in Indiana.

On Karl's mother's side of the family, Andreas Weisbecker was born January 12, 1873, in the Niederrad suburb of Frankfurt-on-Main in central Germany. Andreas married Apollina (Lina) Rodius. Their daughter Maria Franciska Weisbecker turned out to be Karl's mother, who took the name "Mary."

Arnold Timmermann raised a family of ten children. He was about 5-feet, 2-inches in height and sported a red billy-goat beard, which became decidedly gray in his old age. A farmer in Germany, he also farmed at several locations in the Pebble Creek Valley section of Cuming and Dodge Counties, Ne., some 70 miles northwest of Omaha, and southwest of the Cuming County seat of West Point. Large families were in vogue on the farm because that meant more farm hands and cooks to meet the appetites of those who did the back-breaking work without the advantage of modern, labor-saving conveniences.

Arnold celebrated the arrival of his son (Karl's father) who first saw the light of day on July 28, 1884, at the small Cuming County hamlet of Monterey. Although later in life he went by the name of John Henry Timmermann, the birth certificate and all census records up through 1910 listed him as "Henry John Timmermann."

Anna Wortman and Arnold Timmermann, Karl's paternal grandmother and grandfather.

Henry had an idyllic childhood. He soon started working on his father's farm, and never seemed to be lacking in some wage-earning opportunities. Later he helped his father in Arnold's livery and seed business. Henry in his youth quickly developed into a ladies' man, and he flitted from romance to romance during his adulthood. He seemed determined to escape matrimony well into his thirties.

At a dance, Henry was jumped by two men, one of whom accused Henry of stealing his red-headed girl friend. It was a case of mistaken identity, but it nearly cost Henry his life. By his own recorded account, verified by Mrs. Lena Kraft (his sister), one of the men pulled a knife and slashed Henry across the back of the right side of his neck. "My shoes were full of blood when I reached the doctor," Henry explained. "The doctor told me if I had waited ten minutes later 'you'd be dead.'"

Happy-go-lucky in his approach to life, Henry also thoroughly enjoyed his beer-drinking buddies. His father tolerated his son's behavior but when Arnold got drunk on hard liquor he frequently beat up Henry although Henry

Karl's father (second from left) and three of his brothers in Snyder, Ne., prior to World War I.

was inches taller. Neither Arnold nor his wife were well educated and unlike many parents who lacked a good education, neither of them insisted or made a high priority of good schooling for their children.

[In an interview with Joe Wortman, one of Henry's cousins, I learned that one of Henry's classmates used to tell how Henry was frequently put back with the beginners, because he was a slow learner.]

"On one occasion on the farm my kneecap was shattered," Henry told me in a recorded interview. "It was really Dad's fault. We were on horseback and my Dad hollered at me. I looked back and the horse reared backward. I couldn't get out of the saddle. I spent six months on my back in the hospital and was on crutches after that." Henry had a limp from then as his knee cap never fully mended. He also suffered a double hernia.

During wartime many Nebraska farmers were reasonably prosperous. Arnold owned his own threshing machine and made good money from his farming neighbors who came to use it. But after peace broke out on November 11, 1918, the bottom fell out of the market and many banks went under. Henry had been operating his own farm and started to borrow on it. He persuaded his father to co-sign his mortgage notes and when hard times came Henry went into debt.

Then in 1919 when Henry wrecked his car, he was suddenly faced with a financial crisis. At the age of 35, Henry had been able to escape the draft, also because he was deferred because of his age and occupation. Henry suddenly decided one day to join the peace-time Army because he was totally unable to pay his debts. According to his sister, Lena Kraft, Henry was not seen for several days. Then a note he had left on the kitchen table was found, in which he cryptically wrote that he was "going back to the old country."

[In 1954, I recorded an interview with Karl's father in which he described his mood when he decided to enlist. "I didn't give a damn for my life at that time. I didn't give a damn for nothin' because I had lost so much money."]

Henry (John) went to Omaha and he put up at a hotel. A man named Frank Nichols was just packing to leave when he offered Henry a drink. Nichols, from Chicago, hit it off immediately with his new-found friend, with whom he went to Fort Crook to enlist as "John Henry Timmermann." During their service, they slept in double-decker bunks with Henry always in the uppermost one. In the Army, John was known as "Dutchie."

They went to Fort Crook in Omaha and were immediately shipped to Fort Logan, Colorado, where they formally enlisted. John then enlisted as "John H. Timmermann" (the name he kept for the rest of his life) on April 9, 1919.

John told me: "On April 10, they read us the Articles of War. The next thing I recall is that on April 22, they loaded us on a train east to Camp Meade, Maryland. Then all of a sudden we were sent to Hoboken, N.J., to board a ship overseas. When I got to Camp Meade, Md., I telephoned my father. He didn't have any idea that I was joining the Army.

"He asked me: 'Are you going across?' He sounded angry with me so I answered: 'I'm not sure I'll ever come back!' He didn't even respond.

"At three o'clock in the morning they got us up to go to the Port of Embarkation."

Timmermann's unit boarded the small transport ship *Great Northern* on May 14, 1919, arriving at the French port of Brest on May 21. They were temporarily stationed at Pontorson, France. From July 24 to July 28, he was confined to the evacuation hospital. The hospital records state: "Patient indicates he had pain and tenderness in right lower quadrant of abdomen for past two weeks. Dull ache in right lower abdomen. Two weeks ago while at Brest, France, while running an orderly detail patient slipped and fell, striking his abdomen. Two days later there was discomfort while lifting heavy objects and this has gradually increased. Pain is relieved by pressure (diagnosed as 'Adhesions')." The unit was then shipped by forty-and-eight box cars to Bendorf, Germany, for eventual assignment to occupation duty at Koblenz, Germany.

Pvt. John Timermann in the World War I Occupation Army.

John Timmermann complained bitterly to me about his commanding officer, Capt. George W. Gering.

[Was John exaggerating? I thought I should track down Capt. Gering to find out. He had already retired when I found him at this home in Damascus, Md. He did not recall John Timmermann personally, but he had a crystal clear memory of his unit in the 8th Infantry. "Biggest damn bunch of undisciplined, untrainable screwballs I ever met in the army," Gering exploded. "We loaded 17 officers and 851 enlisted men into these box cars on the trip to Germany. Some of them had openly threatened to jump off en route, so we locked the box cars and whenever we had to stop, the officers were armed with clubs along the tracks so nobody could escape. Unfortunately, there were no toilet facilities aboard, so you can imagine the stink inside. At least we got to Germany full strength," Gering chuckled with pride.]

Timmermann described Gering as "That fat-ass Captain who didn't know nothin' about right face, left face, about face. I felt like telling him if he turned around I would put a bullet in his back." John got along well with his fellow members of Company M, 8th Infantry. Early in September, a group of soldiers in the outfit began to talk about what might happen if they skipped out. They began to make serious plans, one feature of which was to time the changing of the guard, which might furnish the chance to leave. John himself was one of the ringleaders in the bull sessions, because back in Nebraska he had been a free spirit all of his 35 years. He was also a betting man, and about all of the disgruntled troops started to make bets as to who could stay out the longest before being apprehended.

Finally the magic day arrived: September 2, 1919. About forty men successfully eluded the guards and boarded a train in Koblenz. When the train stopped north of Frankfurt at Oberwald, they got out and walked back to the city where they figured they would melt into the urban throngs and also find a place to stay.

The meat grinder of trench warfare had killed the flower of German manhood, leaving behind tens of thousands of war widows unwilling to spend their future grieving their loss. American soldiers were actively courted, and the happy

AWOL escapees from Capt. Gering's outfit had little trouble finding places to stay.

John found the pickings so much more liberal than his forays back in the Cornhusker State, and he enjoyed a continuous series of successful one-night stands as 1919 faded into 1920.

Maria Weisbecker, born October 2, 1902, in the Niederrad suburb of Frankfurt-on-Main was in her late teens at the time the mass exodus had occurred in Koblenz. Her parents doted on this beautiful young lady, giving her every advantage in education and work opportunity in a local delicatessen, as a chambermaid and a nearby factory. Maria, known as "Mary" to American friends she met, had dreams of glory with relation to her future Prince Charming who she hoped would own a long, black limousine, lived a life of luxury and wanted to raise many children. One of her older brothers, Carl Weisbecker, had taken up residence in Suffern, N.Y., from which he wrote of the freedoms in America where everyone could become a success.

On the extreme left, Karl's mother as a spirited early teenager with shoulder-length hair. Apollina and Andreas Weisbecker, Karl's maternal grandmother and grandfather are seated in the center of the above photograph..

THE YEAR WAS 1921. The month was February. Nobody remembers the day, so let's just pretend it was February 14 because that makes it a better Valentine's Day love story. One of Maria's many suitors asked her for a date at "La Croix," the local dance hall. Although she accepted, she had already decided that this particular boy friend was not going to be her Prince Charming of the future. As luck would have it, John Timmermann decided to sample the female wares at the very same dance hall.

Over a quarter of a century before Ezio Pinza advised men what to do when they observed their true love on Some Enchanted Evening, Maria Weisbecker gazed "across a crowded room" and her approving eye saw what she wanted in John Timmermann. "She was pretty as a picture," he related to me, "and she deserted her boy friend to come over and ask me to dance." He held her closely and at the end of the evening Maria said, "Let's get out of here," and asked John to take her home. That was the start of a torrid love affair.

The Weisbeckers lived on the second floor of a huge apartment building in an upscale suburb of Frankfurt named Niederrad. There was a balcony where they raised vegetables, rabbits and chickens behind their building. There were three rooms for 13 people. As members of the family left to get married, there was plenty of room for Maria and John to set up housekeeping.

Andreas and his wife Lina were devout Catholics and respected the institution of marriage. As a World War I veteran Andreas did not cotton to the

Apollina (Lina) Rodius Weisbecker and Andreas Weisbecker, Karl's maternal grandmother and grandfather.

The Weisbecker family; Karl's mother is at upper left.

idea of having an army deserter for a son-in-law. Despite the fact that John had been successful at working for a local forester, then driving a wagon to haul coal and finally working for a company which made briquettes, before long he was laid off from all of these jobs as the post-World War I German economy collapsed.

As 1922 dawned, John was dependent on the Weisbeckers for food and shelter and soon it was obvious that Maria was in a family way. "I did not want to get married," John told me many years later in his recorded interview. He had always succeeded through an excellent gift of gab to get out of scrapes by convincing promises and excuses. These served him well until early April of 1922. By now Maria was in her sixth month and the Weisbeckers were running out of patience.

What happened next was ugly. The development was verified by a letter written by F.T.F. Dumont, the American Consul in Frankfurt, who stated that John "had a quarrel with his wife's family and was thoroughly beaten up by her father and brothers."

The beating finally changed John's mind. On April 15, 1922, John and Maria were formally married on Easter Sunday.

Almost all of the Weisbecker children had been delivered by an extremely able midwife, Mrs. Becht. Mrs. Timmermann told me some years later:

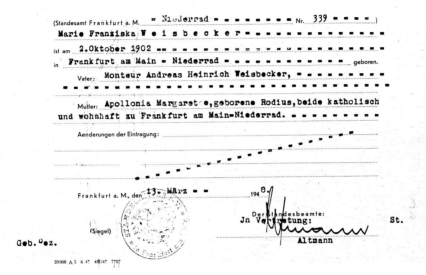

Karl's birthplace on second floor of this apartment house in Niederrad section of Frankfurt, Germany.

"I had worked in the munitions plant on Saturday, but when Monday morning came I had a lot of washing to do, so faked being sick. I washed baby clothes and other things most of the day.

"Toward evening I started getting chills. I wrapped a raincoat around my shoulders and started walking back and forth and mother heard me. She said, 'We should call Mrs. Becht.'

"I said 'No, I have another month yet.' I was stubborn, as always, with my mother. She got my father to go and get Mrs. Becht. When she arrived,

Karl had started to arrive also." On June 19, 1922, Maria gave birth to a 7½ pound healthy boy who was named on the German birth certificate "Hans Karl Heinrich Timmermann"—destined to be the Hero Of The Rhine. The Weisbecker family allowed their daughter to return home for the birth of their new grandson, but just as soon as Maria had recovered, she and John were evicted.

Now entered a period of extreme difficulty for the new parents. Without a source of income, John related, "I had trouble finding a place to live. I went from place to place, frequently sleeping on the floor." Relations with his new wife became strained when she discovered his age from the marriage and birth certificates to which he had to swear. At their initial meeting, John told Maria he was 23 years old, when in fact he was 37.

IN THE SUMMER OF 1923, John's luck began to change. He called on a true angel of mercy, a British Quaker named Marion C. Fox, who had come to Frankfurt several years earlier to help organize the Quaker efforts to feed and clothe Germans who were starving as the result of the deep depression in the post-war economy and the strictures of the blockade which crippled efforts to import needed commodities.

In the early months of 1923, when Karl was less than one year old, he suffered from life-threatening malnutrition. One of the first things which

Marion Fox, about 1935.

Marion Fox did when she met the Timmermann family was to work on restoring Karl's health, and also enabling John and Maria to survive by giving John the job of carrying packages of food and clothing to the most needy families in and around Frankfurt.

Marion Fox's central mission was to help feed and clothe destitute Germans. Why she decided to spend considerable time and money on the family of an American Army deserter is a puzzle I have attempted to solve. I am convinced from the circumstances that had Marion Fox not intervened, baby Karl would have perished from malnutrition. Had Karl somehow survived, the Army authorities would have closed in and administered a stiff sentence to John Timmermann, far beyond the tap on the wrist which they ordered in 1928. Marion

Fox effectively shielded the Timmermanns from the military authorities. She also shielded them from the German police, who for six months had labeled John Timmermann as an "undesirable," liable for prosecution.

Finally, had the Timmermanns escaped all these horrors, they never would have gotten steamship passage back to America and Nebraska except, as we shall see, the dedicated and determined initiative of Marion Fox in weaving her way through the bureaucracy to achieve a miracle.

I was so impressed by the compassionate genius of Marion Fox and her fellow Quakers at the American Friends Service Committee in Philadelphia that in 1954, when I started collecting material on Karl Timmermann, I decided to fly to England to interview her personally. I wrote her the following letter:

May 4, 1954

Mrs. Marion C. Fox
The Bower
Wellington
Somerset, England

My Dear Mrs. Fox:

I am not at all certain how to reach you, since the last address I have for you is 1925, and many things have happened since then.

I am writing a book about a courageous family-- the Timmermanns of West Point Nebraska. Mrs. Timmermann showed me correspondence from you, and Mr. Timmermannk told me that after the first World War you were most helpful to them and helped them get over to this country from Frankfurt, where you were working with the Quaker Embassy. Mrs. Timmermann's boy Karl was an outstanding hero in World War II, being the first officer to cross the Remagen Bridge on the Rhine.

I plan to come to Europe at the end of this month, leaving here about May 20. I realize the time is short, but I would very much like to talk with you if I can locate you, and possibly see some of the things you may have about the Timmermanns, since you more than any one else helped them get over to this country. Please write to me if you have the chance, and if I do not hear from you I shall make an attempt in any event to stop by and inquire when I am in England.

Sincerely yours,

Dr. Kenneth W. Hechler

Address reply to 1800 Eye St., N.W.,
Washington 6, D.C.

Before leaving for England, I received two prompt answers in May from Marion's sister:

My dear Dr. Hechler

I opened your letter to my sister Marion C. Fox & must tell you that she died 5 years ago at the age of 87. I am afraid I can't help you with information about her dealings with the Timmermanns. It was so long ago & most of the Quaker workers at Frankfurt have died.

Mrs. J. Bradbur of Moylan Avenue, Moylan, Pa., USA is still alive. She & her late husband worked with my sister there.

Also Miss Hidurg Lion of Flat C 15 Sinclair Gardens West Kensington, London. She was a school teacher in a poor quarter of Frankfurt & knew a great many of the people whom they helped. It is cheering to hear of many having made good in happier surroundings.

Miss Lion is herself a refugee from Hitler's regime.

Sincerely yours,
Margaret W. Fox

Dear Dr. Hechler

I am writing on the chance of catching you before you left for England. I should be delighted to see you here, & could probably provide some background (no Timmermann letters).

There is a very nice little hotel nearby opposite my old European house in the main street. The house is very peaceful with a beloved little garden at the back. I do hope you will be able to come. If you can't manage it, I must suggest that you go to Friends House, Euston Road, London. In the book shop there you should be able to get a copy of "Marion Fox, Quaker," compiled by our nephew (a retired naval officer), an account of her life mostly from her own letters and journals . . . It shows how she became the person she was.

If you come here I can show it to you.

Sincerely yours,
Margaret W. Fox
My sight is very bad but I try to make my letters legible.

While in England in 1954, I had several very productive conversations with Marion Fox's younger sister, Margaret Fox, plus the other people she mentioned. I also traveled to interview one of Marion's cousins, Elizabeth Fox Howard. Mrs. Howard had been in Frankfurt with Marion, and she kindly autographed a copy of her book *Across Barriers*, which revealed much of the background and details of the noble work of the Quakers in Frankfurt.

I learned a great deal of Marion Fox's life, personality and motivations from these interviews. Margaret told me: "The people at the War Office could not seem to understand the burning desire of Marion to go to Germany. They warned her of the treatment she might incur there, but she persisted.

"She loved little things and little people. Whereas I was a gardener, she was a horticulturist. She would get the first violet or the first little flower in spring and send it to somebody in a match-box.

"She had courage underneath her pleasant and friendly exterior. She was a slight woman, barely over five feet tall. She saw and tried to cultivate good in everyone through love.

"If she despaired of anything, she hardly ever said so in words, but her silence and her tolerance shone through. She could pack a great deal of wisdom in a few words, and could suddenly flash on you a crisp humor all her own. When she spoke in meetings, her messages were generally brief and to the point. She was never taken in by deception. She overlooked all human foibles and seemed to want to make all people worthy of her trust. She especially loved young children, and she loved to pop little sweets into the mouths of squalling children, some of whom had never tasted a sweet. She was brought up in rather sheltered circumstances, and only in later life did she become awakened through the discovery of Quaker principles."

Up until the time I visited England and talked with Marion Fox's sister and friends, I did not fully appreciate why she saw something special in the Timmermanns among the tens of thousands of those in need. Only then did I understand the herculean efforts she made to take care of them in Germany, to arrange the seemingly impossible in getting them back to the United States, and for several years exchanging handwritten letters with Mrs. Timmermann on Karl's progress in this country.

THE SAGA OF HOW John, Mary and Karl were able to get to Nebraska started with the following letter dated September 6, 1923, in the National Archives in which the American Consul General in Frankfurt, F.T.F. Dumont, describes John Timmermann's visit to his office.

Secretary of State
Washington, D.C.

Subject: John H. Timmermann,
a deserter from the United States Army.

Sir: I have the honor to report that one John Henry
Timmermann, residing at Niederrad near Frankfurt-on-Main,
presented himself at this office on September 5th and stated that
he had deserted from Company M, 8th Infantry, American
Forces in Germany in 1919. He asked that he be taken into
custody and returned to the United States with his wife, whom
he married April 15, 1922, and their child born June 21, [sic]
1922. Timmermann has never before reported to any American
consulate. It appears that the reason for his doing so at the
present time is that he is absolutely without funds. He had a
quarrel with his wife's family and was thoroughly beaten up by
her father and brothers. He is a man of very inferior mentality
and his return to the United States, unless required by law, is of
no value. It appears that he is the son of one Arnold
Timmermann of Snyder, Neb.

I have the honor to be, sir, your obedient servant.
[Signed] F.T.F. Dumont

At this point, the Secretary of State asked the War Department for advice.
On October 8, 1923, the Acting Secretary of War reported in a response which
was forwarded to Consul Dumont in Frankfurt:

My dear Mr. Secretary:

I have your letter of the 1st instant, enclosing a communica-
tion from the American Consul General, Frankfurt-on-Main, in
which it is noted that one John H. Timmermann reported to him
with a view to securing transportation for himself and wife to
the United States.

The records of the Department show that one John H.
Timmermann enlisted April 9, 1919 and deserted September 12, 1919,
at Coblenz, Replacement Depot, American Forces in Germany.
[John actually went AWOL on September 2, but was not listed as a
deserter until September 12.]

It is not the policy of the War Department to accept the
surrender of deserters in foreign countries, to furnish transportation or to take any other action in their cases until they are
again under military control under the jurisdiction of the War
Department.

When Wilbur J. Carr on behalf of the Secretary of State forwarded this
response to Frankfurt on October 13, it would seem to most people that they
had completely slammed the door against any possibility of returning the
Timmermanns to the United States.

Not so to Marion Fox.

She thought about the problem awhile, and came up with the thought that
if she could raise the money for steamship passage it might somehow soften
the bureaucratic insistence that it couldn't be done. Realizing that raising the
funds might take some time, she decided without consulting her superiors that
one ploy would be to make the rash promise to pay the total cost while asking
the Timmermann family in Nebraska to reimburse the money.

Her next step was to persuade one of her friends to write an affidavit to
Washington to float this idea. The American Vice Consul at Frankfurt,
Maurice W. Altaffer, then sent this affidavit to Washington, D.C., clearly
marked "Opinion of Officer Taking Affidavit" with reference to John H.
Timmermann:

Affiant, a native-born citizen deserted from the American Army in Germany at Coblenz, in 1919. He came to Frankfurt on the Main, and has been
here since, where he married a German woman. He has produced evidence
to show that he was married previous to September 22, 1922.

Since the prevalence of unemployment in Germany, the affiant has been
out of work and altogether dependent on local charity to keep himself and
his family from starvation. For the past six months the police officials
have threatened him with deportation as an undesirable, and they have
only been kept from carrying out their threat because they had no money
to pay the expenses connected with deportation. His family has been in
such pitiable plight that the Frankfurt branch of the Quakers (British) have
taken his case up. They are paying his passage to the United States, and for
the issuance of a passport. The Department referred to its instructions in
this case dated October 13, 1922, in which it is explained that the War
Department has no interest in him as a deserter until he reports within the
jurisdiction of an army post. He has no birth certificate or other evidence
to support his claim to citizenship, but it is considered beyond a doubt
that this man's story is true.

It is recommended that a passport be issued to him and his family for
their return to the United States.

Now it was time for Marion Fox to notify the American Friends Service Committee in Philadelphia of her efforts, and to enlist their support to help raise the funds to cover the cost of steamship passage, and also to contact the State Department in Washington to make arrangements to obtain the necessary passport.

After a preliminary letter on November 1, 1923, Miss Fox sent the following letter on November 14, to Philadelphia:

American Friends Service Committee
20 South 12th Street
Philadelphia U.S.A.

Dear Friends,

Referring to mine of 1st 11. 23 I have further to report that John Henry Timmermann and his wife have been several times in our office, not having received any more letters from the father Arnold Timmermann, Snyder, Nebraska U.S.A.

I have had a talk this morning with the American Consul here who understands the circumstances.

He says that the German Government cannot deport to the U.S.A. without paying fares, but they can arrest Timmermann for being here without a passport.

If they were married before September 1922 the wife and child can go over on his passport as American citizens. The passport would then cost ten dollars. If she married after that time she and the child are Germans. The extra passport costing a further ten dollars can be got on affidavit from the consulate. If they are not married they can go on affidavit, but they would be forced to marry at Ellis Island.

He thinks the whole fare and passport as far as New York would cost if she is American about three hundred dollars if she German about three hundred twenty-five dollars. In any case $350. would cover the expenses. If we can furnish the dollars the Consulate will get them off.

He asked me to write to you to ask the Department of State to cable to the American Consul Frankfurt a.m. to issue an emergency passport.

Your friend sincerely,
Marion C. Fox

P.S. I will write again when I know about the date of marriage.

Meanwhile, in response to a personal request by John Timmermann, the German authorities in Frankfurt confirmed that John's wife Maria had lost her German citizenship by reason of her marriage to an American. The translation of the German authorization follows:

Frankfurt/Main, 16 November 1923

Mr. John Heinrich Timmermann
Niederrad

With reference to your request of the 15th of this month, which you made in person, I herewith wish to inform you that a certificate to the effect that your wife is an American citizen can be issued solely by the authorities of your country, i.e. by the American consulate having jurisdiction in your area of residence.

However, I can confirm that, after you have entered into matrimony with Marie Franziska nee Weisbecker, born on 2 October 1902 at Frankfurt/Main-Niederrad, according to the marriage certificate which you presented here, the latter, in accordance with Paragraph 17, Chapter 6 of the Reich Law of 22 July 1913, has lost her Prussian citizenship and thus also her German citizenship.

[Signed] Fringler

To HIS GREAT CREDIT, Wilbur K. Thomas, the Executive Secretary of the American Friends Service Committee in Philadelphia, immediately recognized and appreciated the need for speedy action to raise the funds necessary to bring the Timmermanns back to the United States. Thomas fired off a telegram and a letter to John's father, Arnold, in Snyder, Nebraska, as follows:

Wilbur K. Thomas.

November 15, 1923

Arnold Timermann,
Snyder, Nebr.

Dear Friend:

We have just received a letter, a copy of which is enclosed. We immediately sent you the following Day-Letter:

LETTER FROM OUR OFFICE IN FRANKFURT SAYS YOUR SON JOHN HENRY TIMMERMANN AND WIFE IN DESPERATE CIRCUMSTANCES AND MUST GET TO AMERICA BY DECEMBER FIRST THEY NEED FIVE HUNDRED DOLLARS WE WILL CABLE AMOUNT FOR YOU UPON RECEIPT YOUR CERTIFIED CHECK PLEASE ADVISE US IMMEDIATELY LETTER FOLLOWING GIVING FURTHER EXPLANATION.

I think that the letter from Miss Fox in Frankfurt explains itself. As was said in the telegram, we shall be very glad to cable the money to our office in Berlin, and have them forward the amount to your son.

The American Friends Service Committee is a relief organization, having carried on reconstruction work in Russia, Poland, Austria and Germany since the war. We, the Quakers, were in Germany from 1920 to 1922, and we fed as many as a million children a day at the height of the work. We are about to organize a similar relief work for German children this winter. General Henry T. Allen, who was in charge of the American forces on the Rhine, is Chairman of the national Committee which is raising funds to be administered by our committee.

Please advise us immediately concerning your plans for bringing your son home. We are writing a similar letter to his wife's uncle: Carl W. Weisbecker, Suffern, N.Y.

Trusting to hear from you as soon as possible, I am

Sincerely yours,
Wilbur K. Thomas
Executive Secretary.

Not surprisingly, Arnold Timmermann did not respond very enthusiastically to this and subsequent appeals for funds. His answers were prepared by others and he signed them, expressing sympathy. But there were two reasons why he did not immediately send the necessary reimbursement for the return of his son, German wife and new grandson. First and foremost, Snyder and farm communities throughout the nation had been rocked by economic depression after World War I, the same financial collapse which ruined the haberdashery enterprise undertaken in Kansas City by a future President of the United States, Harry Truman. Arnold had not heard from his son for over three years. Furthermore, John's precipitate departure for the Army in 1919 had made Arnold saddled with thousands of dollars of mortgage notes John had co-signed. Maria Weisbecker had a successful brother, Carl Weisbecker in Suffern, N.Y., from whom Arnold tried to enlist for help, without success. Arnold's initial response follows:

Snyder, Nebraska Nov 22 1923.

American Friends Service Committee.
Philadelphia Pa.
Attention. Mr Wilbur K Thomas.
Executive Secretary.

Dear Sirs.

Your telegram together with your letter dated Nov 15th 1923 received and answer has been delayed on account of our not being able to raise the money.

We are doing everything possible to raise the money and have the promise of some help in the near future.

Would you be so kind as to advise us at once if you have heard from the Mr Carl W. Weisbecker of Suffern N.Y. and if so is he is doing anything. If he could furnish a part of the money necessary it would be much easier for us to raise a part. As it is we are without funds whatever and can only rely on our friends to help us out which is pretty uncertain the way conditions are here at this time.

Wish you would please advise your office in Frankfurt to advise our son that we are doing everything possible to raise the money. Please advise us quick.

Many, many thanks for the help and interest you are showing us.

Yours truly, Arnold Timmermann

Thomas then sent a second letter to Arnold, followed by a telegram to the State Department on November 24, 1923:

Arnold Timmermann,
Snyder, Nebraska.

Dear Friend:

We received your letter this morning and also a letter from our representative in Frankfurt.

Miss Fox reports that Timmermann and his wife have been in to see her several times and that they have heard nothing from his family in America. The American Consul in Frankfurt is interested in the case and thinks that $350. would be the amount necessary to get him and his family home. It so happens that the German Government cannot deport to the United States unless they pay the fares. In that case we need only pay for the passage of his wife and child. We wired you this morning as follows:

"OUR WORKER ADVISES US THREE HUNDRED FIFTY DOLLARS WILL COVER EXPENSES STOP WE HAVE HAD NO WORD FROM WEISBECKER STOP SEND TO THIS OFFICE TWENTY SOUTH TWELFTH STREET PHILADELPHIA WHAT MONEY YOU HAVE COLLECTED AND YOUR NOTE FOR THE BALANCE STOP WE WILL ADVANCE NECESSARY BALANCE AND CABLE WHOLE AMOUNT TO FRANKFURT"

If you send us what money you have and your note for the balance, this Committee will be glad to advance the balance and to cable to the Frankfurt bank the $350. necessary for Timmermann's expenses. We are asking the State Department to help us with this case. Timmermann needs an emergency passport; and the American Consul will give it to him if Washington cables accordingly.

We have heard nothing from Weisbecker. We are doing everything we can to get the money to him by December 1st and we will thoroughly appreciate all that you can do to help us. We were very glad to hear from you so favorably this morning and to feel that you understood the situation.

We will write you just as soon as we have something definite to report from Washington.

Very sincerely yours,
Wilbur K. Thomas, Executive Secretary

November 24, 1923.

State Department, Washington, D.C.

JOHN HENRY TIMMERMANN AMERICAN SOLDIER IN LAST
WAR MARRIED GERMAN GIRL NOW RESIDENT FRANKFURT
a/M MUST BE DEPORTED BY DECEMBER FIRST STOP WE ARE
ADVANCING PASSAGE EXPENSES FOR HIS FAMILY STOP CAN
YOU PLEASE CABLE AMERICAN CONSUL FRANKFURT TO ISSUE
EMERGENCY PASSPORT TO TIMMERMANN UPON INVESTIGA-
TION STOP PLEASE ADVISE US AT ONCE

Wilbur K. Thomas
Friends Service Committee, Philadelphia

The State Department responded unfavorably, to which Wilbur Thomas responded with still another telegram which he trusted would become persuasive:

SA WASHINGTON DC NOV 26-23
FRIENDS SERVICE COMMITTEE ANS.
AMERICAN CITIZENSHIP JOHN HENRY TIMMERMANN MUST
BE ESTABLISHED BEFORE AUTHORIZATION GRANTED TO
ISSUE ANY DOCUMENT FOR TRAVEL PURPOSES
G L BRIST
CHIEF DIV PASSPORT CONTROL

G. L. Brist, Chief Division Passport Control,
Washington, D.C.

AMERICAN CONSUL FRANKFURT a/M HAS DOCUMENTARY
EVIDENCE HENRY TIMMERMANN'S AMERICAN CITIZENSHIP
STOP UNLESS CONSUL HAS AUTHORITY ISSUE PASSPORT HOPE
YOU CAN AUTHORIZE HIM ISSUE TEMPORARY PASSPORT IF
DOCUMENTARY PROOFS SUFFICIENT

Wilbur K. Thomas
Friends Service Committee
Philadelphia

On December 7, 1923, Thomas again attempted to persuade Arnold to help raise the necessary funds:

> Arnold Timmermann,
> Snyder, Nebr.
>
> Dear Friend:
>
> We have heard nothing from you in reply to our last tele-
> gram and letter which we sent you on Nov. 24th.
> We have not been able to do anything from [sic] them as yet.
> We feel that we must have more definite information from you
> before we can advance the money for Mr. Timmermann's
> expenses; also, should they come to New York, what would you
> plan to do with them? The $350. would be their expenses only
> to New York City. You must have extra money, of course, for
> their carfare to Nebraska.
> We shall be very glad to hear from you concerning this case.
> Please understand that we would be very glad to help you if we
> felt that we could do so, and perhaps if your next letter encloses
> a check for the sum of money or for only part of it and a note
> for the balance with satisfactory arrangements made for their
> transportation from New York to Nebraska, this Committee
> may be able to be of assistance to you.
> We have heard nothing as yet from Mr. Carl W. Weisbecker.
>
> Sincerely yours,
> Wilbur K. Thomas
> Executive Secretary

A bright light now shone on the protracted proceedings as the State Department on December 12, 1923 sent a cablegram to its American Consul in
Frankfurt: "Issue emergency registration certificate to John Henry Timmermann
including family, endorsed good for immediate return to United States or if
necessary obtain emergency passport."

F.T.F. Dumont immediately responded on December 15, 1923:

Subject: Return to the United States of John Henry Timmermann.

"I have the honor to acknowledge receipt of the Department's cablegram
of December 12, 1923, directing that an emergency registration certificate be

issued to John Henry Timmermann, including his family, endorsed 'good for immediate return to the United States.'

"Immediately upon the receipt of the Department's instruction, Mr. Timmermann was notified and appeared at this office. He was furnished with a certificate of registration endorsed 'good only for return trip to the United States on December 29, 1923' for which date Mr. Timmermann has secured passage on the S.S. George Washington.

"I have the honor to be, sir,

Your obedient servant,

F.T.F. Dumont, Consul General."

IT IS UNFORTUNATE that history does not record the details of the joyful celebrations which this tremendous news touched off in Frankfurt and Philadelphia. We can only imagine that Marion Fox, who greeted most good and bad news somewhat phlegmatically, must have jumped in the air at least half of her 60-inch height.

Back in Philadelphia, Wilbur Thomas must had had moments of sudden depression when a stern-faced and breathless messenger rushed in to thrust into his hand a forbidding-looking envelope with still another urgent message from the Department of State. Wilbur must have opened the envelope gingerly.

The message read:

December 18, 1923.

Friends Service Committee,
Philadelphia, Pennsylvania.

Under date of December 12, 1923, the Department, upon your request, incurred an expense for a telegram to the American Consul at Frankfurt in regard to John Henry Timmermann and family amounting to $4.06.

In settlement of the amount you will please forward check drawn payable to the order of the Disbursing Clerk, Department of State.

I am, Sir,
Your obedient servant,
For the Secretary of State: Wm. McNeir

The American Friends Service Committee, realizing that several hundred dollars would enable them to move forward on several worthy projects, made two more attempts to encourage John's father to help. Their letters follow:

December 20, 1923.

Arnold Tmmermann,
Snyder, Nebraska

Dear Friend:

We have heard from our worker in Frankfurt that John Timmermann and his wife are being allowed to remain there for two more months with the understanding that efforts will be made to bring them home from Germany. Thinking that this advance in time will give you further assistance towards making the remittance necessary for their expenses, I am therefore sending this information on to you.

We do not know how we can possibly advance the money ourselves for Timmermann and his wife. It would seem most uncertain that the boy himself could repay us within a few months, and as we explained in a previous letter, we would not know how to take care of them after they reached New York.

Sincerely yours,
Wilbur K. Thomas, Executive Secretary

December 27, 1923.

Arnold Timmermann,
Snyder, Nebraska.

Dear Friend:

We have just had a letter from our representative in Frankfurt in reference to your son, John Henry Timmermann. The United States Government has given him an emergency passport; and he and his wife and child are leaving Bremen for New York either on the 29th of this month or on the 30th. Our representative there has advanced him $270., which is the total amount of his expenses from Germany to New York City. We shall have to ask you to please send us the necessary money to cover his carfare and that of his wife and child from New York to Nebraska; and, of course, we shall expect you to refund us the $270. just as soon as you can do so. I am sure you must have some friends there who can advance you the money; and then let your son pay you back when he is working.

Please reply to this immediately; as we must hear from you in regard to the money.

Very sincerely yours,

Margaret E. James, Secretary

In his response, Arnold Timmermann asked Bob Young of George Stockmans' Refectory and Opera House to write on his behalf.

Kind Friends Society of Service:

Mr. and Mrs. Timmermann have brought your letter to me to read and wish me to write this reply to you.

They would like to see their son and wife and child in better circumstances and wished that they could arrange for stipulated amount to send them but claim that they are in such shape that they cannot, but hoped that if they could get to this country they might be able to raise money enough to get them back to Nebraska. These people at one time were well-to-do. This boy just before he left the States cost them some six thousand dollars that he fooled away in notes. They have another son who is married with some four children and wife who has been sick with bone out of the leg. Red Cross gave a hand toward that and think doctors are still unpaid. Looks like leg will have to be amputated.

These people had an affidavit to fill out from Washington last week showing the son to be American born. I think it was Mr. Blix out of General Counsel's office. Thank you for your good work and cooperation. Kindly address any news or good tidings to the Timmermanns.

/signed/ Bob Young for George Stockman for
Arnold and Anna Timmermann.

ON DECEMBER 26, John, Maria and Karl packed their belongings and drove to Bremen to prepare for the December 29 voyage to New York. Maria (who became "Mary" in the States) was still persona non grata to the Weisbecker family, so she did not even say good-bye to her folks. On the stormy voyage across the Atlantic on the S.S. *George Washington*, 18-month-old flaxen-haired Karl was an active favorite of the passengers and crew. A. W. Randall, the master (captain) took young Karl all over the ship, from the bridge to the engine room. His mother was deathly seasick for the entire voyage. She was so sick that she could not even breast-feed her second child after it was born. Their ship did not dock in New York until January 9, 1924.

Some years later, Mrs. Timmermann said to me:

"I was two years on the ocean."

Puzzled, I asked her: "How was that?"

"I left in 1923 and didn't get here until 1924," she smilingly recounted.

[See the entries in the ship's log as the appendix to this chapter.]

The new arrivals spent two days in New York at the Leo House in New York named after Pope Leo XIII who had responded to a group of German businessmen to contribute to a haven for German Catholic immigrants. On January 12, they took the train to West Point, Neb., after which they took a taxi to Snyder, in neighboring Dodge County, six miles southwest of West Point (cost=$1.50). Upon arrival, Mary's child (Anna) was born but lived only 36 hours because of malnutrition.

DEAR READER, WE INTERRUPT this program with a special announcement. Nobody ever repaid the American Friends Service Committee for advancing about $270 to bring the Timmermanns back to America. That $270 could have been used for many worthy projects by the AFSC over the years. How much is it worth to you to allow the Hero of the Rhine to help capture the bridge at Remagen? Get out your checkbook and thank the American Friends Service Committee at 1501 Cherry Street, Philadelphia, PA 19102-1479.

If this were a novel, I would cook up an emotional, Frank Capra–type sentimental ending, with Karl Timmermann on leave in London during World War II visiting a bedridden, aged Marion Fox. As Karl, followed by dozens of news-hawks, enters her bedroom to the tune of popping flashbulbs, Miss Fox's tired eyes glisten over as she reaches out to grasp Karl's hand. "My hero, my hero," she proclaims over and over.

The S.S. George Washington *of United States Lines, the ship that brought 18-month-old Karl and his mother and father from Bremen to New York, January 9, 1924.*
COURTESY OF MARINER'S MUSEUM, NEWPORT NEWS, VA.

Of course it didn't happen that way. In fact, there is no evidence that Karl's mother or father ever shared with Karl the full extent of Miss Fox's herculean efforts on behalf of the Timmermann family. Her nephew, Hubert Fox, in her biography entitled *Marion Fox: Quaker* makes no mention of the Timmermanns. To his dedicated aunt, this was just one of the thousands of unselfish and Christ-like actions which characterized her life.

It is within the scope of this book to speculate:

Surely, there must be a very special place in heaven for Marion C. Fox.

Ship's Log, Dec. 29, 1923–Jan. 9, 1924

I WAS ABLE TO OBTAIN a copy of the log of the S.S. *George Washington*, which reveals how stormy the crossing proved to be.

Proceeding from Bremen to Southampton and Cherbourg, the seas were relatively calm from December 29 to January 1st, but at 4:00 P.M. on that date the log reported: "Fresh westerly breeze, rough sea."

Subsequent entries explain why Karl's mother was so seasick, but Karl seemed to enjoy the pitch, the roll and the pounding:

January 1, 12:00 midnight: "Squally, fresh westerly breeze. Rough sea."

January 2, 4:00 P.M.: "Squally, strong southwesterly breeze. Rough sea."

January 2, 12:00 midnight: "South southwesterly gale. Rough sea."

January 3: "Day commences overcast. South southwesterly gale. Rough sea."

January 3, 2:30 P.M.: "Reduced speed 5 revolutions to eliminate pounding."

January 4, 4:00 A.M.: "Vessel taking heavy spray fore and aft throughout the watch."

January 4, 12:00 noon: "Overcast and squally. Heavy sea."

January 4, 8:00 P.M.: "Squally westerly gale. Heavy sea. Vessel taking heavy spray fore and aft."

January 4, 12:00 midnight: "Squally westerly gale. Heavy sea."

January 5, 4:00 A.M.: "Squally, west northwesterly gale. Heavy sea."

January 5, 7:25 A.M.: "Sea moderated. Resumed standard speed."

January 5, 12:00 noon: "Partly cloudy. West northwesterly gale. Rough sea. Vessel taking heavy spray fore and aft."

January 5, 12:00 midnight: "Overcast. West Northwesterly breeze. Moderate sea."

January 6, 4:00 A.M.: "Overcast and snow. Moderate northeasterly breeze. Moderate sea."

January 6, 4:00 P.M.: "Overcast and snow. Fresh westerly gale. Rough sea."

January 6, 7:24 P.M.: "Reduced speed 10 revolutions to eliminate pounding."

January 6, 9:10 P.M.: "Sea moderated. Resumed standard speed."

January 7, 4:00 A.M.: "Cloudy. Strong west northwesterly breeze. Rough sea. Vessel pitching easily and taking spray forward."

January 7, 8:00 A.M.: "Overcast. Strong westerly breeze. Rough sea."

January 7, 10:00 A.M.: "Herbert Klovague, German, found stowed away. Placed in brig for safekeeping."

One-year-old Karl, with his mother and father in Germany.

January 7, 4:00 P.M.: "Squally, moderate westerly gale. Rough sea. Vessel pitching easily and taking heavy spray forward."

January 7, 8:00 P.M.: "Overcast. Moderate westerly gale. Rough sea."

January 8: "Day commences partly cloudy, fresh northwest breeze. Rough sea."

January 8, 8:00 A.M.: "Cloudy. Moderate west northwesterly breeze. Moderate sea."

January 8, 6:00 P.M.: "Arrival Ambrose Light."

January 9, 9:23 A.M.: "Passed Statue Of Liberty."

January 9, 9:47 A.M.: "Passed Battery."

January 9, 10:00 A.M.: "Arrived off Pier 4, Hoboken and proceeded into berth assisted by tugs."

January 9, 10:45 A.M.: "Dismissed tugs. Gangways in place. Commenced discharging passengers and luggage."

On this voyage there were 196 U.S. Citizens (including the three Timmermanns), 1,285 Alien passengers and 608 Crew Members on board.

THREE

Growing Up in Nebraska

THE WINTER WIND WHISTLED and howled across the treeless Nebraska prairies as 18-month-old Karl and his mother and father took up residence in Snyder on January 14, 1924.

Mrs. Timmermann looked around her scantily furnished small room on the second floor of 205 Pine Street, thinking about the "palatial estate" her husband had gulled her into believing he owned in America. As for John, he was welcomed rather coldly by his father, Arnold, who still resented having to assume the mortgage notes which his son had left him to pay in 1919.

For seven months John was out of work and penniless. Under modern circumstances, his wife would have gone to a hospital or at least seen a doctor in her weakened condition as she was expecting her second child. But the Timmermanns could not afford it, and shortly after they arrived in Snyder the baby was born, suffering severely from malnutrition. She only lived 36 hours, barely enough to be named—Anna Maria.

Mrs. Timmermann was overcome with grief. She told me that while she was growing up in Germany that if she ever had a problem she would take a long walk in the peaceful woods which extended behind her home. She bemoaned the fact that Nebraska did not seem to have the kind of wooded retreat where she could repair to restore her soul. She also sorely missed the amenities of urban life—indoor plumbing, plenty of fresh water instead of using an outdoor pump, and enough electricity to run all labor-saving domestic chores—advantages which an isolated rural community could not provide. While growing up in Germany, she loved to swim and cycle, none

Karl's first home in Nebraska at 205 Pine Street, Snyder.

Karl at an early age in Snyder.

of which seemed possible in Snyder. She was also hungry for German food. On one occasion she wrote to her family in Frankfurt how much she missed "Blutwurst" and pleaded that they send her Blutwurst.

Above all, Mrs. Timmermann was terribly lonely for nearby friends with whom she could openly share her problems. I am grateful to Alex Meyer of Scribner, who researched and conversed with many of the Dodge and Cuming County residents who related details of the Timmermann experiences for a series of articles from January to March 1995, in the newspaper *The Dodge Criterion*. In the February 16, 1995, article is noted that "Dora Schneider Schroeder loved to socialize and being good at Mary's native German language became her good confidant. Walter Schroeder recalls making many trips with his mother Dora to visit with Mary at the Timmermann home." There was a difference between "high German" and "low German" which made it difficult to understand Mary in Snyder.

The famous water tower that signals the approach to Snyder, Nebraska.

After several months of unemployment, John finally got a job with Carl Schneider. "I was paid $50.00 a month," John told me. "I fed cattle on the Schneider farm and worked at his sawmill." Later, John also earned $50.00 a month on Fred Yarnak's farm. He also earned compensation as a member of a railroad section gang in West Point, and painting and cutting weeds at a cemetery. One of his associates reported: "John wasn't too easy to work with because he wanted to be the boss and order his fellow-workers around."

Since Mrs. Timmermann could no longer correspond with her father and mother, both of whom violently opposed her liaison with John, she decided after arriving in Snyder to write a series of letters to her English Quaker benefactor, Marion Fox. None of Mrs. Timmermann's letters to Miss Fox have survived, but her responses reveal something of the life of Karl and his parents in Snyder. The first two Marion Fox letters were written, as was Mrs. Timmermann's, in German. Text of the German letters are translated as follows into English, followed by the text of the subsequent letters.

[ENGLISH TRANSLATION FROM GERMAN]

The Bower-Wellington-Somerset-England

June 27, 1924

Dear Mrs. Timmermann:

In receipt of your letter, for which I heartily thank you.

I am very sorry to hear that Karlchen's little sister only lived 36 hours before she passed away, and also that Karlchen was ill with scarlet fever.

You yourself have suffered much in the recent months, and I hope that it goes tolerably well with you.

I am happy that your husband has work now. I know how hard he can work. He has helped us so very much.

No, surely I will not be angry with you, and will have much patience with you. You have survived hard times.

Next week I hope to return to Frankfurt. It is now getting better, but very expensive, and much unemployment. One can now buy milk.

Hopefully you are making progress and will write an English letter one of these days! In a few years Karlchen will be able to write an English letter.

With warm greetings to the entire family.

Yours,

Marion C. Fox

It was also very cold and wet here, but it is better now.

[Evidently Mrs. Timmermann had overlooked the above response, even though Miss Fox's letter in German was in her files. This explains the references in the following letters from Marion Fox, written originally in German but translated into English.]

Public Training InstituteFrankfurt/Main,
4 November 1924
(Volksbildungsheim)

Dear Mrs. Timmermann:

Today I received your letter of 22 October. I regret very much that you did not receive any reply from me and that this saddened you.

I do not have any knowledge as to who might have written to Mr. Georg Stockman in Philadelphia. It is not true that I was unaware of your whereabouts and the circumstances in which you find yourself. I have received several letters from you and there is no hurry as far as getting back my money is concerned. I am not mad at you at all and am firmly convinced of your honesty! I also know that up to the present time you have been unable to repay me.

I was happy to learn that little Karl is doing fine and has grown into a beautiful and nice boy and trust that the entire family is doing well.

Here in Germany, as well as in England, there is widespread unemployment and it is raining day and night. Yesterday there was a flood in the old city. I just came from the Fahrthor and the Leonhardthor (two medieval gates in the old city) and saw the flood myself—it is amazing and is supposed to be about one and a half meters high.

Karl's mother with Fritz, Mary (on her
mother's lap) and Karl (on right).

Karl (right) and his brother Fritz (center)
with their mother in Snyder.

Fortunately, we have had some sunshine today.

Wishing you a Merry Christmas, I remain,

your friend

SIGNED: Marion C. Fox

BETWEEN 1922 AND 1930, Mrs. Timmermann bore six children, four of whom survived. Fred ("Fritz") was born on April 5, 1925, and Mary ("Molly") on March 25, 1927, both in Snyder and both baptized at the St. Aloysius Catholic Church in Aloys, Nebraska. John Rudolph Timmermann ("Rudy") was born on October 1, 1930, after the family moved to West Point, Nebraska. Another son, Walter like Anna Maria, died early in life. Walter passed away from pneumonia.

While he was very young in Snyder, Karl came very close to being killed in a farm accident which has been documented by several different sources. According to Alex Meyer's article in *The Dodge Criterion* of February 16, 1995: Ruth Schneider Beck recalled that her father, Carl Schneider, owned a farm on which Karl's father worked. One day when Schneider was stacking hay the rope broke and nearly buried little Karl who along with his mother were close by. Carl Schneider got very excited and yelled to Mrs. Timmermann to "take that little boy home right away."

Snyder Elementary School where Karl attended first grade.

Karl entered the first grade in the elementary school across from his Pine Street residence. On December 12, 1927 John and Mary Timmermann along with their three children (Karl, Fred and Mary) moved first to Arlington, then Stanton, back to Snyder and six miles northeast to take up residence in the Cuming County Seat of West Point. The weekly newspaper, the *Snyder Banner* contained this entry in its school news section: "Monday was Carl (sic) Timmermann's last day at school. He is going to West Point. We all were sorry to see Carl go."

Asked why he decided to move to West Point, Henry (who assumed the first name "John" upon his arrival) explained that "I had trouble with my folks. They said I should always give money to them. (Probably to help repay the debts they had assumed on his mortgage notes when he left for the Army in 1919.) I had three kids to feed and clothe."

Perhaps a better reason for leaving Snyder to go to West Point was the fact that Karl's father had been working for Anton ("Tony") Meyer on his farm. When Tony got married he decided he did not need the services of his farmhand, forcibly persuading the Timmermanns to move. The family's first residence was in a house by the railroad track near the lumber company. They then moved into a house which was formerly an office for a local physician, Dr. I. L. Thompson, for whom John worked for awhile. Subsequently he worked for a bridge gang, and hauled lumber around Cuming County.

The story goes that when John's father Arnold first came to this country from Germany he dropped the second "N" on the Timmermann name. John is supposed to have restored the second "N" because he and a cousin also named John were getting each other's mail. In any case, John's family name was used interchangeably with one or two "N"s, but always with two after the family moved to West Point.

Karl did not start school at Guardian Angels Elementary School in West Point until the fall term of 1929, when he entered the second grade. The record is unclear as to where he finished the first grade—some sources contend he continued across from his Pine Street home at the Snyder Elementary School, while other sources indicate he attended elementary school in Crowell, Nebraska, close to Snyder, or at a Catholic school connected with St. Leo's Church in Snyder.

Not long after the Timmermanns moved to West Point in December 1927, John's conscience began to bother him about the stain on his military record. He had a few conversations with friends who had served in the military, and because of his inability to write he persuaded a retired Army Captain to pen a handwritten letter to the Adjutant General in Washington, D.C. dated July 2, 1928 as follows:

> Honorable Adjutant General, Washington, D.C.
> Sir: I enlisted in April 1918, and was drafted, enlisting in the infantry at Omaha, Nebraska in July of the same year. I took A.W.L. leave at Koblenz, Germany, going to Frankfurt A.M. returning after four years to the United States. The American Consul furnished me papers to return to the U.S.A., but I have no discharge papers and ask you to kindly advise me what to do in this case. In other words, I desire to give myself up in order to revive my full citizenship of the United States. Upon further correspondence I am glad to state a full review of how this happened and hope to get it all straightened out to satisfy everyone.
>   Very Respectfully,
>   John H. Timmermann
> P.S. I was born in Cuming County, Nebraska.

Of course, John was incorrect in contending that he had been "drafted" in 1918, since he actually enlisted in April 1919 after the war was over. Searching his own records, The Adjutant General discovered a memorandum from

Edmund W. Hill, Captain, Commanding the Replacement Depot, American Forces In Germany, dated November 23, 1919, transmitting the records of John H. Timmermann to the Adjutant General, along with his Service Record, his Notice of Discharge (Form 333), one descriptive list of deserters and three reports of desertion.

For the War Department, not known for excessive speed in acknowledging and answering communications which did not involve appropriations, some kind of record was broken when on July 13, 1928 The Adjutant General sent a personal letter to "Private John H. Timmermann, West Point, Nebraska." The letter stated peremptorily:

> With reference to your letter of July 2, 1928, you are directed to report without delay at the nearest military post for disposition of your case and to avoid apprehension.
>
> By Order of the Secretary of War
> F. L. Whitley
> Adjutant General.

> Fort Crook telegram 3:15 P.M.
> July 17, 1928 to Adjutant General,
> Washington, D.C.

> Pvt. John H. Timmermann Army Serial Number unknown an alleged deserter from Company K Second Battalion Overseas Replacement Depot American Forces in Germany Coblenz Germany since July in Nineteen Nineteen surrendered this station this date. Request disposition.
> C. A. Trott

John was immediately confined to the stockade at Fort Crook. A few days after his incarceration, Mrs. Timmermann swung into action. She paid a personal visit to Col. Trott at Fort Crook and argued vehemently and persuasively that she was not working and had three children to feed—Karl, Fritz and Mary and a fourth on the way (Walter, who subsequently died an early death from pneumonia). In essence she confronted Col. Trott with this challenge: "As long as you are requiring me to feed my kids through welfare, you are costing money to the taxpayers. And as long as you keep my husband here, that costs money too. Why don't you let him go so he can come home to take care of me and my children? What good is he ever going to be for the Army?"

John asked for an immediate trial and definite sentence, but Col. Trott disagreed. He sent a recommendation to The Adjutant General in Washington, dated July 28, 1928, as follows:

1. It is recommended that Private John H. Timmermann, 6411294, a deserter from the Replacement Depot, American Forces in Germany, Coblenz, Germany since September 12, 1919, be discharged from the Army, under the provisions of Paragraph 48 a, A.R. 615-360.

2. Private Timmermann admits his desertion, as endorsed by the enclosed affidavit, and trial by court-martial is deemed inadvisable for the reason that he is not physically fit for service.

It took several days of negotiation with The Adjutant General and completion of the paperwork before John was issued what is known as a "Blue" Discharge Certificate ("Other Than Honorable"), dated August 16, 1928.

By the time he was released to return to West Point, John had spent a total of 28 days in the Guard House (Stockade)—certainly far less than had the Army apprehended and court-martialed him in Germany. His discharge was not "Dishonorable" and also confirmed the fact that his desertion was not committed during combat. These facts were never fully recognized by Karl's detractors in West Point. Nevertheless, his father's war record inspired Karl with a strong determination to clear the family name by joining the Army. Actually, knowledge of his father's military record not only strengthened Karl's character but also underlines the courage he displayed at Remagen.

On April 20, 1931, Dr. I. L. Thompson, the family physician for the Timmermanns, penned the following letter:

War Department
Attn: Adjutant General

Dear Adjutant General:

Find enclosed a Discharge and letter of advice from Adjutant Dudley, concerning this man.

On behalf of John H. Timmermann I make the request for an exchange of discharges.

What is his status with respect to his receiving his bonus allowances?

This man is unable to write, has a family of 4 children. They are paying money on a little home and any money received on his bonus would surely be of help to them. Thanking you, I am

Yours Truly,
I. L. Thompson
(Their Family Physician)

O. H. Bridges
Major General
The Adjutant General

May 7, 1931

Dear Sir:

I have your letter of April 20, 1931, with enclosures herewith returned, relative to former Private John H. Timmermann.

The records show that this soldier was discharged at Fort Crook, Neb. On August 16, 1928, by reason of desertion admitted and physical unfitness for the service and that he was furnished a Discharge Certificate on Form No. 526, A.G.O., which is commonly called a Blue Discharge and is neither Honorable nor Dishonorable but one that sets forth the facts of discharge.

As the former soldier was discharged in accordance with Army Regulations, the War Department is without authority to alter or amend its records to show him discharged otherwise than as is now shown by the records, or to furnish him an Honorable Discharge.

As he did not enlist in the Army between the dates of April 6, 1917 and November 11, 1918 he is not entitled to Bonus on account of World War Service.

In 1955, I made still another attempt to get John Timmermann's Discharge changed to "Honorable." I appeared personally before the Army Review Board and also enlisted the support of Nebraska U.S. Senator Roman Hruska. I used the argument that Karl Timmermann had brought outstanding credit to the Army and the nation through his heroic feat of leading the capture of the first crossing of the Rhine at Remagen, Germany. I also elaborated on the argument of Karl's sister Mary that the Timmermanns were indeed a "Five-Star Family"—Karl, the winner of the Distinguished Service Cross; Fritz, in combat with the 158th Engineer Combat Battalion in the European Theater of Operations; Rudy, who served as a paratrooper in the Far East; Mary, who served in the WACS; and her first husband, Victor Roberts, who served in combat with General Patton's 3rd Army.

The officers serving on the Review Board listened to me, stony-faced, and asked no questions. Shortly after my appearance I received the following conclusion from the Army Review Board:

16 September 1955
AGRC-WA 201 Timmerman, John H.
6 411 284 (12 Sept 55)

Dr. Kenneth W. Hechler
1800 Eye Street, Northwest
Washington 6, D.C.

Dear Dr. Hechler:

In connection with John Timmerman's application, the Army Discharge Review Board, established under the authority of Section 301, Public Law 346, 78th Congress, approved 22 June 1944, has reviewed the type and nature of his separation from the service.

After a careful review of the entire case, the Secretary of the Army has directed that his request for a change in type or nature of separation be not favorably considered.

Sincerely yours,
David H. Arp
Colonel, AGC
Commanding

KARL WAS A PRECOCIOUS youngster. He began talking when only nine months old, and by the time he was only one year old in Germany he was talking in complete sentences, such as: "I want a piece of bread with jelly on it."

When Karl entered the second grade in 1929 at Guardian Angels Elementary School in West Point, his grades were as follows, starting September 2, 1929.

	First Term	Second Term
Deportment	85	80
Effort	85	80
Christian Doctrine	80	92
Bible History	76	89
Arithmetic	90	88
Reading	84	88
Spelling	90	97
Language and Grammar	80	88
Drawing or Art	80	87
Music	82	87
Physical Training	80	90

Karl's first acquaintance with his lifelong and closest friend occurred when he spotted first-grader Gerhard Willms in 1929.

According to Gerhard:

> Our parents had met earlier, but my first meeting with Karl was when we enrolled at school—Guardian Angels (GA).
>
> I'd re-enrolled in the first, he . . . in the second. (I had a learning problem the year before, in 1928, with English.) He stood just inside the doorway entrance, slightly slouched and grinning; a healthy towheaded boy in clean bibs and a denim shirt, who was 7 years old, 5½ months older than me. I was in my seat when he saw me. He walked over—smiled and said "Hey, du boob." (Hey, you boy.)
>
> I had very little contact with him in that first year. I remember having a struggle learning and getting help from other boys, who helped me with the language and taught me how to play their games. There were the White boys, my neighbors, who helped me to deal with other kids, who were giving me a bad time. I came in contact with Karl occasionally, when I came near his home, and ran into his two chums, the Morgan boys who were good scrappers. I tangled with the younger and licked him. Karl was impressed and took a liking to me. After my stint with the Morgans I earned my first respect from the kids in Karl's block.
>
> In June 1930, the first day of school vacation, Karl dropped by and said: "Let's go swimming." Barefooted, dressed in bibs, we rambled down to the river, a quarter mile from our house.
>
> The site we chose to swim was a covey shoreline, near a bend laid out in cottonwoods. The river's current flowed softly there so we spent the rest of the summer—swimming and browsing on a sandbar nearby. Our young bodies became a dark brown and our peers named us both River Rats, when we showed up down town. We swam in the nude—sat on the banks and retold the German fairy tales our parents had told us as little brats. Some were spooky.
>
> We enjoyed counting the snakes as they swam past down stream. We had a favorite cottonwood that we climbed, and pretended we were apes and monkeys.

IN THE COTTONWOOD GROVES by the Elkhorn River, Karl and Gerhard's background were quite a contrast from the German families who had settled there earlier. Other families were more oriented to the new customs and culture. Gerhard felt that "our two families had a heritage still fresh in folklore that other children had not received. The other people spoke the language. Karl mastered it in grade one. I flunked it. Today, I know the reason. I had a Polish mother, who placed religion over language. The Timmermanns placed more emphasis on the language."

Gerhard related: "Both our families had been reared in fairy tales, stories introduced by the Grimm Brothers—tales that paint a timeless world where fantasy, and sometimes brutal reality, converge. In the grove by the Elkhorn

Gerhard Willms, Karl's boyhood friend.

Karl and I created a little world of magic all our own, not in German folklore but in western movies and dime novels. In the grove, where we isolated ourselves from taunts of our tormenters we created a world we wanted to see and feel. Karl thrived in it and we envisioned it as our reality. It all came true."

When Karl was growing up, his mother was the glue which held the family together. There were loud and bitter arguments between his mother and father as to how to bring up the Timmermann children. Armed with his razor strap, Karl's father administered what he deemed were the necessary corporal punishments. As he put it "to make men out of Karl, Fritz and Rudy." He only conceded to Karl's mother the disciplining of Mary. Mrs. Timmermann on the contrary believed in babying and inspiring character in all their children. To Karl's father, the most serious transgression was to be late for the evening meal, always scheduled at 6:00 P.M. sharp.

There was no such thing as "sex education" either at home or school when Karl was growing up. One summer he befriended an older boy in the neighborhood named "Ham," who had gotten a new bike and sold his old one to Karl for $3.00. Ham had an older, rowdy friend named Denny and the

The Elkhorn River.

two of them briefed Karl on the mysteries of conception and procreation, including the appropriate gutter language. According to Gerhard Willms, Karl at the tender age of eight picked up more than he should have, which got him into trouble. In their cowboy fantasies, Gerhard and Karl had a girl named Nina who had been in a movie starring Bob Steele. Gerhard related that "our heroes seldom kissed the girls, but Karl and me had a drink (sarsaparilla) with Nina occasionally."

What got Karl into deep trouble was a buxom young lady whose home place he passed by and blurted out a forbidden epithet. She was standing in the yard with her mother one day, full-blown and inviting, Karl yelled: "I'd like to kiss and _____." He sang out an obscenity. The young lady, urged on by her mother, swiftly approached Karl, while Gerhard quickly advised "run, run." But it was too late. She grabbed Karl by the nape of the neck. By now both of her parents were shouting, "Whip him! Whip him good!!"

Wham, bam, wham bam, backhands and forehands until Karl just hung limp, and then she shook him and yelled: "There, you foul-mouthed German bastard, that will teach you to open your big mouth!"

The railroad tracks divided West Point between the "better people" and those like Karl and Gerhard who lived in the Third Ward, characterized by those on the west as "the wrong side of the tracks," sometimes labeled "the bloody Third Ward." Fist fights were common in the Third Ward. Karl himself was frequently challenged into a fight. He won some and he lost some.

He would fight at the drop of a hat. Although he walked over a mile from his spotless home at 635 South Oak Street up the hill across the tracks, across the main street and up another hill to Guardian Angels School, he always knew he was entering territory where he would be subjected to taunts and challenges by those who repeatedly addressed him as "Dutchman."

In retribution and defiance, the young residents of the Third Ward looked on those on the other side of the tracks as "invaders" if they tried to share in their private hunting ground down near the Elkhorn River. Karl even lumped the invaders together as "sissies" who shunned the manly art of fist-fighting.

According to the graphic account by Gerhard Willms, "We were playing in an alley with Duke Wagner when a sissy from uptown came by on a bike and gave us a razzberry. I grabbed the bike and Duke slapped him across the mouth. I slapped him. He started to howl, so Duke said 'let him go.' That wasn't enough for Karl. He reared back and hit this kid right in the nose and the blood flew. Duke and I were terrified. The sissy started screaming. Karl just walked away and went home as if nothing had happened. Duke's mother had to clean this kid up. It was another Timmermann mess.

"Twelve years ago, in September, 1991, I took in the County Fair in West Point. I was eating a hot dog, and a guy sitting next to me kept giving me mean looks. 'You know me?' I asked. 'Oh, yes,' he responded. 'It was you and that Timmermann that caused all the trouble. We couldn't play anywhere near that river. We had to look behind our backs when we went to school. You two were a nemesis.'

"It was the sissy, still bitching after half a century."

Scene in Neligh Park, West Point, one of Karl's playgrounds in the Third Ward.

During the depression years, when Prohibition was still on the statute books, the Timmermann family became bootleggers in order to raise enough money to feed their expanding family. They did not have a "moonshine still," but in the basement of their Oak Street home they manufactured and sold "home brew" to a steady stream of customers. When the New Deal repealed the 18th Amendment, John Timmermann signed up for the WPA. He worked on public bridges and for a time served as a guard at the Fair Grounds. According to Mrs. Mabel Pflueger, who headed the Relief Office in West Point, "John couldn't seem to hold a steady job, and so he was a very frequent visitor to our office. Pretty soon he became such a pest that our employees would hide when they saw him coming."

Gerhard Willms recalled with some detail how he and Karl were influenced by the cowboys who intrigued them on the silver screen.

"My first two summers romping with Karl just flew by. We lost ourselves in nature . . . playing cowboy drama, as we saw it on the screen. We took on actors' names, imagined ourselves in ten-gallon hats, pearl handled pistols and fancy boots. We made sketches of our garb on paper, created a dance hall girl called Nina. She lived in the thick plumb brush along a barbed wire fence that we called a hitching post, near a saloon. In the bar we always drank sarsaparilla until a third member joined our group who drank red eye.

"Naturally, cowboys who catch outlaws, herd cows, need ropes, guns, and horses. At the city dump, we found rope, wood to carve out hand guns, and long poles to straddle for horses . . . usually tied up by the hitch, by the saloon. Sometimes we'd stop by at the slaughter house, and use one of my dad's knives to carve . . . very unhandy. He'd send us to the hardware store to buy nails. Inside the store, while I bought nails, Karl would slip a couple of pocket knives in his pocket, when the clerk wasn't looking. We couldn't take this loot home; so, we took half gallon coffee cans, buried them in the plumb thicket with Nina, and called it our cache. All our heroes on the screen had one."

Talking pictures had not yet arrived when Karl first came to West Point in the 1920's. His first "talkie" heroes were cowboy stars like Ken Maynard, Buck Jones and Hoot Gibson and of course, Bob Steele. As related by Gerhard Willms, "most of us try to find real truth. Karl and I tried to forget truth and rediscover it in fiction."

To raise the pennies to take in a Saturday night movie, Karl and Gerhard would pick up junk, hunt pop bottles and beer bottles then sell them. Karl was too young to get any thrill out of Clark Gable drooling over his leading ladies, nor did he ever appreciate the likes of Jean Harlow or Myrna Loy. He loved

J.P. Lannan's Nebraskan Theater, where Karl and Gerhard Willms distributed hand bills.

films like "The Charge of the Light Brigade," "Captains Courageous" and "San Francisco", but was completely bored by "Those two upper-crust Sunday singers," Nelson Eddy and Jeanette MacDonald. Karl also loved swashbuckling villains like handsome Basil Rathbone and Douglas Fairbanks, Jr.

Karl's mother told me that "Before Karl entered high school he was very good with helping with the dishes, sweeping the floor, fetching water, pouring the slop for the pigs and things like that. I still remember the day after he graduated from the eighth grade and was about 14, after he had finished the dishes one night he threw the dish towel at Mary and said, 'This is your job from now on—I've graduated from it.' And then he stopped helping with the dishes and would only do the rough, physical work."

Both Karl and Gerhard got their chance to see movies four times a week instead of just on Saturday nights when they got a job distributing handbills for J.P. Lannan's Theater at a very modest salary. They also cleaned his auditorium and ballroom floor. Lannan, a hard-shelled conservative, lectured Karl sharply when his mother had the temerity to ask Lannan for a modest raise. Theater-owner Lannan berated him because his mother made the request, turning Karl down with the conclusion; "Always remember, it's not what you earn, but how much you save."

Karl was a great admirer of Will Rogers and his characteristic wink when Rogers smilingly described how he could rope flies with a string. On a hot day in August 1936, Karl and Gerhard were helping Shell Brothers put up a circus tent just to earn a free admission, when the tragic news arrived that Will Rogers and Wiley Post had been killed in a plane crash in Alaska. It was a shock to both youngsters and their circus venture turned into a requiem of silence.

Among other movies, Karl and Gerhard dramatized "Trader Horn" and the Tarzan movies. They turned their wooded area in the Third Ward into a jungle. They would climb a tree, build a little hutch, tie a rope to a limb and slide to the earth as an ape. Karl always played Tarzan.

They also closely absorbed developments in the comic strips. They loved Flash Gordon, Captain Easy and Tim Tyler. According to Gerhard, "Karl played Flash and I played Prince Berin. This called for fencing and by age nine we were quite skillful," reported Gerhard.

When Karl and his classmates studied Caesar and his Commentaries in Latin, this inspired more fantasies for Karl and Gerhard to play out. Karl of course became Caesar and this resulted in Gerhard acting the role of the Gallic rebel Vercingetorix—despite Karl's reluctance to realize or condone the eventual execution of Vercingetorix by Caesar. Gerhard would ride up on his "stick horse," throw a spear between Karl's legs as he was sitting on a log and shout "Hail, Caesar, I surrender and proudly await my fate!" Karl would laugh, and fall off the log in a frenzy of laughter.

Karl's boyhood was not monopolized by serious re-enactments, pleasurable though they proved to be. He spent most of his spare time down around the Elkhorn River, which dominated the landscape of the Third Ward. Fed far to the Northwest by the Powder River in Montana, when the Elkhorn

Pictured is the Guardian Angels School eighth grade class in 1936. The eighth graders made their solemn Holy Communion in the spring before they finished eighth grade. Karl is on far left, second row.

reached West Point it was a miraculous magnet for Karl in all types of weather. During the winter it was an attractive place to skate. As the temperature plunged, vehicles could even drive across the frozen Elkhorn from shore to shore. Some of their winter recreation included sledding from the top of Selection Hill across the tracks and ice skating in the park. They carved their initials on the water fountain in the park.

But summertime was the biggest attraction for skinny-dipping, Karl and his friends to swim, sun themselves and think up all types of hi-jinks in and out of the occasionally muddy stream. Karl loved to walk the narrow railing and wave at cars crossing the bridge along Highway 22. He would artfully stand on his head or swing from an overhanging limb of a cottonwood tree before plunging from on high into the swirling waters below.

The Elkhorn River surrounded Gerhard's home on three sides because when it reached West Point it took a sharp turn to the North, then formed a bow, doubling back on itself as it meandered southward toward the Platte River, long before the bow was straightened out in 1949 and 1950.

Gerhard relates that "Karl and I used to hunt rabbits, squirrels, pheasants and catch catfish, bullheads, carp and frogs, shoot sparrows, pigeons and if nothing else shoot the neighbors' tame ducks. We were no angels, you know." He added that "we feasted on wild plums, mulberries and gooseberries for dessert." Karl bought a .22 caliber, single shot gun which later enabled him to qualify as an expert rifleman in World War II.

During the terrible drought of 1937, they watched the Elkhorn form a large sandbar in the center as the river narrowed to a trickle. They waded out to the middle of the river and started a sand fight.

The Timmermann residence at 635 South Oak Street, West Point.

The Third Ward kids pretty much stuck together as a clan. During the summer evenings, they would go to band concerts and watch the people dance to the music. In 1933 the entire clan hiked eight miles to the national corn husking contest near West Point. According to Gerhard Willms, "we saw real tribes of Indians and Barney Oldfield's racing car. At Halloween we upset outhouses; our record was 22 in one evening. Deke Welding, who later became County Sheriff, joined us when we fished, but the lake that had the best bullheads was off limits. It was known as Hunke's Hole. We had to sneak into the lake, toss in the lines, catch a couple fish and then be prepared to run, because Mr. Hunke would always see us, and take after us with his buggy whip. Karl, Deke and me slipped in one afternoon and fished. The fish were biting well. We didn't see Hunke anywhere, and assumed he'd gone to town.

"Suddenly! Out of the brush, over the bank, he loomed over us—shouting: 'Aha, now I've got you!' And flaring his horsewhip.

"We just ran. Karl and me straight along the shoreline for home. Deke cut to the left, just out of reach of Hunke and sprinted into the high weeds and hid. He told me later that Hunke circled the high weeds for an hour trying to find him. Finally, he just bolted out and ran home. We lost our fishing poles and about 12 fat bullheads."

Gerhard recalls: "In 1936 our families had medical bills with Dr. Thompson; the doctor's family had a farm where Karl and I were sent to work off the bills. Karl thought he'd get a chance to ride horses, but all we did was pitch hay and shovel corn. The food wasn't too tasty, either."

Karl had no compunctions about climbing a tree without a stitch of clothes on, and waving at female golfers starting at hole one on the nearby golf course. He regarded it as a good day if he could get one of the golfing ladies to smile and wave back.

A nearby watermelon patch was always a favorite spot to raid when the melons ripened.

For some reason, Karl and Gerhard got a kick out of stealing pigeons, especially the pure white ones which neighbors collected and usually penned up behind their houses. Gerhard would knock on the front door, asking for spare pigeons, and while he was getting a negative response Karl would be around at the back "liberating" several choice pigeons.

Karl trained a dog whom he called "Pete." He was very proud that Pete, a Rat Terrier, was what he termed a "one-man dog." Karl was devastated when Pete was run over by a neighbor's car. Karl buried Pete personally and even fashioned a stone over his grave, clearly labeled "Pete."

One hot day in June 1930, just after Karl turned eight, he had jaunted up river with Gerhard to collect some long, stiff willow branches to shape into spears by sharpening the tips. Suddenly they saw some scrawny-looking horses, followed by two wagons with swarthy-skinned and mean-looking people dressed in gaudy colors. They talked a strange language, but one of them spoke a little English and offered to trade some shiny stones to Karl for his pocket knife. Karl declined, despite the promise that the stones were "very valuable and had magic in them."

The County Sheriff, Art Shelton showed up. He told the Third Ward parents: "We don't want them here too long. They steal like hell, ya know. Besides it's a city ordinance. They can't camp inside the city limits." They were Gypsies.

Karl was disappointed because he wanted to ride one of their ponies. The next day the Gypsies were gone, but they were soon rediscovered across the river in a private park owned by Anton Pesota and named "Coney Island." Pesota insisted it was off limits from the city ordinance. Gerhard reported: "Karl and I got to ride those horses through the rest of June, but we paid a little price. We had to give the Gypsy boys our pocket knives, two good sling shots and we had to take the boys swimming three days a week. After two days on those bony flea-bags, we had sore rear ends."

The Third Ward where Karl grew up was always known as the "Bloody Third Ward" and with good reason. Arguments among Karl and local youngsters were always resolved or resulted in fisticuffs with both parties bloodied.

In 1933, an even bloodier incident added to the reputation of the Third Ward. Ed Forks, a man of 45, ruddy and strong, was having family problems which he would air in detail when he had a few drinks. Karl and other young observers could see at firsthand why Ed Forks was upset. Whenever Karl and some of his Third Ward friends would walk to school up the hill to Guardian Angels, they would pass the homes of Ed Forks and Charlie Moulton who lived on a corner block across the alley from each other. They would frequently see Charlie and Mrs. Forks sitting on the grass together, engaged in obviously very friendly conversation. Many others in the neighborhood noticed it too, and pretty soon this obvious display of affection became the central subject for gossip all over town.

One night Ed Forks visited one of Karl's neighbors and consumed just enough extra whiskey to embolden him to put an end to Charlie Moulton's philandering. He went home, placed two shells in his 12-gauge, double-barreled shotgun and sat by the kitchen door until Charlie emerged. Ed stepped out his doorway and yelled: "Now, you son of a bitch," then aimed and gave Charlie both barrels.

Ed methodically set the gun down in the doorway and went to the Court House to give himself up. He was sentenced to life and died 20 years later in the Lincoln Penitentiary.

Long after the deaths of both Charles Moulton, Sr. and Karl Timmermann, it was Charles Moulton, Jr. who gave the dedication address to name Timmerman Field on Memorial Day 1965, despite the fact that the name on the scoreboard was misspelled with only one "N." The younger Moulton in 1965 was serving as post commander of the Veterans of Foreign Wars.

But in the summer of 1935 Karl at the age of 13 had a run-in with Bob Moulton, another of the murdered Moulton sons. Both Bob and a 20-year-old companion were considerably older than Karl and Gerhard. Bob had a reputation as a "burly bully" and it soon became apparent he was itching to display his wares. He acted while Karl and Gerhard were splashing around in the river.

On the river bank, Moulton picked up Karl's shoe and yelled defiantly: "Timmermann, I'm going to piss in your shoe." According to Gerhard, "He did, and then threw the shoe full of urine into the river along with all our clothes. While we frantically flopped through the water recovering our clothes, he stood on the bank, naked, and hee-hawed with glee."

Fortunately, a friend of Karl and Gerhard, Andy Wenge, was present and became enraged at Moulton. Andy picked up a glob of wet sand and threw it hard at Moulton's wet bottom, stinging him smartly. Then they sprung at each other. Although Andy was smaller, he later became a Golden Gloves champion and quickly drew blood with a tattoo of fast right and left cross punches.

Although Gerhard was Karl's closest friend, they did have differences from time to time, as Gerhard explained: "It was late fall. Karl and I were browsing around in the willow brush, near the riverbank. Old Hans flowed by in his skiff —pushing it up stream with a long pole. He was a river man who fished with traps and set lines. Once we had tampered with them and Hans really chewed us out. 'If you don't stop it,' he warned, 'I'll cut your ears off.'

"We avoided him after that, but he always kept a peering eye on us when he floated by. Surveying him as he rowed on—Karl said: 'Let's build a raft, so we can move on the river, like Hans.'

"'How about logs?' I argued. 'There's nothing here but willows!'

"'I know where there's one log,' he offered. 'It's a foot thick and six feet long. We can use two willow poles, six feet, six diameter for the other pontoon.'

"'And flooring?' I asked.

"'There's plenty of old lumber at the city dump,' he assured me.

"To me, the plan of construction of the raft appeared slightly undersized and crude, but Karl went right into action with zeal and determination.

"For two rainy weekends we sawed and hammered, and it didn't take old nosy —Hans—long to row up—to check out our progress.

"'What you kids doing?' he asked.

"Karl leaned back on his axe and yelled, 'Building a raft, Hans!' Hans stepped from his boat and studied our project for a long moment. I saw a sour, deep frown on his whiskered, leathery face. He stepped back in his boat, turned and said: 'Well, I don't think you'll float that raft, boys,' and shoved off downstream chuckling, 'Ha — ha — ha.'

"I had the feeling . . . Hans was right; he was a real river man, but I knew Karl was determined to float his project. 'I plan to launch!' he shouted.

"We had one weekend left to finish; all we had left was to nail down some planking. I'd concluded Hans was right, so I decided to let him finish himself. He was disappointed, and talked my brother Frank into helping him drag it to the riverbank, where they launched the craft. Yes, Hans was there, drifting by, as a river vulture lurking, as an overshadow of doom to Karl's venture. They shoved the raft in some deep water and the whole structure sank to the bottom. Karl stared at it going down while Hans rowed off gloating.

"They were both at my place, after the sinking, and Karl was not too disappointed. 'We did launch,' he kept reminding me. The next day he mentioned it in class, even to his teacher, who praised his effort. Agitation from his classmates didn't faze him; he'd had his adventure. In his early years Karl had notions of plunging ahead and then dealing with the consequences. He would climb bridges and get a personal thrill out of the height. All I could do was look on in awe, or try to slow him down."

Karl was a compulsive prankster. Even before he was two years old over in Germany, he would delight in ringing the doorbells of neighbors in his apartment house and run for cover before they could come to the door. When he got older, he had two favorite tricks with hats. He would slip into a pool hall where some old fogey was playing rummy. From behind he would pull the guy's hat down over his eyes, and the guy would cuss a blue streak. In church when big shots in the pew in front of him would leave their expensive hats beside them, Karl would wait until they stood up for the Gospel reading and slide their hats over so they were flattened when the parishioners sat down.

In the classroom, Karl was a master at launching paper airplanes and could always sense the strategic moment to send spit-balls or other missiles propelled by rubber bands. He also realized that one of his teachers lacked a sense of smell, which encouraged use of matches to send up smoke signals.

In 1955, I interviewed Father Bosheck, the most popular cleric in West Point, who had a special liking for Karl. When I mentioned his name, Father Bosheck's grizzled features broke into a wide smile.

"He was a real fireplug," he commenced. "He was the quickest student to absorb everything in the classroom, even though he probably studied less than any of his fellow students. He became fascinated with Latin primarily because of Julius Caesar's Commentaries, which he devoured. He was addicted to military developments and loved to study the history of the exploits of Alexander

Guardian Angels High School in West Point.

Some of Karl's teachers at Guardian Angels High School.

The Great. His heroes were military leaders, not politicians."

One day Karl rushed into Father Bosheck's office, seething with anger. With his fists clenched, Karl made a challenge: "The next time any of these blowhards calls me 'Dutchman,' so help me, I'm going to knock his damn block off. I mean it, Father."

The priest asked Karl to sit down. After 30 seconds he put his arm on Karl's shoulder and said "Look, Karl, I was born in Germany like yourself and your mother. I was born in München-Gladbach. As a matter of fact, I was all of 33 years old when I came to this country. You know what I did when people tried a put-down on me for my German birth, I just smiled. Pretty soon they got no satisfaction out of me and treated me like all Americans want to be treated.

"I'll make a deal with you, Karl. At the next assembly I'll tell all the students that it's against school rules to engage in any name-calling. Now your part of the deal is this: Instead of getting upset if anybody calls you names, just smile. The only reason they call you names is they get a reaction which makes them want to repeat. Smile and that takes away their reason.

"Now, will you shake hands with me on that deal?"

Karl shook hands, with a look of skepticism on his face. But he told Father Bosheck several weeks later that it worked.

Father Bosheck arranged for Karl to be appointed Assistant Janitor during his senior year at Guardian Angels High School, enabling him to earn extra money cleaning the classrooms and doing other odd jobs around the school.

Karl played on the second team in basketball and never earned a letter. He was tall enough, but tended to shoot instead of passing. Karl personally felt he was being discriminated against because Coach Schmitt chose one of his classmates for the first team, according to Karl's belief, because that student came from a wealthy West Point family which paid his tuition whereas Karl and his family all attended tuition-free because of their low income.

Karl decided that he wanted to play football his senior year. Because Guardian Angels had no football team, Karl decided to transfer to West Point High School where the coach encouraged him to try out. He had already had a taste of scrub football in pick-up games between Third Ward youngsters and those on the east side of the railroad tracks across town. Karl never played in the backfield, but loved the smack-mouth scrimmages along the line. The West Point High School quarterback, Jim Ferguson, had actually picked out a football uniform for Karl.

When Father Bosheck heard of Karl's plans, he called him in and used his supreme persuasive powers to convince Karl that after all these years of tuition-free attendance he should stay with his fellow students in the Guardian Angels graduating class. Karl reluctantly consented.

The discipline at Guardian Angels was nothing like the movies depicting "Fast Times at Ridgemont High."

Gerhard Willms recalls: "Sister Noel was Irish to the core, and what didn't fit in with the prayer book was taken care of with the yardstick. (I'd heard — sometimes with a choir rope.) The Principal stood just inside the entrance, when we came to class at 8:40 AM: 'SINGLE FILE' she shouted, and she meant single file. Any wavering was corrected with a whack on the ear with the prayer book, or a head shaking that made us so dizzy, we wavered—looking for the classroom; then we were marked tardy."

On one occasion in sodality meeting when one of Karl's classmates arose to speak, Karl stealthily placed a tack on his seat. When his classmate sat on the tack, he suddenly was propelled upward as though powered by many jets.

While Karl was picking up extra pocket change by selling popcorn at the Cuming County Fair and mixing poison to kill grasshoppers, his mother was having a difficult time both physically and mentally. Not long after Karl's youngest brother Rudy was born in 1930, Mrs. Timmermann took a back-breaking, strenuous job as a cook and waitress at the Golden Rod Café on Main Street. Karl and his younger brother Fritz had a red wagon in which they carried garbage and slop from the Golden Rod to feed the Timmermann hogs and chickens and if nothing else John Timmermann was adept at using his axe to butcher hogs to supplement the Timmermann diet. On one occasion

Main Street, West Point, 1955. The Golden Rod Café is located on the left side of the street, just this side of the Rivola Theater.

when Fritz was helping his father split firewood, he failed to withdraw his hand soon enough and John's axe lopped off the ends of Fritz's two fingers. It was a cold day and Fritz didn't even feel the accident until he entered the house and blood was splattered on the ceiling. Fortunately, the fingers were sewn up before Fritz lost too much blood.

Every morning Mrs. Timmermann would walk from her home at 635 South Oak Street in the Third Ward more than a mile uphill to reach her job at 11:00 A.M., a job which would not end until long after midnight. She dreaded the reception she always got when she crossed the railroad tracks and a few town bums would hurl insults at her because of her "Kraut" ancestry. After 1933, when the Nazis seized power, this got much worse when she was greeted by the taunting shout: "Heil Hitler."

At the time, neither Mrs. Timmermann nor her taunters knew that the Weisbecker family were all courageous critics of the Nazi regime. One of her brothers, Karl Weisbecker (who had been baby Karl's godfather in 1922), was so outspokenly anti-Hitler that the Gestapo arrested him one day as he was riding to work on a street car. The next day on May 28, 1941 his body was found floating in the river. Another of Mrs. Timmermann's brothers, Walter Weisbecker, an equally outspoken anti-Hitler activist, was arrested and sent to the infamous Dachau concentration camp in 1941. He miraculously survived the horror of the camp until liberated in 1945 to fight the Russians. But a further tragedy occurred after he returned home as he was working for an organization for the victims of Nazi-ism. An Austrian Major applied for restitution and after Walter denied his request Walter gave him back his papers, for which his superiors roundly criticized Walter. Disturbed, Walter went to the Major's home and forcibly seized the papers, against which the Major brought suit against Walter. Walter hanged himself, leaving a note that he could stand imprisonment for his political beliefs, but not being labeled as a common criminal.

The Timmermann family roundly criticized their family doctor, I. L. Thompson, for the medications he was giving Mrs. Timmermann. John Timmermann told me in a recorded interview that he felt the medications were designed to prevent his wife from having any more children. "Dr. Thompson's medicine made my wife crazy," John contended. "It's none of his business whether my wife has kids."

I spent a great deal of time with Dr. Thompson, but of course do not have the medical knowledge to analyze his prescriptions. But John's most violent criticisms of his wife centered around the amount of money she was sending to her family in Germany. Dr. Thompson as part of his treatment of Mrs. Timmermann had opened an active correspondence with her family. He showed me a letter dated January 15, 1945 in which Mrs. Timmermann's father, Andreas Weisbecker, had written "you will probably have gathered from the newspapers what conditions prevail in Germany today. Injustice is rampant. Whoever has money can live, but a person who has none can die of starvation, since he cannot buy anything on the black market where everything is available. If it were not for my dear and good daughter Mary I would have starved to death long ago. She is very good to me."

The Golden Rod Café was owned and operated by a no-nonsense, pudgy, bald-headed proprietor named Bill Schäfer who was far from lenient in his insistence that Mrs. Timmermann observe strict hours and not rest on the job. To supplement her income, she took in washing and spent considerable time ironing. Karl's little red wagon is what he used to pick up and deliver the laundry. His sister Mary marveled at the endless hours her mother spent on these two jobs. "When the work piled up, she just went with less sleep. I doubt whether she ever slept more than three hours a night," Mary recalled.

The pressures of long work days soon began to take a toll on Mrs. Timmermann. She suffered two nervous breakdowns and actually tried to commit suicide on two occasions, according to a recorded interview with her husband, confirmed by Dr. Thompson. This was the cause of more taunting of Karl: "your mother's crazy, your mother's crazy."

Mrs. Timmermann was truly a heroic woman. Overcoming many difficulties, she succeeded in developing and inspiring character among her children. During his Junior year at Guardian Angels, Karl delivered a five minute talk on "character" in his public speaking class. Holding his head high, with his jaw jutting out, hands behind his back, Karl was very eloquent. He had memorized his talk, and effectively elaborated on his theory that "character is power."

Karl matured greatly in his last two high school years. He developed a taste for good literature, like Charles Dickens' "A Tale of Two Cities." In additions to his military heroes, Karl gained inspiration from Sydney Carton. Among other authors, he rated Zane Grey highly because Grey represented the western spirit. Richard Decker, the editor of the senior newspaper carried a popular column written by Karl and entitled "A Wild West Serial."

Gerhard Willms, Karl's closest friend over the years, gives the following candid appraisal of Karl's strong and weak points: "He had brash ways at times. He was good-hearted and very honest, but he liked to brag about himself. He wasn't a quiet type of fellow. I even told him myself he shouldn't brag so much. However, he would just laugh and say 'why not? I give myself a pat on the back when I brag.' Then he would laugh and walk off in his happy-go-lucky way. He liked his friends to be loyal. He liked people to be honorable and he respected truth.

"He took no interest in learning a trade, or farm work. For those of us who grew up with him in high school, few would question his desire to lead. Even as a high school senior, Karl craved importance. In class, he would deliberately attract attention.

"Karl was a proud boy and he usually had an insult in return for every one he got. He was very temperamental and couldn't take too much ribbing.

"He took in dances, and had a girl friend or two. He was a normal, good looking kid, big and husky—a prankster with a gleam of mischief in his eye.

"Karl liked to play pranks, then he would laugh. He would tell a joke and then be the first one to laugh at it. Sometimes he talked when he should have listened."

On Sunday, May 26, 1940, Karl was scheduled to attend his high school graduation ceremony at St. Mary's Church. The motto of the class of 1940 was "Either find a way or make one." In the graduating class of 23 students, Karl's grade average ranked him 18th. His marks in Latin and History were above average, but he did get marked down for playing hooky, especially when the warm days of late spring beckoned him to join Gerhard Willms on the Elkhorn River.

Bursting with maternal pride, Karl's mother got the night off from her job at the Golden Rod Café to join him as they walked more than a mile up the hill and across the railroad tracks to Karl's graduation at St. Mary's Church.

THE WEST POINT REPUBLICAN, THURSDAY, MAY 30, 1940

GUARDIAN ANGEL SENIORS graduate at St. Mary's church Sunday night

Guardian Angel high school seniors who graduated Sunday night at St. Mary's church are, left to right: Back row, Henry Stalp, Nicholas Wackel, Eugene Uhing, Florentius Parker, Matthias Hugo, Harold Cyrier, Keith Abbott; middle row, Leona Reeson, Richard Decker, Raymond Stratman, Francis Mahlberg, Karl Timmerman, Joseph Knobbe, Norman Boyle, Dorothy Studeny; front row, Marcella Knievel, Bernice Decker, Dorothy Rochford, Helen Feichtinger, Ruth Lueckenhoff, Imelda Kaup, Margaret Fork, Helen Meister.   —Bethscheider Photo

Mrs. Timmermann told me her vivid recollection of that balmy night: "I told Karl that I was proud of him for sticking to it and finishing high school. I told him never to back out on anything in life, and to keep after it. That evening Father Bosheck delivered a beautiful commencement address, the theme of which was 'stick to your guns. Never back out on anything you start. What others can do, you can do too. Don't just lag behind and follow other people, but take the lead. Be loyal to your school and country.' I still remember Karl turning around and smiling at me while Father Bosheck was talking. Afterward he said to me: 'Ma, Father Bosheck told us exactly what you were telling me on the way up to the school.' I smiled and said I couldn't say it anything like Father Bosheck.

"Karl walked up for his diploma looking just like a soldier. He was straight as an arrow. All the others had slumped shoulders or swaggered up self-consciously."

FOUR

"Yer in the Army Now"

K<small>EITH</small> A<small>BBOTT</small>, one of Karl's classmates, noticed something early on about Karl. Whereas the doodles of most students were pointless and meaningless scribblings, Karl was drawing clear images of tanks, artillery pieces and airplanes.

An unlikely friendship developed between these dissimilar characters. Keith's father, a highly respected leader in West Point, had developed a prosperous business as the proprietor of the "West Point Filling Station" on South Main Street. The Abbott Family lived in a large and comfortable house among the "better" people of West Point, far from the roughnecks of the "Bloody Third Ward." Karl respected Keith not only because the latter usually was tapped for leading roles in the school plays or musicals like "Oklahoma," but perhaps more important Keith never engaged in the humiliating put-downs which many students directed at Karl to salve their own personal egos. Later, it was Keith whom Karl asked to be his best man when Karl prepared to get married.

There is no question that Karl's first interest in the military was sparked by his fascination with the Latin Commentaries of Julius Caesar and the exploits of Alexander The Great. It may be too much of a stretch to link Karl's intense interest in Caesar's building of a bridge over the Rhine near Remagen with the later heroic leadership of Karl at the Ludendorff Bridge. Nevertheless, it is evident that Karl became addicted to the military by his exposure to his heroes through studying Latin and History.

On July 6, 1940, Karl was officially inducted into the Army at Fort Crook, Nebraska.

Despite the military triumphs of Hitler's blitzkriegs, Karl developed an early aversion—peculiarly enough because of his German mother—to all dictatorships. Karl took a great interest in the early phases of the Spanish Civil War, which Hitler and Mussolini were using as a testing ground for their weapons of aggression. Conventional wisdom among the faculty at Guardian Angels was to equate the Catholic Franco Government as the "Good Guys" while denouncing those Communist Loyalists who were bombing Catholic churches. Karl had a more maturely independent judgement, viewing the conflict not in religious terms but as a prelude to the inevitable shooting war which would eventually draw Americans into combat.

How much was Karl's attraction to the military the result of his reaction to his father's military record?

The answer to this question involves an examination of human and family psychology. Karl really loved and respected his mother. The string of "Dear Ma" letters was not only a recognition that his father could neither read nor write, but also a demonstration that he realized his father's sense of values did not encompass respect for the military.

There also may have been a lingering pain from the frequently unnecessary welts from the razor strap. Surely Karl could distinguish between the failure of his native-born father to take advantage of the opportunities for a good education versus the determined efforts of his German-born mother to achieve a modicum of self-education. Obviously, Karl's intense desire to clear the family name played a major role in his determination to make good in the military.

During high school, Karl heard about the Citizens Military Training Corps at Fort Crook, and he could hardly wait until he had a chance to join up. On his 17th birthday, Karl hitchhiked to Omaha to join the CMTC. It was a rewarding decision.

For thirty days of intense training, Karl learned the fundamentals of military life and discipline. The trainees lived in tents, ate healthy meals, served as K.P.'s, engaged in physical toughening (body building), learned about the organization of the Army, had endless close-order drills, learned the basics of leadership, spent ten days on the firing range with Army rifles, wore uniforms, learned about Army regulations and court martials, and got a thorough taste of military life from A to Z.

When Karl returned after the summer of 1939, he was more determined than ever to join the Army. In September of 1939, Hitler invaded Poland. It became more evident than ever to Karl that it would not be long before America would be drawn into the war in Europe.

Now all he had to do was to wait for his 18th birthday, which occurred less than a month after his 1940 graduation from Guardian Angels High School. The draft law was still several months in the future when Karl decided to enlist. The record is not clear, but Karl was probably the first man in West Point to enlist. His date of enlistment was July 6, 1940.

Basic training was a breeze for Karl. His boyhood in West Point had conditioned him physically and he had a big head start over recruits as the result of his preliminary military training in the summer of 1939 in the CMTC.

Shooting rats at the smelly city dump had improved Karl's marksmanship and he qualified as an expert rifleman. Hiking 25 miles with a full field pack was easy. Three square meals a day were healthy, and Karl never had to worry about his father's razor strap. Negotiating the obstacle course and under machine gun fire crawling through the mud under barbed wire even seemed simple. Karl had been looking forward to being a full-fledged Army man, and he even took the rigorous discipline in stride.

Out of his meager pay of $21.00 per month, Karl sent $5.00 home every month and tried to keep his mother informed of his location and activities. He also sent money home for his 10-year-old brother Rudy to buy a bicycle.

September 1, 1940, as a member of Company D, 17th Infantry, Karl wrote from Little Falls, Minnesota.

> Dear Ma:
>
> How is everything? I feel fine. I don't know when we will leave Minnesota. I am sending you $5.00, and don't spend it, put it in the bank.
>
> After I had all my debts paid I had $14.35, and now I got $9.35 left. Maybe in October we will get $30.00 a month.
>
> Can Rudy ride his bike already? What color is it? I hope he takes care of it and not wreck it.

Oct. 2, 1940
Co. "D" 17th Inf.
Fort Ord, Calif.

Dear Ma,

Happy birthday! How's everything at home? The payroll is late this month; we won't get paid until next week.

Fort Ord is about five miles from Salinas and nine from Monterey. It is four miles from the ocean. On the way out here, we stopped at North Platte the first night; the second night at Cheyenne, Wyoming; the third night at Green River, Wyoming; the fourth night, Salt Lake City, Utah. We stayed at Fort Douglas, Salt Lake City over Sunday. I climbed mountains all that day. Monday morning we pulled out again and we stopped at Elko, Nevada that night; the next night at Reno, Nevada. About six o'clock the next morning we crossed the California state line. Camp was at San Jose, California that night. Eleven o'clock the next morning we drove into nine every nite. So I get enough sleep. I eat like a bear. Next time you see me I'll be about thirty pounds bigger.

Well, good luck.

Your Son, Karl

Fort Ord.

If anyone in West Point wants my address just give it to them.

All we do now is have machine gun drill every day and take hikes. So-long

Your Son, Karl

On October 15, 1940, Karl wrote:

Dear Ma:

All this week we fire at Germans as targets. Saturday we go to King City, California and have a parade.

Does Pa still say anything about me being in the Army?

Do the people in West Point say anything?

The next letter Karl wrote home follows:

Nov. 1 1940
Co. "D" 17th Inf.
Fort Ord
Monterey, Calif.

Dear Ma,

I am fine and I hope you are alright too. Tomorrow we go on a 15 mile hike. Today, we had machine gun drill in the morning and played base-ball in the afternoon.

To-day, I bought two pair of wool underwear. To-morrow night I'll go to town and have 3 pictures taken (.75) a piece. One for each Pa, Molly and Fritz.

If I had $30.00 I'd come home for Christmas; but I won't come home. No-body will miss me anyway.

Well, say hello to the rest of the family for me.

Auf Wiedersehen,

Deiner Sohn, Karl

Despite his threat not to come home for Christmas 1940, Karl received a furlough from December 21 to January 1, 1941. On January 24, 1941 he received the welcome news that he had received a promotion to Private First Class, and could wear a single stripe on his uniform.

Karl promoted to Private, First Class.

At Fort Lewis, Washington, in 1941 Karl was addicted to pin-ups (prior to his marriage).

February 11, 1941
Company D 17th Infantry
Fort Ord, California

Dear Ma,

I am fine. How are you; how is everything at home? Yesterday, it rained and today the weather is like in May.

We are not going to the Philippines. I don't know where we are going. In your last letter, you asked me what part of the Army I liked best. Well, I like pay-day the best. I like to go to Intelligence school pretty good.

Next pay-day I'll send another package home. Say hello to the rest of the family for me.

Your son,
Karl

On March 25, 1941 Karl's assignment was changed to Company D, 30th Infantry and he was assigned to Fort Lewis, Washington, and later to the Presidio of San Francisco.

On August 7, 1941, Karl wrote his mother:

> Aug. 7, 1941
> Co. D, 30th Inf.
> Ft Lewis, Was
>
> Dear Ma,
>
> I am the same as ever. The weather here is hot and dusty. Yesterday we were on a maneuver and we hiked about twenty-three miles. Last night I went to the show.
>
> It is a good thing that Gerhard didn't join the Army, maybe the Army would make a drinker out of him, or maybe he would make drinkers out of the Army. In your last letter you said that you hope that I don't drink like Gerhard. Well, I might drink a few beers, but never will it be said that I am or ever will be a drunkard.
>
> I am not going to the Philippines, because they won't let me go. We practiced boat landings this morning.
>
> Say hello to the rest of the family for me.
>
> Your Son, Karl

> Oct 27, 1941
> Co. D, 30th Inf.
> Presidio of San Francisco
> California
>
> Dear Ma,
>
> I received two letters from you to-day. I am quite the same. I hope that everything is O.K. at home.
>
> I am through going to gas school. I got my diploma last Thursday. Last Friday our Company Commander asked me if I want to go to West Point Military Academy in New York. I think I'll go, if I pass the examination.
>
> I hope I can get my furlough to start somewhere around the 10th of December instead of the 1st so that I can be home over New Year's too.
>
> Well So Long
> Your Son, Karl

With good Army chow at Fort Lewis, Washington, in the winter of 1941, Karl's weight ballooned to over 200 lbs.

When the Japanese attacked Pearl Harbor on December 7, 1941, Karl was serving in the Northwest Defense Command at Fort Lewis, Washington and explained to his mother why he would be unable to be home for Christmas:

> Dec. 9, 1941
> Co. D, 30th Inf.
> Ft. Lewis, Wash.

> Dear Ma,
>   Of course, you know that I won't be able to come home Christmas. You can blame the Japanese Emperor. I am the same as ever. I hope that you don't worry too about me and this war. I'll be back.
>   You can ask Pa if he is satisfied now that war is started. He always said, he wished there be war so that there would be work.
>   Well Merry Christmas.
>
>   Your Son, Karl

On December 11, Karl again wrote his mother from Fort Lewis:

> Dec. 11, 1941
> Co. D, 30th Inf.
> Ft. Lewis, Wash.
>
> Dear Ma,
>
> I received a letter from you today. I am quite the same. We went into the field Sunday night and been there since. We got our machine gun set up and guarding an air field from Japanese air planes. So far we have not seen any.
>
> So Dicknite is a staff sergeant. Well in my opinion, he wouldn't even make a pimple on a private's rear in the 30th Infantry nor in any Infantry.
>
> Save this Gas Certificate for me until after the War.
>
> Your Son

ON APRIL 1, 1942 (no April fool!) Karl was once again promoted, this time authorizing him to wear three stripes as a Sergeant. Then on April 26, 1942 his entire unit was reassigned to the 81st ("Wildcat") Division at Camp Rucker, Alabama. On May 12, 1942 Karl was stationed with the 323rd Infantry Regiment, Company D, at Camp Rucker.

Karl now applied for Infantry Officer Candidate School at Fort Benning, Georgia. His application was accepted and on November 10, 1942, Sgt. Timmermann left Camp Rucker for Fort Benning OCS.

Karl is promoted to Sergeant.

"Gun will be mounted here."
L'ENVOI

For thirteen weeks you've stood the test
Shined your shoes, done your best,
You've mastered every situation
Up to the day of graduation.

You've learned to sing out loud and clear:
"Gun to be mounted here,
Up to three clicks, now bore sight,
Company A is on our right."
You've placed fire on red scarred hills,
Learned the use of C. C. pills,
Planned the Battalion Aid Station
In every possible situation.

It seemed to work out every time
That your reference point was that lone pine.
The enemy, as you could see
Was very plainly up a tree.

You've learned the one about the WAAC
To tell your unit when you go back,
But the ultimate peak of your evolution
Was the day you hit the school solution.

At rifle cleaning you've worked hard
For Inspector Hall of Scotland Yard,
But then when you came in at night,
"Those shoe laces—not quite right."

And you can easily remember
That dreary day in late November,
When Captain said: "How win this war?
You've eleven gigs and one's a star."

But that's all past, the job's ahead.
Now you're to lead as you've been led.
The day is here, your training's done,
And what's more, you're a man, my son.

"Cease Firing! Clear all guns!"

BENNING SCHOOL SONG

FAR ABOVE the Chattahoochee, by the Upatoi,
Proudly stands our Alma Mater, Benning School for Boys,
O'er the burning sands of Georgia, through its awful rain,
Up the hills and through the gullies, we have learned with pain.
Though we often seem to hate her, curse her name with joy.
We have come to love our college, Benning School for Boys.
As the thirteen weeks go by, in this torrid clime,
They have kept us on the run, with their DOUBLE TIME.
As we rise long 'fore the dawn, midst clamor and the noise,
Shavetails will be born at Benning, BENNING SCHOOL FOR BOYS.

To BETTER UNDERSTAND Karl's experience at Fort Benning, I got in touch with a number of his classmates in the Officer Candidate Class who received their commissions as 2nd Lieutenants on February 16, 1943.

One of Karl's classmates, Warren D. Hardy of Sac City, Iowa, wrote to me: "As I recall Karl and I entered OCS from the same division (81st). We were in the same class, and upon graduation, were sent to the same combat division, the 9th Armored. I suppose Karl and I were acquainted a little over 2 years as soldiers. As I knew him, he was clean cut, unassuming and probably leaned toward a shyness, and the fact that he was the first officer to cross the Rhine amazed me at the time.

"But to go back to Benning, in our training of course, we would race up and down the hill of Chattahoochee, or Upatoi river and someone in each squad had to carry the BAR (Browning Automatic Rifle) which was no mean load, for me it was labor, but for Karl it was a breeze. As you say he was a big boned fellow and strong.

"My first recollection of Karl Timmermann was possibly on a bus which we rode from Camp Rucker, Al. to Columbus, Ga. Both of us being from the Midwest gave us bond for companionship on the new venture. I recall the 'blood sweat and tears' of OCS; the GT's, the obstacle courses, the 'fire a burst of six' etc.—I know we all felt that at the time the pressure was not worth the end result, seems like the original class of 200 odd dwindled to 80 some men on graduation day, so you see only the stout hearted survived."

Another of Karl's classmates Sumner H. Wyman of Hampton, Virginia, wrote:

"Your letter about Lt. Timmerman was forwarded to me here in Virginia where I've been the past few years.

"I remember Lt. Timmerman well, although I did not get to know him very well. While we were in OCS at Ft. Benning, we were in the same platoon.

Each platoon had two sections of 26 men each and we were in the same section but in different squads. Each squad had a little tar-paper shack called the 'hutmut.' Lt. Timmerman lived in the 'hutmut' next to mine.

"Our average day was up at 0500, breakfast, prepare our area for inspection. Often times our TAC officers had to use a flashlight to examine our shoes in the dark. Then to class. We double timed to and from all classes except when we rode trucks or buses. We usually changed uniforms two or three times a day.

"After supper we polished our gear, washed leggings, fatigues etc. and studied until lights out. During my three months there, I only found time to take in three movies and left the post only once."

According to Edward D. Smith of Bend, Oregon:

"I certainly do recall Timmermann although I did not know him too well. My recollection of him is probably fixed better than for others because I remember wondering at the time of the Remagen Bridge seizure whether or not the Timmermann mentioned was my old OCS buddy. None of the publications I had access to ever printed his picture and so I was never sure until your letter arrived yesterday.

"Timmermann lived in the hut just north of the one I lived in at OCS. If your OCS was Benning then you are undoubtedly acquainted with the setup of the company areas. We lived in those tarpaper shacks, a thirteen-man squad per each. One of those names appearing in the Graduation Program, Sutherland was the last name in my hut; Tilly would be the first in the next hut. There were two huts, I believe, between ours and the latrine so not all of the remaining names on the list would have been in Timmermann's hut. I hope some of Timmermann's squad-mates respond to your inquiry for they would have had much more opportunity to become well acquainted with him.

"Timmermann as I recall, was not only tall but had very light hair and a fair complexion. Germanic, I guess you'd call him. He was given to narrowing his eyes and creasing his forehead. His voice was clear and penetrating, sometimes even to the point of harshness. He was not always given to perfect enunciation and the use of the choicest grammar. He was forthright and certain of his opinions. I doubt if he assumed many relative positions usually seeing things as either black or white. His bearing was in the best military manner and I recall him as having as much military pride (in the best sense) as any man in the company. I don't believe he had been a soldier long, but there was no suggestion of the recruit in his manner.

"As you no doubt recall, it was the practice of the tactical officers to make different assignments among the candidates each week. I remember the week Timmermann was the class 1st sergeant. After we had returned to the company area and had been checked out, the 1st sergeant dismissed us. When Timmermann was finally told by the acting company commander to dismiss the company, he would do an about face in a very vigorous fashion, narrow his eyes and roar 'Dismissed.' In his pronunciation it was a word of only two syllables and sounded something like 'DUSS-MUST.' I remember there was another candidate I associate with this recollection. He was a short fellow named Phares and had a very high-pitched voice. He was really on trial for he had a different prominent assignment each week. I may be imagining this, but I think Phares was company commander the week Timmermann was 1st sergeant. The contrast between the pip-squeak voice saying 'Dismiss the company' and Timmermann's 'DUSS-MUST' was very humorous.

"There is a mixture of both gossip and provable truth in this next paragraph but if you have access to any records at all you can find the material which will make the point valid. By the time we got started in November 1942 the pinch for officers wasn't quite so great and, too, I suspect the caliber of candidates was becoming lower, the cream having been skimmed off earlier. At any rate we started in our company (I believe we were company 173) 220 strong. Only about 80 of us were still there in February 16, 1943, and to the original number should be added the 20 or so men we picked up as a result of sickness having caused them to drop out of earlier companies. Since my wife was in Columbus from December on I was able to relax and have a fairly healthy attitude in the knowledge that she could see almost at firsthand how rough the school was and would understand if I got the axe. Hence I consider myself lucky for having got my commission. But for most of the others the strain caused by so many candidates being cut down was pretty severe and anyone else who got through had every right to be extremely proud of himself. Timmermann certainly belongs in the category of the deserving. Despite the tremendous pressure, though, there was an excellent spirit of camaraderie, the men all helping each other in every conceivable way. The overbearing, the cocky, and those prejudiced against our 13 Negroes were mostly eliminated early and those of us remaining were in my estimation a pretty decent lot.

"As I said my wife was in Columbus from the middle of December on and since we were still childless then she was highly mobile. She came out to the post every night we didn't have compulsory study hall. If she couldn't come out I sweated out the PX telephone line for an hour or so to call her up.

On February 16, 1943, after successfully completing Infantry Officer Candidate School at Fort Benning, Georgia, Karl was awarded his gold bars as a second lieutenant.

Weekends I spent in town with her. Consequently I wasn't with the other men as much as the single men were. Actually almost a hundred recollections well up, but I am not sure they would be in the least bit pertinent: the bitter cold nights, the blustery days on the ranges, the one week of almost summer weather when one could lie on the ground and relax during the ten-minute breaks, my surprise at the literate almost college-professor-like lecturers for some of the study units, the compulsory study halls (in which I once got caught with a paperback novel inserted in the manual I had already mastered but was supposed to be studying but for which I was let off with a wink when the lieutenant discovered I was reading Dorothy L. Sayers' *The Nine Tailors*), the sounds at night from the open fields where the candidates practiced giving commands usually to platoons and companies but sometimes optimistically to battalions and regiments, the fact that Lucky Strike green went to war while our OCS class was in progress, the miserable black rainy night we went on our 30-hour problem (I was a scout and my fellow scout was a Negro named Levy. He was continually joking about his invisibility making him a perfect scout, so good that I couldn't even see him at two paces), the extremely thorough inspections that provided demerits for the most minute irregularities, the little German boy named Stern who was watched for possible subversion, the aversion I originally earned for volunteering to help my squad mates in writing their required autobiographies but which I finally overcame when my wife acted as liquor-purchasing agent for our belatedly announced New Year's Eve restriction, etc.

"Stern. This little lad was of German extraction and spoke with a marked German accent. The accent probably was what got him bounced for he was a sharp student and well liked by the others in the squad. (We had to rate each other in the squad at regular intervals: a form of mental torture equal to the best devised by the middle ages.) After I had been in the class for several weeks I was summoned one evening to report to the company c.c. I was told about the army habit of checking up on individuals suspected of subversion (and anything else I guess) and asked if I would be the observer of Stern. My first reaction was one of contempt and I almost said Hell no and prepared to leave the next day. Then I happily realized that if Stern were watched by an unsympathetic observer his chances would be worse than if I accepted the detail. That may have been simply my method of doing what otherwise revolted my conscience, but I accepted the job. Every Sunday night I had to write a letter addressed to an insurance agent with a P.O. Box in Columbus, Ga., the post town. I was to use no return address. I had a pseudonym for signature purposes. I was to begin it Dear Joe and request an extension on my insurance premium payment. In the second paragraph I was to say that I had run into Stern, using however a code name instead of his own, and had the following observation to make on him. Boy did I go out of my way to dream up convincing statements about what a good guy he was etc. But unfortunately he got bounced and I wrote a very sad last report requesting another delay in my premium payment. It is a wonder I didn't get called in for being sympathetic to Germans myself! Perhaps Timmermann was being observed too."

James P. Phillips of Muldrow, Oklahoma recalls:

"I didn't get closely acquainted with Lt. Timmermann, but I clearly remember what he looked like. He was a perfect picture of an ideal soldier. I always associated him and his home town with the 'West Point Military Academy.' He reminded me of the pictures of a West Point Cadet. He was straight, square shouldered and carried himself well. I believe he was one of our first 'acting' company commanders of the class for a week. I know that he made quite an impression on the rest of us as an outstanding leader. After that I don't think anyone questioned his ability or qualifications of becoming an officer. He was very sociable and well liked by other candidates."

Richard S. Steele of Utica, New York wrote:

"I remember Karl; as a matter of fact, I bunked with him during the hectic days of OCS at Fort Benning, Georgia. I especially remember Karl as a quiet, soft spoken youngster, full of down to earth advice; the type we could not afford to ignore.

"I respected Karl during those days for we all knew that he would continue to be an outstanding officer as he was an officer candidate. He was not the flashy or spectacular type; yet he was, I'm sure, respected by both candidates and tactical officers for his leadership qualities.

"I remember a specific instance when he was Candidate Company Commander and I Candidate Platoon Leader. During this assignment I was to march my platoon a short distance, halt them and guide them through commands to face front. Feeling the watchful eye of a 'Tact Officer' I was slightly nervous and, accordingly, gave the wrong command, 'Right Face.' Some candidates in the platoon, recognizing the error, tried to cover up by turning to the opposite direction. I certainly was in a dilemma with men facing both ways. I thought, 'what would the Tact Officer think?' At that, Karl, apparently recognizing my predicament, walked down to the platoon and proceeded to reprimand the men for not following my commands. He told them, 'If I felt like giving them a little close order drill, it was their responsibility to follow my command to do so.' This is what I remember about Karl, always on top of the situation, with a dry, experienced comment to let you know it.

"I have tried not to portray Karl with flowery comments, but hard as I have tried I can give you only this impression, 'Lt. Timmermann must have been an outstanding officer because he was that type of a man.'"

All that Don B. Austin of Henderson, Texas remembers of that OCS class follows:

"As for OCS—I'm afraid my remembrances aren't too military! I attended during a winter session and my most poignant memories are of sitting—

freezing—in the stands trying to concentrate on the demonstrations being run! (and not succeeding too well!). Another thing that fascinated me about those demonstrations—how perfect they always came off! Especially in tactics—where every man on the demonstration team turned up at the right time in the right place with the right weapon! Never seemed to work out that way later!"

Dean T. Jones of Lincoln, Nebraska recalls that "Karl spent innumerable evenings in the woods practicing voice commands. I am sure that since you say you spent time in OCS that you remember the lone wolf calls of an officer candidate in the dim light of the evening dusk.

"Karl and I rode the train together from Fort Benning, Georgia to Omaha, Nebraska upon completion of our OCS training and graduation and I am quite sure that we had but one thought uppermost in our minds and that was to get home and show the new gold bars to our families."

When Karl arrived at his Oak Street home in West Point on February 17, 1943, resplendent in his spiffy officer's uniform, his younger brothers Fritz and Rudy were waiting for him at the door. The area around the Timmermann home was muddy from a recent downpour, so Fritz and Rudy rushed out to carry the new lieutenant across the mud because they didn't want Karl's highly shined shoes to get soiled. Inside, there was a joyous family celebration, featured by a freshly baked cake.

Karl savored the adoration of his family, unaware of the fact that on the next day—February 18, 1943—would take place a great turning point in his life.

```
God and the soldier we adore
In times of danger - not before
Time has passed, things have
righted
God is forgotten, the soldier
slighted.
```

A note Karl carried in his billfold throughout the war and after.

FIVE

Romance

WHEN KARL TIMMERMANN and his buddy Jim Strehle walked into Sass's Drugstore for a coke on the evening of February 18, 1943, romance was absolutely the last thing on Karl's mind. Furthermore, no citizen of West Point would ever dream that such an unlikely couple as La Vera Meyer and Karl Timmermann would ever hit it off together.

After all, La Vera was a confirmed Missouri Synod Lutheran, a graduate of the public high school in West Point, and Karl was a devout Catholic, a graduate of Guardian Angels High School. In addition, these two had experienced serious run-ins with each other in recent years, developing personal animosities which seemed to be deep-seated.

Karl's mother also harbored smoldering resentment against La Vera, based on La Vera's treatment of her while she was working as a waitress at the Golden Rod Café. Mrs. Timmermann told me that on several occasions La Vera and her giggling high school classmates would consistently ask her to repeat in broken English the various flavors of ice cream sundaes and then, to gales of triumphant laughter, La Vera would conclude: "I'd like a Seven-Up."

La Vera had grown up on a farm several miles outside town. Students at both the public and Catholic schools frequently visited a dance hall on North Main Street called "Del Rios," where "singles" could spend an evening for the admission price of ten cents. After dancing once with Karl, La Vera's friends advised her that it was in poor taste to dance with Karl because the Timmermanns lived in a poor household, they had been bootleggers, Karl's father was an Army deserter and there was constant fighting between Mr. and Mrs. Timmermann.

La Vera Meyer

Soon La Vera began to refuse to dance with Karl and when he asked her, she said "no" in angry tones. Once they got into an argument on who had gotten the highest grade in Latin, and Karl walked a mile home to bring his report card to prove he had scored high on his most recent Latin test. When Karl returned with the evidence, La Vera infuriated Karl by refusing to take a look at his report card.

On another occasion when a boy escorted La Vera home, Karl threw rocks at them all the way home, then hung around to make sure her escort did not kiss her good night. La Vera reported "about this time in my life, I believe that I sincerely hated this boy who really could antagonize me."

"I really don't think I saw much of Karl during 1939. Anyway I don't think I thought about him; if I did, it was with resentment.

"I do remember being on the street with a girl friend one day in the summer of 1940 when we met Karl dressed in his Army fatigues. He was with another fellow, and I remember the icy stares that passed between us. I took particular delight in telling my friend what a horrible creature he was, giving her the details of how he followed me home when I was escorted by another fellow."

Jim Strehle told me about his friendship with Karl. "We used to get together a lot down at the West Point Recreation Center to shoot pool. Lots of times Karl would stick around the Guardian Angels Library until five or six P.M. until we could drag him out. He was reading, reading about history, about wars and stuff. As I look back on it now, he was smarter than we knew. He talked about trouble in China and the Orient, and said that the Japs would be after us next.

"When Germany attacked Russia, even before we got into the war, he said that we should first team up with Germany and then turn on Germany. I didn't believe him. He was always coming up with historical analogies. He always talked about joining the Army."

When Karl came back to West Point in his 2nd Lieutenant's uniform, he was shooting pool and walking the streets that evening when he said to Jim Strehle, "Jim, let's go to Sass's for a coke." They walked in and there were La Vera and a friend.

Karl suddenly asked Jim with some surprise as he looked at La Vera: "Who is that?"

Jim answered, "Oh that's La Vera Meyer. She's been around for years."

La Vera related what happened next:

"Our paths didn't cross again until February 18, 1943. By now we were at war, and everyone seemed to feel a little sorry for his plight. I was still keeping busy as a school-marm, and Karl had become the 'spit and polished' soldier that he had dreamed of becoming. I had really forgotten that he existed. Things were very dull in our small town. Most of the boys were in uniform, and those that were lucky enough to avoid the draft were very uninteresting. Since this was a farming community, there seemed to be a shuffle of population in getting Junior back on a farm where he was considered essential enough to avoid the draft. Father, in turn, would move to town and make the necessary retirement. I must also add that this same Junior found the old farm very boring during times of peace and found working in town much much more enjoyable. Perhaps I am citing from just a few cases, but this condition did exist.

"Getting back to February 18, 1943, the day Karl and I met again. It was a Friday night, and a teacher friend of mine came into town with her brothers as they were attending a Knights of Columbus meeting at the church. She wanted me to attend the local movie with her, but as I had previously seen it, I decided to walk up town with her. I did so, leaving her at the movie, and myself stopping at the drug store for a sundae. Sitting at the counter talking with another girl I knew only as an acquaintance, I noticed this tall very good-looking 2nd Lieutenant enter the store with another of the local boys. He looked so familiar, and yet it couldn't be that horrible Karl Timmermann. After several glances, I finally asked the girl at the soda fountain if that were he? About that time he had purchased his package of gum and had started on his way out the door. As I was seated near the entrance, he hesitantly came over and asked if I were still mad at him. Getting in my share of flag waving, I replied, 'Well, since you're now a soldier in uniform, I guess I'll forgive you.' Corny, huh? It was another incident I was teased about in the following years. Anyway, we were speaking again. My sundae being finished about that time, I decided to leave the store, and my acquaintance sitting next to me did likewise. Of course, we walked out with the fellows, and at their suggestions, we all stopped at a café in the next block for refreshments. Karl and I had a bottle of beer (we were only 20 years old), and the other two companions had to settle for soft drinks as they were a few years younger. I remember Karl handing me one of his calling cards which proudly bore the title, 'Second Lieutenant.' It so happened that I had learned the insignia of rank only a few days previously when I conducted a reading examination for my eighth grade students. This was standard literature which was put out by the State to test their reading ability. It went into detail on the different Army ranks, so that is why I recognized a 2nd Louie when I saw one. Karl had been commissioned just a few days ago and came home on a delay en route to his new assignment at Fort Riley, Kansas.

"After our drinks were finished, and conversation was beginning to lag, we decided to go home. We said goodnight in front of the café, and I started to cross the street, when Karl stated that since he lived in the same direction, he would walk with me if it was permissible. I agreed and we walked very slowly home. We were engrossed in quite a conversation about what we had been doing the past few years and the town in general. Before I knew it we were at my door. I didn't ask him in as my parents were in bed, and they were rather fussy about having boy friends in the house. We sat on the steps and talked for awhile. He asked me for a date the next night, which was Saturday, and since I didn't have anything better to do, I consented. There seemed to be a magnetic attraction for one another again, and before he left, he awkwardly asked: 'Well, how much nerve does it take?' Having said this, he kissed me and I might add that it was very well done.

"The next day found me rather confused because of this boy who had come into my life again. I really wanted to date him that night, but I found myself wondering what my friends would say. I had notions of contacting him and calling the whole thing off. However, he didn't have a phone, so I really don't know if I would have called if I could. He came for me very promptly looking fresh and scrubbed, as if he had walked out of a recruiting poster. As he didn't have a car, we walked up town to attend the movie. It was a cowboy shoot 'em up picture, so neither one of us was very interested. He managed to hold my hand before the picture was over, and I think it somewhat irritated me. We didn't stay for the entire picture, but went to the café up the street and drank a few bottles of beer. This was something quite new to me as I wasn't accustomed to much drinking. In fact, neither was Karl. At any rate, it didn't hurt us and probably made us more at ease with one another. We found that we had a great deal in common and really enjoyed the evening. Naturally, he asked me for a date the following evening; and I accepted. We went up town again, stopped for a bottle of beer before going to the Del Rio Hall for a dance. I discovered that Karl was a very smooth dancer. Not the jitter bug type, but quite a waltzer. I believe that he requested the 'Beautiful Blue Danube,' and the manager's wife announced that it was to be played especially for him. It was one of his favorite songs, as were all of the Strauss waltzes. I think there was a great deal ado about our dating; several of the girls in the ladies room commented on how good-looking Karl was. We stayed quite to ourselves though, sitting away beyond the confusion of the crowd.

"I could have seen Karl on Monday night also, but since I had to get up early in the morning to teach school, I thought it best to get a good night's rest for a change; therefore, I told Karl on Sunday night that I wouldn't see him until Tuesday evening. That Monday night I began to do some serious thinking about Karl. I realized that I liked him a lot, and was wishing that I had consented to see him that night, being a little worried that he might find someone else more interesting. (The town was packed with lonely girls dying for a date.)

"Needless to say, I was very happy to see Karl on Tuesday evening. I think we went to the Del Rio to another dance, but didn't stay too long. We found it pleasing to go to our favorite booth in a favorite café and play all our favorite popular numbers on the juke box, talk and . . . drink beer. I don't think our capacity was over three bottles per evening.

"On Wednesday night we saw each other again. I think we just went up town, sat in the same booth, talked, and stared at one another like two people in love. At this time we were rather remorseful about Karl's leave being up as he had to leave West Point on Friday.

"I asked him over to dinner on Thursday evening. Since I was teaching school, my mother and sister prepared the dinner. My sister was staying at the house because she was expecting her first baby at any time and wanted to be near the hospital. They baked a chicken with all the trimmings. I remember Karl asking who cooked the delicious dinner, and my mother and sister wanting to give me a little boost in the eyes of my beau, stated that we all had a hand in the cooking. My little cousin was staying at the house at that time (I think that she was about 8 or 9 years old), and she had taken quite a fancy to Karl, and also wanted to give me a little 'plug' so she added to this conversation by saying quite proudly, 'Yes, La Vera did help. She dished up the pickles.' This incident gave us many a chuckle in later years. With dinner being over, we stayed around the house long enough to be polite, and then took a walk up town to a café to talk and have a bottle of beer. Since parting was near, we were both quite sad. Later on returning home, Karl came into the house, and we went into a rather serious discussion about marriage, religion, etc. He told me that he thought he loved me, but that we had gone together such a short time that he couldn't be sure until we had a little more time together. I felt the same way. That parting on Thursday night was sad as it always is for lovers of any age. He promised to write, and I likewise.

"The first few days that followed were very lonely. Although it was only a few days before I received that first letter, it seemed forever. By then we realized that we were really in love, and that first letter he wrote to me told me that his feeling was for real."

Subsequently, Karl frequently made reference to that chance meeting on February 18, 1943, and how it changed his life. For example, on April 16, 1943, Karl wrote to La Vera from Fort Riley, Kansas.

"Following Jim Strehle's suggestion to go into Harry Sass's Drug Store on the evening of February 18, 1943 was the best thing I ever did. I doubt whether or not I would have found you if it hadn't been for that night. God blessed that night, La Vera."

La Vera immediately answered:

"Yes, Karl, God must have blessed that night we remet in Sass's. We've got Dolores Mahlberg to thank for sort of pulling us together.

"That night Angela Ritter had been at my house. She was going to the show and wanted me to go along. I had previously seen it, but walked along up town with her and then stopped in for ice cream. Was feeling rather lonely and dejected. I remember a conversation Angie and I had on the way. We were discussing our latest dates, etc., and I found myself saying 'Angie, you know, I don't think I've met the right one.'"

On subsequent occasions, both Karl and La Vera recalled their recollection both of February 18th and what happened the rest of that week when

they were together. Sensing that this was a date which to them was as important as their birthdays, wedding date and Christmas, I asked La Vera in 1954
to elaborate on further recollections. She told me:

"On that Friday evening when we went into Sass's Drug Store, we had
only been sitting there a little while when in walked Karl and Jim Strehle.
Karl looked resplendent in his 2nd Lieutenant's uniform (he could *really*
wear a uniform).

"I said to Angie: 'Is that Karl Timmermann? How did he ever get to be a
2nd Lieutenant?'

"Karl poked around a little, looking at various things. Then he sauntered over
and said to me 'I'd like to apologize for throwing those rocks at you that night.'

"He said it in such a noble way. Then we started laughing and joking and
the four of us went outside together. That's when Karl asked me if he could
walk home with me. I lived on Ash Street, which was over three blocks away
from Oak Street where the Timmermanns lived.

"When we sat on the steps of my home, we began to talk about everything under the sun. I was so impressed with his honesty and maturity. I
began to realize that here was a person who was quite different than the Karl
Timmermann I had known as a brash and egotistical person. He impressed
me as a human being who had high ideals. Unlike most young men his age,
he asked me about my own future and what I believed in, instead of trying to
impress me about his own importance.

"I saw a human being who was very wholesome in his approach to life,
who was pure in his beliefs. He talked about the books he read, and what he
had learned from history. We talked at length
about religion, and despite the fact that I was
raised as a Lutheran and he as a Catholic, we
came to remarkable agreement on the principles
of Christianity which transcend all denominations. We even got into areas of love and sex
which most people avoid, and I found Karl to be
the type of person who shared my views on the
sanctity of marriage and the difference between
love and lust.

"At the end of the evening, I readily agreed to
meet him again for a date the next day. When we
parted, I sensed that I was in love, and he gave
me the vibes to indicate that he was also in love
with me."

*In late Februaryf 1943, Karl served
as a platoon leader in the 9th
Armored Division at Fort Riley,
Kansas.*

For years afterward, La Vera and Karl would always recall the magic which brought them together on February 18, 1943.

When he reported for duty at Fort Riley, Kansas, late in February, Karl was assigned as a Platoon Leader in Headquarters Company, 2nd Battalion, 52nd Armored Infantry Regiment of the 9th Armored Division. La Vera asked him how he liked Fort Riley. He answered somewhat cynically; but then went on to tell what was really on his mind:

"How do I like Fort Riley? Well, La Vera, there are only two fairly good army posts for a soldier and those two are the one he is going to and the one from which he just came. The average soldier is never satisfied wherever he might be.

"You know, La Vera, whenever I hear music no matter what I may be thinking about, my thoughts change and I find myself thinking of you. Many times I catch myself daydreaming of you when my mind should be on my work. Please, believe me, La Vera, I haven't ever felt that strong about any girl."

The object of Karl's affection was 3 ½ months older than Karl, having graduated in 1939 in the 59-member class of 1939 at the public West Point High School. Karl's class of 1940 had only 23 in the graduating class. In September, 1939, La Vera had started teaching at a rural elementary school seven miles from her West Point home. She loved her job, although she was paid only $55 per month at the start and described her pupils as "little bundles of mischief." She related that she had to be sensitive to the fact that some of her pupils were children of school board members, but she refused to compromise her standards.

During the snow-blown and frosty month of March, the long-distance romance between Fort Riley and West Point heated up. La Vera's mother cried when she heard the news. On the other hand, Karl's mother immediately overlooked her former reaction to La Vera's teasing, and greeted the news with unalloyed enthusiasm.

La Vera's first letter to Karl was a clear indication that she was eager to ignite the fires of love which Karl had indicated were smoldering:

Wednesday, March 3,

Dearest Karl,

So you think I've already forgotten you? Karl, how could you think that of me? You know that would be quite impossible.

Got your precious letter today. It seemed an eternity before it came. Gosh! It should have been here yesterday for certain. You'd better make that complaint to the Postal Dept., Karl.

Sun. night my feet wandered down to the Del. What a mob!

Soldiers & more soldiers. I danced & managed a smile once in a while, but my heart wasn't there. You kept that, Karl. Take good care of it, will you?

Yes, I find myself daydreaming a lot. How can I help it when you have me so completely bewitched?

Karl, I love you, too. I know it's real. I couldn't feel this way, otherwise. You're A-1 in my heart. Every time I hear "our songs" I'm with you in Dunns, drinking beer & loving you.

As I want to take this up town & mail it I'll say "Goodnight, Karl." I'll be thinking of you & loving you.

Very lovingly, La Vera

During March, Karl was hard-pressed to keep his mind on his obligatory Army duties at Fort Riley, as he continued to express his deepening love for La Vera as often as he could find the time to write.

March 10, 1943, 10:00 P.M.

Hello La Vera,

I intended to write you a letter last night but I had to write a machine gun problem instead. Of course, I had no choice. Did you receive my last letter? I'll try to write you every chance I get.

So you wonder if I miss you as much as you miss me. Well, La Vera, I'm constantly daydreaming of you. I love you—and it isn't anything to be turned off and on, as desired. It isn't a lust or anything that might be called cheap.

Sun. March 14, 4:30 P.M.

Hello "Sweetheart,"

I've had you in on my mind all day & really doubt whether I'm capable of thinking of anything else.

You asked what I've been doing to keep out of mischief. Well, La Vera, there really isn't much to write. Friday morning we went to southern Kansas in armored cars.

Friday, March 19, 9:30 a.m.

Dearest Karl,

Karl, were you such an honery boy when you went to school. If you were, all I can say is this. You turned out to be an ideal man, and I think I'm one of the luckiest of girls to have you love me.

I'm going home now. Wish you were there, but that would be too much of a surprise.

Just me, who loves you, La Vera

Karl didn't have too much trouble answering that question: "You asked if I was an honery boy when I went to school. Boy! You ought to ask some of my old classmates."

As March progressed, La Vera longed to see Karl:

Tuesday, Mar. 23,

Dearest Karl,

Thinking of you, as usual, so may as well write a letter. How are you? Seems like I haven't heard from you in ages. Guess the last time was Friday, but then, that's long when one's in love. I can't relate how much I long to see you again. It does seem ages, though it really isn't so long. I'll say it now, Karl, as in my every letter, I love you. There's no maybe about it either. Course you know that already, but if you're like me you won't ever tire of hearing it.

Karl responded:

Well, La Vera,

My thoughts are the same as any normal man or else I wouldn't be a man but my love [of] you is sure and it's something that will keep forever. (I wouldn't dare write this on paper if I didn't mean every word.)

Karl reiterated his desire and intention to get together with La Vera as soon as possible:

Tuesday, March 16th, 10:00 a.m.

Hello La Vera,

I really should be working. I'm preparing my weekly drill schedule for my platoon this morning.

I received your letter yesterday and I must have [read] it dozens of times since. La Vera, what makes you think that I haven't thought about seeing you again? It so happens that I have been giving this subject very much thought. How could I keep from wanting to see you, when everytime I try to think, drill my men or do any job that is required of me by the Army, I have to first try to get you off my mind and I don't want to. I love you, La Vera, and I couldn't love you and not want to see you. (Please, believe me.)

March 17, 3:00 P.M.

Hello La Vera,

    I really haven't had much time now to write a long letter. I just came over to my room to get my pistol belt and then back to work. I've been thinking of you constantly, La Vera, you know how I feel about you. Don't worry, Sweetheart, I'll see you as soon as it is earthly possible. I'm working the angles now.

So long, as ever Karl

As the whirlwind courtship continued, Karl came up with the suggestion that they might be able to meet in Omaha if he could succeed in obtaining a 3-day pass on Saturday, April 3:

March 21, 4:00 P.M.

Hello La Vera,

    I just finished my Sunday afternoon nap. And I'm still sleepy. I slept about two hours.

    La Vera, I've got an idea. I don't know what you'll think of it, but here goes: I can get Saturday afternoons off and all day Sunday until Monday morning six o'clock. I can be in Omaha on or before seven o'clock in the evening on Saturdays but I wouldn't be able to get to West Point until one in the morning on Sunday and then leave again at nine the same morning. That wouldn't do us any good. But La Vera, if you could be in Omaha on a Saturday night, well—I'll be there. If you like the idea, La Vera, let me know which Saturday. Let me know well ahead. And for your own sake don't tell anyone.

    I love you, La Vera, and I'm as sure of that as I [am] of my own life. I long to see you more than I would ever be able to express on paper. That's why I suggest Omaha.

Reading between the lines, Karl's reason for asking La Vera "not to tell anyone" was his strong determination not to mix love with sex, and his unshakable opposition to pre-marital sex. On March 23, Karl reiterated his strong affection for La Vera:

March 23rd, 10:15 P.M.

Hello La Vera,

   I just got through with my day's work. It was a rather long day. In spire of the fact that I was busy all day, I was constantly thinking of you. La Vera, you know how I feel about you. I long to see you and hold you in my arms more than anything in the world. I'm not giving you "a line." La Vera, please believe what I say, as I know you now and I'm sure that I know you through and through; (I believe that I can judge human nature that well) I love you. No other woman has ever stirred up my insides like this before. My love for you isn't a lust or an animal desire for the opposite sex. Of course, La Vera, I'll be able to get a three days leave within the next month. I'll try my best. Of course, La Vera, you know that I love you and I want to tell you in person.

   La Vera, I really must go to bed. I'm too sleepy.

   Good Night, Sweetheart, I'll always love you, Karl

Karl explained on March 29th why there had been a gap in his love letters:

March 29, 9:15 P.M.

Hello La Vera,

   Tonight will be the first night since last Wednesday that I'll be able to sleep in my bed. We were out "in the field" and we just came back this afternoon. That's why I didn't write last week, I couldn't.

   La Vera, since I had my leave I don't feel like the same person any more. I can't clear my mind. I'm in a constant daze because mentally you're always with me. I can't think of anything else. La Vera, you know I love you—I'll never tire of saying it.

   I'm really sorry but I can't be in Omaha on the third of April. Our weekly drill schedule doesn't permit it. I tried.

On the same day. La Vera exuberantly proclaimed her undying love:

Monday, March 29

Hello Darling,

   I haven't been in school very long yet this morning; however, long enough to taker the chill out of the schoolhouse. Don't know exactly what time it is as my clock refuses to tick more than 60 times without me shaking it.

I feel grand this morning, Karl. I'm not one bit tired and my heart is glad inside. You know why, too. It's because you're there and I'm going to see you soon. It's really spring now & the birds make me feel glad all over. I love you, Karl, more than I ever thought I was capable of loving any man. You seem to be my whole world, everything I'm living for.

April 4th, 8:40 P.M.

Hello La Vera,

I love you, La Vera, more than I'd ever be able to write on paper. I'll never cease telling you. If I get the leave which I asked for I'll be home next Saturday until Monday morning. Whether or not I get my leave remains to be seen.

I long to see you more than anything else in the world. Proposing, yes, La Vera—not supposing. I'm not kidding myself and not giving you a line. I want you La Vera—I want you forever.

What happened next was described to me by La Vera in 1955, who told me that Karl had finally succeeded in getting a weekend pass starting on Saturday, April 10:

"I knew that he was going to propose to me because it was implied in his letters. He arrived on the Saturday night bus about 7:00 P.M. I meant to meet it, but was a little late, so found him in the Golden Rod Café where his mother was a waitress. He was eating dinner, so I sat in the booth with him. After dinner we left and went to another café to have more privacy. It wasn't long before he popped the question and I had accepted.

"There was still a religious difference to be settled, but we knew that we would work it out somehow. Late that evening we returned to the Golden Rod to inform Karl's mother of the news. She was overjoyed and immediately asked me to come to their house for Sunday dinner. I accepted, and the next day I met all of the Timmermann family. [Author's note: with the exception of Mary, who had already moved to Omaha, leaving the class of 1945 at Guardian Angels High School during the tenth grade.]

"Mother Timmermann couldn't do enough for us, she was almost as excited as we were."

When Karl returned to Fort Riley, one of the first things he asked La Vera was "Don't forget to send your ring size."

In addition, on April 14, he wrote: "I've got a solution for 'our Barrier' which I know you'll agree upon. I really have no right to ask anyone to change their religion because I myself have been to church only two or three times since I graduated from high school. I won't ever again ask you to change your religion. Remain as you are and we still get married in June."

April 14, 1943, 8:37 P.M.

Hello Sweetheart,

"A dream mixed with reality" as you put it. Yes, La Vera, a dream—a dream that will come true, one that we'll share together forever. I love you, La Vera, I'll love you and love you forever.

La Vera responded:

Monday. 5:30 P.M., April 18

Dearest Karl,

Say, you've been doing O.K., as I received a letter from you on Fri., Sat., & today. Keep it up, Karl.

Gosh! This whole town knows about us already, but then who cares. People ask me a million questions which I can't even answer myself. But I'm sure of this much, Darling. I love you and we'll marry in June. We've got lots to decide yet, now that our barrier is finally settled. Gee! I hope I see you soon. Betcha I could ask more questions than an army questionnaire.

Your mother invited me to your house for dinner Sunday. Guess I'm going—that is if you haven't plans for Lincoln or something. Did she write & tell you about the silverware she bought for us. She couldn't keep from telling me.

She later elaborated:

Darling, I'm glad you've decided our question. It's good to know that is settled. It had to be that way. You won't be sorry that I'm not a Catholic. I could never be happy as one. I promise I'll make it up to you some way. I love you. And Karl. I've always been so independent, and for myself I don't feel that way anymore. I need you, Karl, I really do. I always feel so secure and restful when I'm with you. I love you with all my heart and it will keep forever.

Your Mother said she'd give you a bottle of Castor Oil so you'd survive my cooking. She was only kidding, of course.

She added:

Tuesday, April 20

Dearest Karl,

I just got home from school, read your letter, & here I am. You express yourself so beautifully, Karl. I read your letters again and again.

Let you do the worrying, is that what you said? I wish that was as easily done as said. I just wouldn't be La Vera unless I had something to worry about. Right now I wish I were safe in your arms. I feel so alone without you.

When is school out? I looked at the calendar and if my judgement is correct, on Sunday, May 23 after the district picnic. I can wave goodbye to a little white school house. It will seem strange, but blissfully so. Funny, I can't realize that out of my 21 years, I spent 16 school years & 1 summer learning & teaching (mostly learning).

That last week of school is enough to throw anyone out of sorts. The school must be cleaned in every nook and cranny, fair work must be finished & mounted, reports galore to make out, and a picnic to plan. So, Karl, if I didn't get a week's rest before our wedding, you'll be getting a No. 1 nervous wreck.

Dearest, I love you as I have never before loved anyone. I love everything about you, your ideals, & oh, Karl, you.

O.K., Darling, I knew a white wedding was impractical all the time, but ever since I was knee high to a grasshopper I had myself in a wreath & veil. I'll just shut my eyes to that and consider as sensible something or other.

What kind of me did you frame? Me, with the big feet. Ha!

What color gold do I like, white or yellow? I'd have to flip a coin & you can do that as easily as I. Must rush uptown and mail this.

Your future wife,

La Vera

Karl couldn't resist taking a poke at West Point:

April 21, 7:45 A.M.

Hello La Vera,

I haven't much time to write now. Of course, I miss you, La Vera. How could I love you if I didn't.

So, nobody was surprised about us. Well, West Point must not be acting normal then. I always thought that in West Point a man had to go with a gal about five years before he proposed or even thought about it. Anyway that's the way some West Pointers carry on.

Two days later, Karl wrote:

> April 23rd,
> 9:50 P.M.
>
> Hello La Vera,
>
> So, the whole town knows about us? What are they saying?
>
> I'll never be able to tell you how much I really love you. Words weren't created big and beautiful enough for that. All I know is I love you with all my heart. I know that I'll always love you, La Vera—forever and ever.
>
> La Vera, do you know why we'll always remember February 18th. Of course, there will be another to remember, the day you become Mrs. Karl Timmermann.

La Vera kept Karl posted on her every move —

> Monday, Apr. 26
>
> Dearest Karl,
>
> I'm about ready for bed, but first must say "hello" to you.
>
> I'm tired and can hardly keep awake.
>
> I was over at your Mothers yesterday for dinner and for the afternoon. She gave me a sheet & a pyrex pie dish. She's certainly good to me.

AT ONE POINT IN THEIR courtship Karl needed this clarification: "Remember that night in the Golden Rod when you started to cry? You never did tell me the reason."

La Vera immediately answered: "Darling, you asked why I cried that night in the Golden Rod. You didn't forget, did you? You see, I was thinking about your leaving the next morning & I guess it was then I realized that I had fallen in love with you. I didn't want you to go, but knew you had to."

Karl and La Vera had planned a June wedding, but there were two question marks which arose. First, it became apparent that the 9th Armored Division would be moving in June to the Desert Training Center in California.

And second, Karl was not sure whether or not he could obtain a 10-day furlough to get married and enjoy a brief honeymoon. Karl also wanted to underline to his future bride the risks of marrying a soldier:

> May 6,
> 9:50 P.M.
>
> Hello La Vera,
>
> As for planning there isn't much we can do until I know whether or not I can get a ten days leave. We might be in southern California by end of June.
>
> I love you, La Vera, love you with all my heart. Because I'm a soldier things are going to be hard on you. There'll be many times when I won't be able to come home. There'll be times when we'll have something planned and my duty as a soldier will interfere. And eventually I'll be sent overseas. Chances are you might become a young widow. Darling, I love you and that's the way I'll always feel. I want you to become Mrs. Karl Timmermann. I know that the name "Timmermann" doesn't mean much in W.P. I used to hate the name "Timmermann" (I must be in a bad mood or else I wouldn't [be] running myself into the "mud.")
>
> I can't think of anything to write. I can 't think of anything. I have you on [my] mind all the time.
>
> I'm so dam[n] discussed [sic] with this world as it is, I can almost bust out crying. I probably would if I were a woman.
>
> > Good night, La Vera
> > I love you
> > Karl

La Vera immediately wrote Karl a reassuring letter which expressed her conviction that love would overcome Karl's apprehensions:

> You must have felt awful when you wrote your last letter. I feel that way a lot too. Of course, I'm a woman, when I feel like crying I cry. I usually feel better then. You know, Darling, I wish right now I were with you already, so I could get you out of that mood. I love you, Karl, and I'll keep on loving you forever.
>
> Please don't worry about me having a hard time as a war wife. Hundreds of women are doing it and they can take it. Why can't I when I'll have the dearest husband in the world to love me and to love.

I won't worry about wedding plans anymore. I'll just wait and hope that you get that furlough. When it comes right down to it nothing else really does matter except "our being Mr. & Mrs."

Darling, I always try to shut my eyes to the fact that you are a soldier and may go "overseas." But if you do, Darling, you're taking my heart with you and don't talk about my being a widow. It can't happen to a love like ours.

So cheer up, my Darling, I love you, and maybe soon those "Lights will go on again all over the world."

Now, don't worry about me, Karl. Just keep loving me and everything will come out alright.

Goodbye for now and I do love you.

Your La Vera

La Vera then recorded her enthusiastic reaction to her engagement ring:

5:00 P.M.

Hello Darling,

Oh, Karl, it's beautiful, it's beautiful. I'm so happy. I can't tell you how much I like it. Gee! It's a whopper of a stone and does it sparkle! If you could see my eyes now, I think you'd say they'd be shining, too. Oh, Darling, I don't know how to say thank you. I like it so very much. And you, Darling, I love you and love you and love you.

I never never expected such an enormous stone. I'm the most happy girl in the world and I shall be happier when I'm your wife.

When I came home from school I stopped for Dad & he said he had a package in Schmidt's safe for me. I opened it in the car going home. Mother & Cedonia Haas saw it, too, right away. I think mother is almost as thrilled as me. Dad, too, thought it a beauty.

Just now I had to stop Alice G & show it to her. She was overwhelmed. You know, Darling, I think I've got the biggest diamond and most beautiful, in town. Will show it to your mother tonight. To boot, I've got the dearest, most wonderful sweetheart to love me. Am I not a lucky girl? It's a perfect fit, too.

The box was broken and in terrible condition. Even the ring case was chipped off on the corner, but I think I can glue it fairly well.

Many, many thanks, Karl. You know I love you & always will.

I can't kiss you, so I will kiss your picture instead.

The future Mrs. Karl Timmermann

On May 9th, Karl responded to one of La Vera's letters in which she wondered whether Karl was getting cold feet about their impending marriage. Karl answered quite emphatically:

> May 9th
>
> 5:30 P.M.
>
> Hello La Vera,
>
> I love you so much that I'll never be able to tell in words. I know that I'll always love you, La Vera, and my love for you increases each day.
>
> Please, forgive me for not writing very much last week. I was quite busy.
>
> Why do you ask whether I'm getting cold feet. My feet could never turn cold. You know, La Vera, I've got our first son named already and you think I'm getting cold feet.

La Vera responded with a description of her visit to Karl's youngest brother Rudy, plus her reaction to Karl's premature naming of a son:

> I was down to your house last nite to say goodbye to Rudy. He told me to take good care of you, and Darling, I'll try to do just that.
>
> I told him I was going to be his sister-in-law, & he was dumbfounded but said he was glad. He said "Oh, boy! Wait till I'm an uncle." I said "Hold on." Not so fast. Ha! He also gave us a gift and warned me not to open it. (Course your Mother told me its contents—6 Towels & wash cloths) Isn't that lovely?
>
> It's time for school again, so, goodbye, my love.
>
> Your La Vera
>
> P.S. What is the name you have given our son? Man, you're getting a little ahead of time, aren't you? (And what if it's all she's?) Ha!

In two separate letters, La Vera revealed her sensitivity toward telling an ex boy friend that she was marrying Karl. La Vera showed that she was soft-hearted and felt that those former boy friends should be allowed soft landings with a parachute instead of being unceremoniously pushed out of an airplane when she handed them their walking papers. On the other hand, Karl felt very possessive and, as his response indicates, opposed any latent sympathy toward La Vera's former suitors.

Last night I went to the Easter dance at the Del. How I wish I could have been with you. My old boy friend is home on furlough & is really "haunting" me. If only he'd accept the fact that I'm going to be married to you & let me alone. I danced several times with him & he (ex) tried his best to make us break up. Darling, no one can ever do that. I love you. I long to have you hold me tight & tell me that again. I'll always want to hear it.

You see I honestly wish I were hard-hearted at times. I'm referring to my ex —. I hate to hurt people, but sometimes it just happens. Last nite doesn't make me feel very noble. I don't know how to express myself, but I feel awful about the whole thing. You just can't go around smashing hearts & laughing. He said to tell you you were a lucky guy. Oh, Karl, I love you so much that I'm afraid— yes, afraid of losing you.

Karl's reaction was immediate and vociferous:

Hello La Vera,

I love you more than anything else in the world. I'll always love you. I even love you, love you when your hair are all mussed up and then put up with pins like that one Sunday morning.

Who is this fellow who has been haunting you? What's his name? What tactics did he use? Please answer these questions, La Vera, because I love you, I want you to be my wife and I've got to protect my interests whenever some one is in the way. I wonder if he'd dare the thing he's tried if I were in West Point. La Vera, you're worth fighting for and that's what I intend on doing if it has to be.

Don't worry, La Vera, I won't ever stop loving you, it isn't possible, I couldn't.

I've got to get back to work now.

I love you
Karl

Nothing further was said by either La Vera or Karl on this delicate subject. Finally, Karl's leave came through starting on May 23, with the proviso that he would have to be back at Fort Riley by May 31 because of the scheduled departure for the Desert Training Center (which did not actually occur for several weeks later in June). Although Karl wanted to get married in

Omaha just as soon as he arrived, now a sudden development on La Vera's part delayed the wedding until May 25 and enabled Karl to return to his home in West Point, as explained by La Vera:

Thurs. May 13,

Dearest Karl,

I love you Karl, and I know I always will. It won't be long now and school will be out. My brain feels like it's going around in circles lately. I've got so much to do.

I'm slightly peeved at one old lady in the district. Just because of her I've got to have a dam picnic on Sunday, the 23rd for the district. It gives me a headache to think of it. Now, sometime yet tomorrow I've got to finish 30 invitations. I was so hoping I could lock this door the 21st and be through. Oh, well.

The town of West Point was a-buzz with gossip about the impending marriage of a Catholic with a Missouri Synod Lutheran after a courtship of only three months. As La Vera explained to Karl: "There's nothing new around here. Guess we're still West Point's latest gossip morsel. People give me a pain. 'Why don't you wait until after the war?', 'Oh, you're so young,' 'What about religion?', 'Why, you haven't gone together very long,' etc. It's a wonder I'm not balmy. I just laugh and go my way."

At last the magic day arrived, as Karl and La Vera boarded the train in West Point at 5:30 A.M. on May 25, 1943 to head for Omaha and their wedding. Perhaps Karl had been over-confident that everything would proceed like clockwork, but many pitfalls developed, as described later by La Vera:

"I knew that I was so excited that I left without taking a coat. Upon our arrival in Omaha, we had breakfast and then proceeded to get our license for marriage. As it was too early for the courthouse to open, we lingered on the street nearby for a few minutes, killing time by weighing ourselves on a nearby scale. Funny how the Judge, (who later married us) witnessed us weighing and remarked to himself that he was sure that here was a couple who were waiting to get a license. After this ordeal was finally accomplished, we picked up our luggage and went out to the home of some friends who formerly lived in West Point. They were Mrs. Edna Lacey and her two daughters, one being a former classmate of mine (Edna Lacey). Mrs. Lacey formerly worked in the Golden Rod with Karl's mother, and consequently knew his family very well. They knew we were getting married in Omaha, and had written us asking us to have the wedding dinner at their house at 115 North 26th Street in Omaha.

When Karl and La Vera were married at Judge Bannen's house on May 25, 1943, the small wedding party included Elvera Fischer (La Vera's bridesmaid) and PFC. Darold Linning, whom Karl had drafted as his best man from the M.P. constabulary in Omaha.

"When we got to their home, I proceeded to unpack my wedding clothes, etc., while Karl went downtown to register in a hotel and contact a friend of his who was going to be best man (Keith Abbott). Together they went to see the priest of the church of which his friend was a member (St. Mary Magdalen Catholic Church). Somehow things went wrong. The priest (Father Rudolph F. Kluthe, who had served at St. Mary's Catholic Church in West Point, 1940–1942) wanted me to take a series of instructions before he would marry us; also I was to make certain promises as to possible children being Catholics, etc. At any rate, things were in complete discord, I was crying and Karl left both the priest and his friend (Keith) in a state of dissension. I never learned the full details, but I know that Karl came back to the house where I was staying as a very unhappy individual. Now here I was with a completely white bridal outfit, complete with veil and all, and where could we be married? I certainly couldn't go to the city hall in a get up like that. There seemed nothing to do but cry, and that I did. Mrs. Lacey came to the rescue

The official wedding photo. May 25, 1943

by suggesting that Karl call Omaha Municipal Judge John W. Bannen and ask him if we might come to his home to be married that evening. He consented, so the wedding was to be at 8:00 P.M. Now we were without a best man (Keith bowed out after the discussion with the priest).

"Karl solved that by going to the M.P. Station and asking for a soldier to appear as his best man. He didn't want an officer, so he was represented by a very well groomed, well-mannered Pfc. My bridesmaid was a girl friend (Elvera Fischer) who was working in Omaha.

"So with all the confusion, we were finally married in the home of Omaha Municipal Judge John W. Bannen at 3556 Woolworth Avenue at 8:00 P.M. on May 25, 1943, and I did get to wear my white bridal outfit after all.

"Besides the bridesmaid and best man and a classmate of mine, no one attended the wedding except of course, the Judge's wife. The wedding being over, we went to the Lacey home where we were treated to a wonderful wedding dinner, complete with wedding cake. After that, we left with our attendants downtown to a night spot (the 'Dugout') where we had a few cocktails. This was our mixed up wedding day. While we were celebrating at the Dugout, three Catholic couples came by and without even congratulating us, they berated Karl for marrying outside the church. They were from West Point.

"We remained in Omaha for several days and then returned to West Point. My mother gave a reception for our immediate families and later on that night we had a wedding dance at the Del Rio hall. There was a huge gathering of friends and relatives, plus curious on-lookers.

"Karl's leave was up the next day, so I in turn accompanied him to Omaha where we said a sorrowful goodbye and parted again. Going back home to West Point gave me a very let down feeling as I didn't know when I would see my husband again. Upon my arrival home, I found that my mother was down in bed with an old leg injury. I stayed at home to take care of her until she was able to be about again, and then I went to Omaha where I took a job at the soda fountain with Mrs. Lacey. It was a long and lonely summer. I had a room which I shared with another left-behind bride. Our letters were the only thing to look forward to, and of course the day when maneuvers were over and we could be together again."

A retrospective on the May 25, 1943 wedding was provided by bride La Vera in the June 3, 1943 issue of the West Point Republican (home addresses added by author).

"Miss La Vera Meyer and Lt. Karl Timmermann were united in marriage in Omaha May 25 by Judge John W. Bannen. The single ring marriage was used. Miss Elvera Fischer and Pfc. Darold Linning were the bridal attendants.

"The bride's dress was of white organza made in floor-length with the full skirt gathered to a fitted bodice. Her veil was held in place by a lace tiara and her accessories were in white. A crystal necklace and a bridal corsage completed her costume.

"A wedding reception was held at the home of Mrs. Keith Wiley, 14082 William Street, with the wedding cake baked by Mrs. Edna Lacey.

"Mrs. Timmermann attended Wayne College and has taught in a rural school four years."

La Vera sent Karl an anniversary card with the following message:

> Hello Darling,
>   Well, this is it—our 1st anniversary. I want to thank you, Karl, for a beautiful year. I hope the others are even more so. And I know they will be.
>   I love you, Dearest, a million times more than I did a year ago. I love you with all my heart. I want you to know that you've made me a very happy wife.
>   Yours forever,
>   La Vera

SIX

From Desert Training Center to Camp Polk

WHILE KARL WAS STILL at Fort Riley in the week before his wedding, he received the following from a very alarmed La Vera:

Sunday, May 16,

Dearest Karl,

I had begun a letter to you previously, and Alice just came over & told me about the Fort Riley tornado. Darling, I hope you're not hurt. You just can't be. I'll worry every single minute till I hear you're alright.

Although the Wizard of Oz had visited Kansas, in political terms Karl assured La Vera: "That tornado didn't touch the part of Fort Riley where I'm stationed. It struck at the Republican Flats Area and I'm in the Camp Funston Area."

Karl had been ordered to cut short his honeymoon and return to Fort Riley no later than May 31, 1943—six days after his marriage—on the supposition that the 9th Armored Division would be moving on that date to the Desert Training Center in California.

On that date, Karl dispatched a mournful letter to his new wife:

8:05 P.M.

May 31st

Hello La Vera,

I didn't want to leave you at the station yesterday. I wanted to stay there and kiss away your tears. La Vera, I love you, love you with all my heart. I didn't want you to cry when I left and when you did, I didn't want to leave you, but I had no other choice. La Vera, you're so sweet and lovable. I know that I have the finest and best woman in the world for my wife. I long for you so much, La Vera, that I could cry, if I'd let myself.

I'm going to bed early tonight. I didn't sleep much last night.

What is your house number?

Good night, La Vera,

I love you

Karl

Threatened with departure as each day dawned, the 9th Armored remained at Fort Riley until mid-June of 1943. Reflecting on the interruption of his honeymoon to force his early return Karl was told by his Fort Riley buddies that was one of the customary army "SNAFU"s, which in unexpurgated army lingo meant "Situation normal, all fucked up." Applied to Karl, they said that every SNAFU is followed by a more family-type sequel to read "hurry up and wait!"

Nevertheless, Karl wrote a love letter every day to La Vera excerpts of which follow:

June 1, 1943

9:15 P.M.

Hello La Vera,

You're on my mind constantly. I'm always thinking of you. La Vera, I love you, love you with a love that is forever increasing. I doubt whether any man could love a woman as much as I love you. La Vera, I love you so much that I'm afraid that my chest will burst . . . .

We went on a fairly long hike today and I'm quite tired tonight. I lose weight every summer from sweating. I wish that this summer were over already. That would bring "our being together" closer. You know. La Vera, you're my very life. You're everything.

I found out today that I'll be needing the clothes which I left behind. I'm sorry but you'll have to send them as soon as possible.

I think that I'll go to Junction City tomorrow and buy about three or four pair of coveralls to wear in the desert.

Did you get the package which I sent from Kansas City? Are we still the latest gossip in West Point?

June 6, 1943
4:00 P.M.

Hello, Sweetheart,

Last week at this time we were on our way to the Union Station. Two weeks ago you had your school picnic and I was in West Point probably drinking beer. That was when we lived in the present. Now we live in the future and past. La Vera, our real future will be when I can say I'm to stay and that we'll never have to separate again. I know that I'm the most fortunate man on earth to have a wife so sweet and lovable as you. La Vera, I love you, I love you with all my heart.

I got another short haircut. I look funny now.

Goodbye for now,

La Vera, I love you, Karl

June 7th
8:55 P.M.

My La Vera,

We made an eighteen mile hike today through rain and mud.

How is the gossip in West Point? I hope that our Mother Meyer is well again for now.

Good Night Sweetheart,

I love you,
Karl

June 8th
9:15 P.M.

Hello La Vera,

My clothes came today, thanks! The box was beat up a bit. Now, La Vera, please send me a box of moth balls. I can't buy any around here.

June 11, 2:35 P.M.

Hello Sweetheart,

I'm the "Commander of the Guard" tonight, so therefore I'm not getting much sleep. I intend to get a couple hours as soon as I say "Good Night" to my wife.

The cookies arrived yesterday morning. They're wonderful. Thanks a lot, La Vera.

I love you, La Vera, I love you with all my heart. If you could count the stars in the sky on a clear summer night then perhaps, you could begin to measure my love for you. I love you, La Vera, a million times more than I can ever say.

Good Night La Vera,

I love you, Karl

June 11th

7:35 P.M.

My La Vera,

I've got a terrible headache from the heat and sun today. We went on a long hike and it was "hotter than hell."

June 12, 10:30 P.M.

Hello Sweetheart,

I just came back from Junction City. I ate supper in town, did some shopping and went to the show.

You say that you'd like to torment me. Now, what could you possibly do to torment a big boy like me? Nothing.

I know that my love for you will always increase. I know that I have the best wife in the world and I knew that she would be before I ever proposed. If there had been any doubt in my mind I would have never proposed. And La Vera, if you ever want to get spanked and have it hurt, just tell me that you doubt my love for you.

June 13, 5:00 P.M.

My La Vera, I've felt like a fish out of water ever since I left you at the Union Station two weeks ago.

My back is sunburned and it hurts. I wish that you could take care of it for me.

We will be leaving Kansas any day now for the West.

June 14

9:20 P.M.

It's rather strange that you didn't receive any letters from me last Friday because I've written a letter every day. Maybe you received two letters on Saturday?

La Vera, your husband loves you more than he could ever say. He loves you more than life itself. He knows that he has best and sweetest wife in the world. La Vera, his love for you isn't something that can be turned off and on. It's turned on to stay forever and ever, because to him, you're the only woman that exists.

La Vera, you've asked if your husband was happy. Remember this always, La Vera, because he loves you and loves you with all his heart, he can't be happy unless you're with him. He needs you. Without you, he is nothing; he might as well die. La Vera, you know your husband better than he knows himself.

It was hot here today. I wish that it would rain. We should have left for the west a week and a half ago. I can't tell you why we were delayed. Don't send any more letters to Fort Riley. This is my new address and it must be written out in full.

Headquarters Company, 2nd Battalion

52nd Armored Infantry Regiment

A.P.O. #259

In Care of Postmaster:

Los Angeles, California

Say "hello" to Mother Meyer for me.

Good Night, La Vera,

I love you and I'll love you forever,

Your Husband

Karl's outfit finally arrived at the Desert Training Center on the evening of June 20, 1943, as indicated in his following letter:

June 21

8:30 P.M.

Hello La Vera,

I love you, I love you, La Vera, more than anything else on earth. You're the sweetest and best woman any man could ever expect. I love you with all my heart.

We arrived here last night. There are mountains on four sides of us, but they are from seventy to seventy-five miles away. The closest town is Needles, California which is about twenty-four miles away. Los Angeles is about 300 Las Vegas, Nevada is about 90. It doesn't seem as if I were still on the planet of Earth. Everything seems so strange.

It will be a long time before we are together again. But when this mess is over, La Vera, we live.

> Good Night. Sweetheart,
> I love you,
> Karl

June 25, 7:35 P.M.

My La Vera,

It was quite hot today. The heat seems to sap my strength. I have to take twelve salt tablets per day.

"How much nerve does it take?" I should have had that engraved in the wedding ring. But I guess the ring would have been too small for all those words.

Thanks, La Vera, for the hair brushes. They're wonderful and you're wonderful. Now if I only had some hair.

I had my teeth inspected to-day. They were alright, except for one small cavity which was filled in about ten minutes.

What is the news in the great little city of West Point? Who are they talking about now?

Good Night, La Vera, your husband loves you and he knows that his wife is a real treasure.

> La Vera, I love you,
> Karl

June 25,
7:35 P.M.

My La Vera,

Last month at this time, you were still Miss Meyer, but not for long.

I wish that it would rain. This dam desert will get the best of me yet.

1715

La Vera, I love you. Of course, you know why.

1801

I haven't been back to our base camp since Sunday, so therefore I haven't been able to receive or send any mail. I'll go back to
the base camp next Friday.

DESERT TRAINING CENTER   •   CALIFORNIA

July 4th
8:05 P.M.

Hello Sweetheart,

Two of my men and I crossed part of the desert, a range of
mountains and some more desert to go swimming in the Colorado
River. We made the 64 mile trip in a "jeep." We came back about
an hour ago and we left here seven this morning. We shot several
desert jack rabbits on the way.

We won't be at our base camp during the next week, so therefore I won't be able to write.

July 7th
8:08 P.M.

My Beautiful Wife,

I love you, love you and love you. I'll always love you, La
Vera, forever and ever. I'm sorry that I didn't write in the last few
days, but it really was impossible to write. We were camped on
the west bank of the Colorado River. Along the river is the only
place in this wasteland where there is green vegetation. All the
rest of it is unfit for life of any sort.

Tell Mother Timmermann and Mother Meyer that I'll write as
soon as possible. I get up so early in the morning that some times
I meet myself going to bed.

July 10th 7:40 P.M.

My La Vera,

It's quite hot here every day. The temperature today was about 142°. Yesterday it was about 149°. It's almost unbelievable.

So you don't know what a gila monster is? Guess I'll have to tell you then. It's a large lizard which is found in the Southwest. It's very pretty, has a yellow tail, orange belly and a ridged back. It's the only lizard in the United States whose bite is poison and it's worse than a rattlesnake, but not so aggressive.

Good Night, La Vera,

I love you,

Karl

Karl mentioned that he was putting in for a transfer to the Air Corps:

July 11th, 8:00 P.M.

My Dearest Wife,

It was quite hot today. I've got a headache from the heat and sun. I took 18 salt tablets to-day. That's about the average amount that I take every day.

It will seem almost too good to be true if I leave this desert and get into the Air Corps. Then we can be together, La Vera and until then keep your fingers crossed.

On July 19, Karl reported on his progress in applying for a transfer to the Air Corps:

July 19th

Hello Sweetheart,

Last night I went to March Field, Calif. And took the examination to become a pilot in the Air Corps. I passed in every way. I hope that it's "Goodbye, Armored Force."

The reason why Karl became disgusted with the Armored Force was the prejudiced treatment he personally received from the battalion commander Lt. Col. George E. Seeley. Although Karl would never put this in writing, La Vera frequently told me that Karl deeply resented the fact that it was obvious both officers and enlisted men got ahead and got the best assignments when they resorted to "brown-nosing" the irascible colonel. Several battalion officers reported to me that "Lt. Timmermann would frequently argue with Colonel Seeley when he felt that the battalion was doing something wrong, and, furthermore, that 'Lt. Timmermann was the kind of officer who would not kiss up to anyone, no matter what his higher rank!'"

In addition, several enlisted men who received senseless restrictions at Col. Seeley's hands would depend on Lt. Timmermann to go to bat for them with the battalion commander, who was further infuriated with the great popularity which Timmermann had among enlisted men.

Col. Seeley, reputed to be the oldest Lt. Col. in the U.S. Army, had a very low boiling point and a short fuse, and his temper was so fragile that he would always shout and get a very red face when he wanted to get a point across or discover that anyone differed from his edicts.

Col. Seeley got his revenge on Lt. Timmermann by giving him an abysmally low efficiency rating that contrasted with the universally high ratings which Karl received from all his other commanding officers.

At the outbreak of the Battle of the Bulge in December, 1944, Col. Seeley had a heart attack and was replaced by his battalion executive officer, Major Murray Deevers, whose personality and *modus operandi* were diametrically opposite from his predecessor.

Behind his back, Col. Seeley was popularly known as "The Bull," which several officers pointedly translated into "The Bully". One wonders if whether Lt. Timmermann would have received the same high honors for being the first officer across the Bridge at Remagen had Col. Seeley been the battalion commander on March 7, 1945.

Evaluations of subordinate officers are customarily included in the lower-ranking officer's 201 file. Unfortunately, there is never an opportunity for a subordinate officer to rate and appraise those who supervise. Col. Seeley tangled personally on many occasions with Lt. Timmermann, who was never bashful in pointing out to Col. Seeley's face where he thought the battalion commander was wrong. This made Karl a hero to the enlisted men, and lowered the esteem of Col. Seeley for Karl's outspoken independence.

It is therefore no surprise that Col. Seeley gave Lt. Timmermann the following critical appraisal for the period July 1, 1943 to October 8, 1943: "An opinionated young officer with little military knowledge. Shows reluctance to accept new ideas; always has an alibi. He performs duties assigned to him, but is satisfied with commonplace results. In comparing this officer with all officers of his grade known to me, I would place him in lower third."

After he had been in the desert for thirty days, Karl wrote:

July 20th 7:45 P.M.

Hello La Vera,

    I feel weak tonight. I had a shot in each arm today. One was for typhoid, the other was for yellow fever, I think. Plus these two shots I got vaccinated for small pox.

    Throughout the entire day I'm thinking of you La Vera. I catch myself thinking of you when I should be thinking of my work. As soon as I get off of this desert we can be together.

On July 21, Karl scratched out a letter while out on a problem:

July 21st
2:00 P.M.

Hello Sweetheart,

    We are about ten miles from the "Base Camp" and we'll get back some time tomorrow. I'll mail this as soon as I get back.

    I received six letters from you yesterday and each one was postmarked on a different day. I don't know why my letters aren't postmarked.

    I applied for a transfer to the Air Corps. I passed all the examinations required to become a pilot. Maybe next year at this time I'll be wearing a pair of silver wings. I hope that my transfer isn't delayed and comes through soon. As soon as I get off of this desert we'll be together, La Vera.

July 25th 7:30 P.M.

My La Vera,

    I believe that it's just a matter of time now, before I'm in the Air Corps.

On July 25, Karl reported with some optimism on his Air Corps application. It is extremely doubtful if Col. Seeley gave him a boost:

July 25th 7:30 P.M.

My La Vera,

    I believe that it's just a matter of time now, before I'm in the Air Corps.

The next day Karl wrote, in response to a poem by La Vera:

> Here's a poem about the desert:
> "Day after day in the desert
> sun, sun, sun
> day after day in the desert
> wind, wind, wind
> day after day in the desert
> dust, dust, dust!
> (Monotonous, isn't it?)"

He added: "Your poetry really is wonderful maybe because it was written by the most wonderful woman in the world or are you a natural born poet?"

On July 27, Karl wrote:

> So certain people in West Point think that I should be worrying about my "stepping out," as they say, because I am 2,000 miles away. Some of the frail-minded people of West Point will never understand. I'm constantly thinking of you, La Vera; I love you more than anything else on earth.
>
> We just came back to our base camp. I'm sorry that I won't be able to write to-night. I have to work.
>
> > I love you, La Vera
> > Karl

On the last day in July, Karl wrote:

> > July 31st 7:35 P.M.
> My Darling Wife,
> I love you, La Vera. I love you. Of course you already know that, but I'll never stop telling you.
>
> We'll be together soon, only if my transfer to the Air Corps is approved and there is no reason why it shouldn't be. I'll transfer to the Air Corps in grade. I won't be losing anything, but gaining.

On the first day of August, Karl reported good financial news: "I've saved $276.71 in the last two months. That's enough for a down payment on our car."

Karl at desert training center August, 1943.

On August 2, Karl wrote:

August 2nd

2:30 P.M.

Hello Sweetheart,

We're back out in the open desert today again. I'll mail this letter as soon as I get back to the base camp.

5:55 P.M.

I'm hungry, sleepy and thirsty. I hope that we eat pretty soon. We'll probably go back to our base camp tomorrow.

On August 3, Karl again expressed hope that his transfer to the Air Corps would come through soon:

> I think that I'm losing weight now because I'm sweating too much, but it's weight that can easily be gained back once I get back in a moderate climate. At present, you do the weight gaining for both of us.
>
> Isn't my writing awful? I'll bet you can't hardly read it.
>
> I hope that my transfer comes through soon. What part of U.S. do you want me to be stationed in next? Of course you know that I haven't any choice. When I transfer to the Air Corps I'll transfer in grade,

On August 5, Karl pointed out:

> Aug. 5th
>
> 2005
>
> My La Vera,
>
> During the last two days I've crossed the Nevada-California State line four times. I've, now, crossed the California line fifteen times.

Once again, he reminded La Vera of the significance of February 18, less than six months earlier: "Before February 18th a wonderful woman like you only existed in my dreams and now that I have you in reality I'm the happiest and luckiest man on earth for having such a wife, such a *wonderful* wife."

Karl still had uppermost in his mind getting into the Air Corps and away from Col. ("The Bull") Seeley:

> August 8th
>
> 7:50 P.M.
>
> My La Vera,
>
> I wish that I could write on paper that which is in my heart. La Vera, you know that I love you. As soon as my transfer to the Air Corps is approved and comes through, we'll be together. Keep your fingers crossed, Sweetheart, I hope that I get stationed near or in some large city. And I hope that I don't get sent to the South. I spent ten months down there and I hate it. But, where I get sent doesn't matter much as long as we'll be together.

On August 11, Karl explained why his beard was so tough it required a new razor blade (Pre-Bick) every day:

Aug. 11th 7:15 P.M.

My La Vera,

I received the sunglasses and the razor blades and shaving soap today. Thanks. You sent me enough razor blades to last for fifteen days. I use a new razor blade every time that I shave. So, La Vera, remember to keep me supplied with blades.

On August 14, Karl reported an amazing story of lost-and-found:

August 14th

2000

Hello, Sweetheart,

Last week I lost my identification tags in the desert. Today, I got them back; a sergeant in the 3rd Battalion found them on this very desert. It's really a small world.

We hiked 40 miles in the last two days. It was dusty and hot. I thought of you all the time. The narrow-minded people of West Point have never seen a soldier in his drill uniform, they have never seen him tired, sweaty, dusty, and so sick at heart that he could cry. The only way they've ever seen a soldier, is in dress uniform when he's on leave. And West Point is only one little hick town in the United States.

By mid-August, Karl was expressing his anticipation about getting out of the desert:

August 15th 1935

My La Vera,

Every night about 2030 a trans-Continental air-liner flies over our camp headed east. I wish that I were on it.

On August 16, Karl reported:

Aug. 16th 1510

Hello La Vera,

At 0400 today it began to rain and it rained until about 15 minutes ago. We left our base camp in the rain this morning and traveled until about an half an hour ago. We've now stopped to dry out because the sky is clear again. Everything is beautiful and fresh, but by noon it'll be hot and miserable again.

There was a gap in Karl's letters until August 27, as he explains:

> August 27th   1005
>
> My La Vera,
>
> I'm sorry that I didn't write this week, but I really couldn't.

On August 29, Karl wrote:

> How would you like to live in Manhattan, Kansas? We might live there soon. As soon as we leave this desert, you and I can be together. So, until then, Sweetheart, keep your chin up. I haven't heard anything from the Air Corps yet. I hope that I get to transfer soon.
>
> This desert must have been an ocean floor in pre-historic times because the rocks, mountains and valley have such weird shapes. There are lines which run along the sides of some of these mountains which I believe to be water lines.
>
> I'm thirsty for a nice ice cold drink. I'm constantly thirsty.
>
> So long for now,
>
> > La Vera, I love you.
> >
> > Karl

By September 1st, Karl hoped his outfit might be going back to Fort Riley:

> Sept. 2nd   1503
>
> Hello Sweetheart,
>
> I've never felt so miserable before in my life, both mentally and physically. This desert is getting the best of me. I feel bad enough to be a 4-F. I wonder how much you'd love me if I were 4-F.

By the next day he was expressing great disillusionment, perhaps because he had heard nothing from the Air Corps: "There isn't much to write about the desert. All the days seem alike. It won't be many more days and we'll be leaving this desert. I figured that it would be about fifty more days and I think I'm right. Then, I hope that we go back to Fort Riley."

In his September 3 letter, Karl showed his displeasure with a question from La Vera:

> La Vera, you've asked a very silly question and for that you get spanked. You asked whether or not I was sorry that I married you. If I would regret marrying you, it would mean that I don't love you. And, La Vera, you know as well as I do, that I love you and love you more than anything else in the world. No man could ever love a woman as much as I love you, La Vera. (But, you're still going to get spanked.)

The next day Karl's disillusionment with the Army once again boiled to the surface:

> Sept. 4th 1905
>
> My La Vera,
>
> It's the end of another hot day. I hope that this will soon be in the past. I'm so darn fed up with this Army, it's awful. Two years ago I was an ideal soldier. I was a Private 1st Class, making $36.00 per month and I liked the Army. Now, I say, "To hell with it."

By September 5, he expressed optimism both about the state of their finances and the prospects for leaving the desert:

> We've now got $202.00 in the bank and I've got $150.00 with me. We'll spend it when we get old—several months older than we are now.
>
> We'll be together again some time in November. It might be sooner, that is, if my transfer to the Air Corps comes through.
>
> I won't be able to write very much during the next six weeks, because we're leaving our base camp tomorrow and won't be back until late in October. And then we'll leave the desert. I think that we might go back to Ft. Riley. Of course, La Vera, we've both got our fingers crossed for the Air Corps.
>
> Today is another hot day. This is the worst place in the United States.
>
> Have you been gaining any weight? You'd better!
>
> La Vera, you know that you've got a couple of spankings coming from your husband and they're going to hurt too.

Sept. 6th   1230

My La Vera,

We left our base camp at 0900 this morning and we won't return until late in October. I wish that these desert maneuvers were
over, better yet I wish that the war were over. Then we could live
and be happy.

On September 7th, Karl showed his anger at a protest from La Vera:

Sept. 7th   1205

This morning I received your letter where you stated that you
were angry because you didn't receive any letter from me. Well,
La Vera, if you're angry at me, then I'm angry too. You know as
well as I that the mail situation is "on the blink." Every letter I
write has to go west to Los Angeles and then back track to the
east over the same route. La Vera, you have no reason for anger
whatsoever. I write every time that I get a chance. I love you more
than life itself and <u>you're</u> angry.

On September 9 Karl wrote:

I didn't have time to write yesterday. Blame the Army.

La Vera, how would you like to have a fur coat for the winter?
You may have one after November 1st.

By Saturday we should be near the Mexican Border. Don't
worry, La Vera, we'll be together again.

I got some battery acid on my back yesterday. It ate several
holes in my coveralls and blistered my back. It's O.K. now though.

La Vera, I'll try to write every time I get a chance; you know
that.

I love you, La Vera,
Karl

Sept. 10th   1400

My La Vera,

I haven't much time to write now, because we're going to move
again soon. I haven't received any mail since Sunday and to-day is
Friday. I suppose that it will all come at once.

On September 14, Karl mentions a friend who graduated from West Point High School, Dean Kerl.

Sept. 14th 0907

My La Vera,

We are now in the corner of California which is near the borders of Arizona and Mexico.

I've been losing quite a bit weight lately but I'm not worried because it's weight that can be easily gained back when I'm back in a temperate climate again.

I saw Dean Kerl last week. He's much taller than I.

It's another hot day today. It was about 145° yesterday.

On September 16, Karl eagerly anticipated his departure from the desert: "I'll be glad when I leave this 'pre-historic ocean floor.' If I stay here many more weeks, I'll probably go nuts."

On September 21, after writing that the temperature reached 140°, Karl had a concerned note:

Sept. 21st 0700

Good morning, La Vera, I didn't sleep much last night because we traveled most of the time. I wish that these desert maneuvers were over.

I'm losing too much weight lately. It's got me worried.

There was some more definite news on September 28:

Sept. 28th 1130

My La Vera,

We start leaving the desert on the 16th of October. We'll either go to Camp Barkeley Texas or to Camp Polk, Louisiana. I hope that it's Camp Barkeley, but if its Camp Polk conditions won't be any better than what they are here. I wish that my Air Corps transfer would come through soon. If this outfit goes to Camp Barkeley we'll live in Abilene, Texas.

In December, I'm going to ask for a 10 days leave, that is if I'm not in the Air Corps by then.

You know how much I love you, La Vera, I long to take you in my arms and never let you go. I'll always love you forever and ever.

It's dinner time.

So long for now, I love you, Karl

Sept. 29th 1930

Hello Sweetheart,

This outfit starts to leave for Camp Polk, Louisiana on the
16th of October. Here's what you do. Go to Leesville, Louisiana,
which is near Camp Polk, find a nice apartment for us there. Make
sure that it's near the bus line which runs into Camp so that I
won't have too far to walk to catch a bus in the mornings. I don't
know what Leesville is like, so therefore you'll have to do a lot of
inquiring when you get there. And La Vera, leave for Louisiana as
soon as possible to find an apartment before the rush.

La Vera, I know that you won't like it in Louisiana but I'll be
going into the Air Corps soon and then everything will be wonderful.

Enclosed is a check; cash it as soon as possible. Get all my old
checks from the bank and find out how much I have in the bank
because I really don't know.

A few days later Karl wrote:

I was way up in the mountains yesterday afternoon. From where
I was I could see Arizona, Nevada and the Colorado River wind-
ing like a snake. While I was up there, I shot a gila monster.

Good-bye for now, La Vera

I love you, Karl

Then on October 6, Karl reported:

Oct. 6th

My La Vera, We are packing and getting ready to leave this
darn desert. We'll probably leave sometimes after the 16th.

I'm all packed to leave already. I travel rather light in compari-
son to other officers.

La Vera wrote on October 14:

Thurs, Oct. 14,

My Darling,

I just finished a few crazy cards to people back home. Gosh, I hope you arrive soon. I long to be in your arms, close as I can be. I love you, Karl. It's been so long since I've received any word from you. I'm still keeping my chin up with hopes of finding an apt. No luck today either. It's hard to look alone. I need you.

La Vera's October 14 letter, in order not to upset Karl, papered over the horrendous demeaning experience which an Army officer's wife suffered in Leesville on her fruitless search for an apartment for two brave souls less than a year before Karl was shipped to combat in the European Theater of Operations.

Let La Vera describe her treatment in Leesville as she looked back on it in 1955, with all the torturous details:

"Karl found out that he was going to Camp Polk, La. He advised me to go on ahead of him so that could find a place to live before he arrived. I packed my bags so fast, and returned to West Point to get the rest of my belongings and see my family before my trip to La. I was so excited, and there was no doubt in mind but that I would have no trouble finding a nice apartment near the bus line as Karl had advised. Upon my arrival in Leesville, La., I intended to check into a nice hotel until I found suitable living quarters. What a laugh that was! Finding a seat on the train out of Kansas City was impossible. I sat on my suitcase in the aisle. It was on this nightmarish trip to Leesville, La. that I soon found out what I was to expect on my arrival. *Look* Magazine had written an article branding this town as the worst army town in the whole U.S. People were living in converted chicken coops or anything that had a roof just to be near their soldier husbands. In other words, rooms were as scarce as finding an oasis in the desert.

"When the train got into this horrible city at about 8:30 P.M., it was one frightened army wife that got off that train. I checked my belongings in a locker, and proceeded with another wife in the direction of town. Soldiers were thick as flies, and it had to be a Saturday night. We tried to get rooms at the hotel, but that was impossible. Being unescorted, every lone soldier tried to pick us up. I might add that all this would not have happened had I written for a reservation at the camp guest house. I didn't know there was such a thing, and Karl didn't think it would be necessary, then having a wife was a novelty for him, and he just didn't think of the problem that confronted me. How I got thru that night, I'll never know. As luck would have it, I ran onto an old boy friend from West Point. He tried in vain to get me a room, but no luck, and he had to report back to camp at midnight, so thought I would be safest in the lobby of a hotel. But it was a mistake to think that I could remain there for the night because shortly after midnight, the manager cleared everyone from the lobby. I didn't know where to turn, so decided to stop in an off limits restaurant for a bite of food. I was too panicky to eat, but went thru the motions and tried to figure out how to spend the night. I decided to return to the train depot, so did so and found that I wasn't alone, for there were two other army wives who had nowhere to go. We spread newspapers on the concrete floor of the depot and tried to catch a few winks of sleep before morning. It got cold during the night and by morning I had a terrific cold. By then, I was so disgusted that I didn't much care. These wives had reservations at the Enlisted Men's Wives' Guest House at Camp Polk starting in the morning, so they were considerate enough to take me along. Upon our arrival there, we were assigned to rooms and after cleaning up, went to the mess hall for breakfast. I then found out that I could stay at the Officers' Guest House, so transferred my belongings. I was quite sick with a cold, but the same day I caught a bus into DeRidder, La., a nearby town, to look for an apartment. I made quite a canvass of the town, and finally located a nice room for $14 per week. Apartments weren't to be found at all, but by now I was happy to find a room to rent.

"Several days later I moved out to the room in DeRidder. The family who owned the home were very friendly, and I believe that I was there about 2 weeks before Karl finally did arrive. It was a long, lonely wait, and the day finally arrived when he was with me once more. Those were really happy days, altho they were filled with fear of another separation, as we all knew that the 9th Armored Division was getting ready to go overseas.

"As it happened, I believe that we were only together 2 months when they were sent on maneuvers again into Texas and I could see no point in remaining in La. when I wouldn't be able to see Karl anyway, and the rent was a terrific price. So back home I went again to mama. I took a job in a Dry Goods Store as a saleslady. I remember arriving home just in time for Thanksgiving. I was home all through December, and it was heck spending our first Christmas apart. I know that Karl was really miserable and unhappy on these maneuvers. The weather was cold and damp, and everyone was weary of the army and the war.

"Finally in January I got the 'Go' signal to join him again. This time I had sense enough to write ahead for reservations at the Guest House. I decided to look for a room in Leesville, La. this time as it was closer to camp, and bus service would be faster. Karl wouldn't have to get up quite so early in the morning to make it to camp on time. Here again I spent several days searching for that 'Apartment', but finally settled on a room. This time the rent was $10 per week. It wasn't nearly as nice as the DeRidder one, but all I could find. It was quite dirty when I moved in and I really went to work disinfecting the place. Also made curtains and had them up before Karl arrived. I think I waited a week or so before he arrived. I remember that I wanted to be all prettied up when he arrived, and then he came and surprised me, and naturally caught me scrubbing and my hair pinned up . . . and he didn't mind a bit!

"Since we had no cooking facilities, we ate all of our meals out. That really got tiresome. It was awful hot there during the summer months. The town had 3 movies, so we saw every one that came to town. Our room was stifling so it wasn't too pleasant spending much time at home. Then, too, we enjoyed movies. I remember one Sunday when we saw the double features at two consecutive movies. We were very much in love and worried that each day would bear the news of the inevitable going overseas.

"In July we moved into a large white house, that was converted into 3 large bedrooms with a kitchen. Here we lived with 2 other couples, sharing the kitchen. Our rent was $15 per week, but we did have the kitchen and could cook our meals, which we did in a fashion. However, sharing a kitchen with other couples had its problems too. Sometimes we pooled our food, and other times we cooked in shifts. What a mad, crazy life everyone lived during the war. As long as we were together nothing else seemed to matter.

"Then one day in July I learned I was pregnant. I was so ill that I got down in bed for several days. Couldn't eat and didn't even have the energy to dress myself alone. I was so ill that when the news came that our guys were going overseas, I was too weak and sick to care about anything. Karl was very happy about the coming baby, but it was tough for him to see me so ill just before they left. It was the last part of August when they went overseas. I left camp a few days before the boys were restricted so that I would have a better chance getting a seat on the train back home. I knew that most of the girls would stay until the last day, and I was afraid I wouldn't make it as it was. I think I was about the most forlorn person in the world at that time. I had lost so much weight and couldn't keep any food on my stomach at all. Karl was the sweetest, most considerate husband ever, and now when I really needed him, we were thrown apart.

"Somehow I arrived home in one piece. The depot agent took me home from the station. My mother was at work, and no one was there when I arrived. I immediately went upstairs to my old bed, leaving my luggage in the middle of the kitchen floor. When my mother came home and found me in bed, she took one look at me and immediately surmised what was wrong. I did a lot of crying then for awhile. After a few months had passed I began to feel better and take an interest in the coming event. Karl's letters, always sweet and filled with love for me, really were an inspiration. I wrote him daily and sometimes twice a day. He wrote whenever he could, and I averaged about four a week. I followed the war from the papers and radio reports and with his letters I usually knew about where he was. He wrote me from France, Belgium, Luxembourg and then Germany.

"The time I really did some worrying was during the 'Battle of the Bulge', and rightly so, because they were in immediate danger at that time.

"That winter in '45 was a long one for many people, but we really sweated out the days. Our letters were filled with dreams of the unborn child. Karl was so certain that it would be a boy that we never did decide on a girl's name. Our boy was to be called James Karl, only when he was born, he was a she, and she came early, 3 weeks early, on February 28th at a few minutes before noon. It was wonderful to have a daughter, and I just couldn't get used to the idea. Couldn't decide on her name, whether it should be Diane Gay or Gay Diane, but with Timmermann being so long, the shorter first name won out. My birthday, March 6th was spent in the hospital, and I went home the next day.

"It was a wonderful feeling to be a Mother, almost unbelievable. Gay was such a tiny baby, weighing only 6 lbs. and 1 oz. I felt badly because Karl wasn't there to share the joy of a newborn baby, all ours.

"It was on the evening of March 7th, when a very exciting event reached our ears. I was in bed at my Mother's house, had just finished eating, when Mother Timmermann rushed into our house in a state of excitement, trying to tell us the glad news that Karl had charge of the company that had made the first crossing of the Rhine at Remagen. In her mixed broken German and English dialogue, it took quite some time to realize what had happened. It seems that a reporter from the *World Herald* had called her telling about the first crossing of the Rhine and that Karl was a hero. With all this excitement, here I was flat on my back with not even a phone in the house. The whole town was buzzing with excitement and I couldn't even be a part of it. With my new baby and the anxiety for Karl's safety and his heroism, I don't believe that I slept a wink that night. I couldn't wait for the morning edition of the paper. I sent my Dad up town early for the morning *Herald*. How proud I was to read about my hero husband's national fame. Then, too, there was a letter of congratulations to Karl from Nebraska's Gov. Griswold. Those moments will always be treasured. It seemed so unbelievable to be in the headlines, to know that the whole world was reading about Karl and about Gay's birth. *Stars and Stripes* and all papers everywhere carried this wonderful story and it seemed like a dream to see our picture in the papers. Friends everywhere were sending articles from their city papers, along with letters of congratulations. It was one big dream and I so often had to pinch myself to see if I was awake. It seemed that Karl stayed in the limelight continuously. There was always an article in another paper or magazine adding something a little different to the story.

"After this big day on March 7, I couldn't wait to hear from Karl his own version of the crossing of the Rhine. Funny thing, that he barely mentioned it in his letters. His main concern was his new daughter and his longing to come home to be with us. It is interesting to learn how Karl finally knew his daughter was born. After the crossing of the Rhine, he was given a pass to Paris. While there, he picked up an edition of *Stars and Stripes*, and lo and behold, he saw a picture of me holding Gay when she was 10 days old. He immediately went to the newspaper office, and got a large photo of us. This is how he found out that he was a father.

"And so the days passed very slowly. I kept busy with my new baby. The war news seemed better after the crossing of the Rhine, and then the war in Europe was finally over."

On October 9, as in all the "light" armored divisions like the 9th Armored, the heavy 52nd Armored Regiment was split into three separate regiments before leaving California. The 1st Battalion became the 60th Armored Infantry Battalion, the 2nd Battalion became the 27th Armored Infantry Battalion and the 3rd Battalion became the new 52nd Armored Infantry Battalion. Karl was appalled to discover that his nemesis Colonel Seeley became the new commander of the 27th Armored Infantry Battalion.

Karl remained optimistic that the chance to be together with La Vera would exceed the difficulties of his absences on military maneuvers and was worth the risk. In his last letter from California, Karl wrote:

October 17th

My La Vera,

Next week at this time we'll be together, that is if nothing unusual takes place between now and then. So, keep your chin up until then, because this week will pass quickly. I can't tell you exactly when we'll arrive at Camp Polk, but you can figure on us being together next Sunday.

La Vera was blunt in her feelings about Louisiana in the following letter to Karl's sister Mary:

Saturday, Oct. 30

Dear Mary,

Received your letter & was glad to hear from you.

Karl is with me a week yesterday & we're really happy to be together again.

I still have the same room. Won't find an apartment around here. I really don't know how long I'll be here as Karl may go on more maneuvers. I hope not: he's still waiting for his transfer to the Air Corps, He's so dissatisfied with his branch of the service. I really hope he is transferred soon. It will be nicer for us both. Then I can have an apt too.

Louisiana is lousy. I'm growing used to it but never can really like it. The South is unsanitary in every way. This is a small town. Nothing to do here but go to the Officer's Club at Camp. We've usually seen all shows before too.

Karl saw Fritz the other day. I think he's coming to De Ridder to see us tomorrow. However, Karl has to work, so I think I'll go out to Camp in the afternoon. I hope you received the gift alright. It's really hard to find anything nice in this dump town. It's 10 times worse than West Point.

Well, write again. Best regards to both of you.

La Vera

In subsequent letters from Camp Polk, Karl during his absences tried to stay in touch, despite the fact he was out in the field, not only in Louisiana but also in Texas:

Nov. 23rd

My La Vera,

It's warm today and I hope that it stays like this and doesn't rain. You know, La Vera, that I'll write every time that I have a chance.

How was the trip back to Nebraska? Did the money last?

Send me a comb or else I have to get my hair cut again.

So long for now.

> La Vera, you know that I love you.
>
> Karl

Enclosed is $100.00. Use as you see fit. Save whatever you don't need. We have a home and car to buy after the war.

You know, Sweetheart, you don't have to work. I make enough money to support us and then some. And besides, I told you that you were to gain weight while I was gone and not be losing it. La Vera, you probably know me better than I know myself. What do you think my thoughts are throughout the day? I love you and long for you more than any thing else on earth. I'm always day-dreaming of you.

Good Night, La Vera,

> I love you,
>
> Karl

> Dec. 12th 4:30 P.M.

My La Vera,

Thanks for the cookies and olives. I received the package about 12:00 today. La Vera, you're wonderful.

We're back in Louisiana again and we're camped about three miles north of Leesville. We'll be located here about 24 hours.

We've had fairly nice weather in the last two days.

The same day Karl wrote to his wife, La Vera wrote to Karl's sister Mary:

> Sunday, Dec. 12,

Dear Mary,

I think I owe you a letter, so will attempt an answer. Gee! I hate being home again. Karl & I had such wonderful times together in La. Of course, I hope to join him again as soon as these maneuvers are over which should be about the 1st of Feb.

I'm not working anywhere, but here at home where I find plenty to do. We live across the street from Fischers in the house where Wortmanns used to live. It's a small house, but rather cozy.

Well, Christmas will soon be here. I sent Karl cookies, olives, popcorn balls & a fruit cake. Then, too, got him a good ring.

You'll be home for Christmas, won't you? I wish Karl could be too.

Fritz looks very nice in his uniform. I saw him several times when he had his furlough. There's not much for a married woman to do around here. I stay at home most of the time. I hate West Point.

We've been having nice weather here yet. I hope it lasts. Is it cold there?

How do you like your job in the drug store?

Your Mom is anxiously waiting to be Grandmother, so you better get started, kid. The flag's still waving here.

Well, there isn't much to write about. Anyway I'll be seeing you soon, so cheerio.

Love, La Vera,

Hello to Vic.

On January 8, Karl wrote to La Vera about moving to North Camp Polk:

Jan. 8, 4:40 P.M.

My La Vera,

The 9th goes to North Polk in two weeks. Leesville is a "dry" town since Jan 1st and De Ridder is "wet," so therefore Leesville is the better place to live. So, La Vera, leave for Leesville as soon as possible.

Co. "A" 27th Armd. Inf. Bn.
A.P.O. #259
Camp Polk, Louisiana

My La Vera,

I'm sorry that I haven't written during the last week. In another week we'll be together again

Somewhere in Texas
Jan. 22nd

La Vera,

I finally received a letter from you. I was a bit worried. La Vera you know how very much I love you, I love you more and more each day. I could never be able to tell you in words how much I love you, La Vera.

Forgive me for not writing but I didn't know the address. I
think that we'll move into North Polk around Febr. 7th but, I'm
not sure that I'll see you before then. So, La Vera, please keep
your "chin up."

FULLY SIX YEARS before Wisconsin Senator Joseph McCarthy pranced across
the national landscape with his bankrupt charges of disloyalty in high places,
including the United States Army, the future Hero of the Rhine was igno-
miniously required to prove that his birth in Germany did not make him
loyal to the nation against whom we were fighting.

At least Karl Timmermann was not unceremoniously thrown without trial
into a concentration camp like countless thousands of Japanese-Americans
interned during World War II. But shame on those narrow-minded authorities
who required this future hero to prove that he was a loyal American.

5 JANUARY 1944
TO LT. KARL TIMMERMANN:

BEFORE ANY FURTHER CONSIDERATION CAN BE GIVEN YOUR CASE
REGARDING YOUR CITIZENSHIP STATUS, IT IS REQUESTED THAT A COM-
PLETE PERSONAL AND FAMILY HISTORY, INCLUDING DATE OF YOUR
ARRIVAL IN THE UNITED STATES, AND WHETHER OR NOT YOU HAVE
BEEN BACK TO GERMANY, BE FORWARDED THIS HEADQUARTERS.

Karl was then required to submit the following affidavit at Camp Polk,
dated on Lincoln's Birthday, February 12, 1944:

Affidavit of Citizenship
Enclosed is an affidavit outlining my family history in detail. It might be
added that neither of my parents have any ties to Germany that could in any
way restrain my doing my duty for any branch of United States service.
John Timmermann married Mary Weisbecker April 15, 1922.
Karl Timmermann born June 19, 1922.
Arrived New York January 9, 1924.
John Timmermann never intended to relinquish his American citizenship,
and his residence in Germany was due to the fact he was unable to get clear-
ance for immigration purposes from American and German governments.
John H. Timmermann born July 26, 1884, son of Arnold Timmermann
and Anna Wortman of Monterey, Nebraska.
Baptized at Church of St. Charles, Nebraska August 15, 1884.

IN SUBSEQUENT MONTHS, Karl's outfit continued the "Louisiana Maneuvers" until shortly before they began to prepare for embarkation to the European Theater of Operations. " P.O.M." (Prepare For Overseas Movement) took place during May, June and July 1944, and involved three 25-mile marches within eight hours, three 9-mile marches within two hours, and three 5-mile marches within one hour.

On August 5, 1944, Karl's outfit left North Camp Polk, Louisiana by train for Camp Kilmer, New Jersey arriving on August 7.

Then on August 19 they arrived at the New York Port of Embarkation to board the transatlantic liner *Queen Mary* for the 5-day trip to England.

SEVEN

After Remagen in ETO in 1945

WHEN THE COMMAND OF Company A, 27th Armored Infantry Battalion was thrust on Karl Timmermann late on March 6, he barely had time to reflect that he was being honored on his wife La Vera's birthday. He wondered about their expected offspring, not realizing until weeks later that his daughter Gay Diane had already been born on February 28.

La Vera was at home in West Point with their daughter when Karl's mother excitedly burst in to report the dramatic news of her son's heroism at Remagen.

The intense fighting plus a wholesale media invasion kept Karl so occupied that he had to explain to La Vera the gap in his letters.

Although the seizure of the Ludendorff Bridge was accomplished by Karl's company with no casualties, the tough fighting occurred on the east side of the Rhine, especially in scaling the 600 foot basaltic cliff, the "Erpeler Ley" which the G.I.'s aptly termed "Flak Hill." Supported by the 14th Tank Battalion the 27th Armored Infantry Battalion had tough going on the east side of the bridge. Hitler rushed reinforcements in a futile attempt to eliminate the bridgehead.

So many rifle company officers in the 27th Armored Infantry Battalion had become casualties that a surplus of captains were sent as replacements to the battalion. One of these officers, Capt. Ralph Williams, was sent down to take over Company A on March 12, 1945. He was replaced by 1st Lt. Hayward Luckett on May 12, 1945.

A horde of news hawks, photographers and Army publicists kept the fighting troops busy with first-hand accounts repeated *Ad Infinitum*.

Karl bemoaned the fact that no mail was coming through from his sweetheart. As late as March 14 he was still speculating when the baby would be born, unaware that the blessed event had long since occurred:

> 14th March 1945, 8:30 p.m., Germany
>
> My Darling La Vera,
>
> Another day has gone by and no letter. I hope that I get one tomorrow.
>
> How's our baby getting along? It won't be long now and we'll be parents.

Karl was given a pass to Paris, where he got the big news about Gay Diane when he picked up a copy of the G.I. newspaper, "*The Stars And Stripes.*" There was an Associated Press wire photo of La Vera and Gay on the front page!

On April 2, Karl wrote another piece of exciting news:

> 9:30 P.M., 2nd April '45,
> Germany
>
> La Vera, the papers of the United States promoted me to a 1st Lieutenant and not the U.S. Army.
>
> I'm still a 2nd. But, I'm sure that before you receive this letter I'll be promoted. I'm supposed to get a medal too.

By April 6, Karl was reporting changes in officers which made life in the Army far more pleasant. "The 'Bull' is in Arizona," he told La Vera (having suffered a heart attack at the outset of the Battle of the Bulge). Col. Seeley could no longer harass Karl with bluster, bombast and bullying; his successor as battalion commander was easy-going Murray Deevers, of Hagarville, Arkansas, who had a reputation as "a fine southern gentleman."

Captain Karl Saulpaw, who commanded Company A in the states and used to predict that "Combat will separate the men from the boys," had shown he had none of the "right stuff" when fired on. According to fellow officers, he would park a tank over his fox hole for extra protection, and was evacuated during the Battle of the Bulge for what the official record listed as a "stomach disorder," but another officer reported he had "gone over the hill." Karl reported on April 6 that Saulpaw was no longer with the 9th Armored, having been "reclassified."

This famous photo in the G.I. newspaper Stars and Stripes *alerted Karl to the fact that his daughter Gay Diane was born on February 28, 1945.*

At 9:00 p.m. on April 6, Karl wrote La Vera: "By the time you receive this letter, I should be promoted to 'first.' I was presented the Distinguished Service Cross yesterday. That is the second highest award that can be given. The Congressional Medal of Honor is the highest."

In every letter, Karl asked about Gay. On April 20, he wrote: "How's our 'Little Princess' getting along? I hope that I get to see her before she graduates from high school."

He fired repeated questions about her height, her weight, the color and nature of her hair, her teeth, when she started to talk, what did she say, what did she like to eat, and how well she slept.

Good news came a few days later:

> 23rd April '45, 9:00 P.M.
> Germany
>
> My Darling La Vera,
>   They finally promoted me. I'm a 1st Lt. now.

On May 8, Karl wrote matter-of-factly of the sensational news of V-E Day.

> 8th May '45, 7:00 P.M.
> Germany
>
> My La Vera
>   Today, the war in Europe is supposed to be over. I hope so. I hope that the war in the Orient is over soon too.

On May 20, Karl reported his transfer from A to Headquarters Company with this new assignment: "The town in which I'm located at present is Pegnitz. It's not very large, about the size of Fremont. We're in the Army of Occupation now, but I don't know how long."

On May 25, he described his new assignment: "I can't get my mail every day because I'm on detached duty with the Military Government. It sure is a pain in the neck. We're sending all slave laborers and prisoners of war to their own country."

At the end of May, Karl reviewed the precious number of "points" he had accumulated to return to the states, and took time to refute one of the rumors in West Point that another soldier crossed the Rhine before he did:

> At present, my geographical location is Bayreuth. At one time it was a beautiful city.
>
> I have 102 points. 56 for time in the Army, 9 for time overseas, 12 for Gay Diane, 5 for the D.S.C., 5 for the Purple Heart, 15 for Battle Stars which are the Rhineland, the Ardennes and Central Germany.
>
> So, Le Roy Rief's mother doesn't like me, so what—tell her to jump in the lake! The 3rd A.D. <u>never</u> crossed the Rhine at Remagen but at Cologne and it was after we crossed in the south. What are some of the people trying to do? Smear some of the "old mud" back on the name "Timmermann"?

In his next letter Karl mentioned what he'd been reading: "I've read two books since I've been overseas. They were 'Mutiny on the Bounty' and 'Geography in Human Destiny.' I started to read 'Mutiny on the Bounty' on the 16th of February and finished it somewhere around the 8th of March."

It is difficult to imagine what La Vera wrote to Karl about West Point which set off the following diatribe:

> I knew that sooner or later the Catholics in West Point would start their "mud throwing" campaign. It's funny that they didn't start two years ago. I'll probably kill some of them, when I get back to West Point. The people of W. P. aren't happy unless they're talking and gossiping. They're all too narrow minded to think. There isn't one of them that could have taken my place in battle for one single second. And there's one question that my men and I can ask anyone in the United States; that question is, "<u>What did you do to help win the war</u>?"

In his next letter, Karl relays the latest rumor about his return, and his attitude toward the Army:

> The latest rumor is that the 9th A.D. will leave for the States in the first week of September. I hope that I get relieved from this job with Military Government so that I can get back to the States with the 9th.
>
> Five years ago today, I enlisted in the Army. Five years is too darn long. I liked my first 2½ years in Army. As an officer, I've hated it.

On July 15, Karl reported his new location and the hope he could return to the 27th Armored Infantry Battalion: "I haven't written in several days, because I've been quite busy and I was on the move. I'm still with Military Government and I'm located in Bamberg now. I've put in several requests to be returned to the 27th."

On July 19, Karl reported good news: "I rejoined the Battalion this afternoon—good-bye to Military Government. I'm now located at Wunsiedel which is northeast of Bayreuth. Bavaria is the most beautiful part of Europe, that I've seen so far. Everything is so green."

In addition, Karl reacted to La Vera's request: "Of course, I agree with you La Vera, we won't have any more children for a long time to come. And if you say so we'll never have anymore—It depends entirely upon you."

On July 20, Karl wrote from Wunsiedel, Germany: "The city in which I'm now located is about 20 kilometers (that's about 12½ miles) from the Czech border. It never was bombed or shelled. I'll try to get some perfume for you, La Vera. I tried to get some when I was in Paris. All the perfume is on the 'Black Market' and at terrible prices."

On July 27, Karl reported:

> I have an appointment with the dentist in the morning to have my teeth checked. I might be able to get a bridge of two teeth put in. The bridge will have to be bought from a German dentist, but the Army dentist will fit it and put it in.
>
> I've read a few books lately. They were "G for Genevieve" that's about the Polish Air Force; and two plays by Shakespeare, "Julius Caesar" and "The Merchant of Venice."

Karl reported good news on July 29: "Tomorrow I'm going back to 'A' company. They finally let me do something I want."

Then on August 1st: "Monday, I moved to 'A' company which was at Weissenstadt and yesterday we moved to Haidt. We're on the border line of the Russian zone. Haidt is four kilometers from Hof."

On August 11, Karl reported enormous profits from selling watches to the Russians: "I bought five money orders yesterday, $500.00 at $100.00 a piece. I've still got $200.00 cash money left. I'll send the $500.00 in the next five letters."

More profit on August 13: "I made another $90.00 off of the Russians today. They like to drink better than I do."

> 16th August '45,
> 9:30 A.M.
> Feilitzsch, Germany

Good Morning, Darling,

> I just came back from A.P.O. #76 (76th Inf. Div.). I bought $550.00 money orders. I'm mailing them to you this morning along with $90.00 money order that I got several days ago. Within the last week I sent $1,140.00 to you. How much have we got in the bank now? It should be well over $2,000.00. Enclosed is another $50.00.
>
> I was to the dentist too already this morning. He filled two more teeth and gave me three new "store" teeth.

On August 20, in response to La Vera's question, Karl wrote that he was no longer A company commander, since that position had been taken over by a Captain and later a 1st Lieutenant. On August 21, he wrote: "The 9th A.D. was alerted today for shipment back to the States. I should be back in the States in the first part of October."

He reported further on August 23 on what he was reading:

> I've been reading nearly all day. The book is "Men Against the Sea." It's written by the same author who wrote "Mutiny on the Bounty." . . . "Men Against the Sea" is based on a sub-plot of "Mutiny on the Bounty."
>
> I go back to Ft. Leavenworth, Kansas for discharge. (I hope.)
>
> Darling, soon, I won't have to write "I love you." I'll just take you in my arms, drown you with kisses and say that I love you. I'll always love you, La Vera, forever and ever.
>
> Good nite, Darling,
Karl
>
> Kiss Gay for me.

In his last letter from Germany, Karl wrote:

> We first go to an assembly area named "Camp San Antonio." It's near Rheims, France and about the 17th of September we go to the port to sail. I should be home early in October.
>
> Gay will be a little over seven months old when I get to see her. I hope that she isn't afraid of me.
>
> I'll probably go to Ft. Leavenworth when I arrive in the States. Then I'll get 30 days leave. . . .

Karl and his outfit reached Camp San Antonio near Rheims, France on September 9, traveling by train and motor convoy. On September 19, they left for the staging area at Calais in the vicinity of Marseilles, France.

They boarded the *U.S.S. Mount Vernon* on October 4, arriving in New York on October 12. To finalize his discharge, Karl traveled to Fort Leavenworth, Kansas, and after becoming a civilian he had a reunion in Omaha on Tuesday, October 23.

La Vera describes the mix-up in their meeting in Omaha:

"He sent me a wire to meet him in Omaha at the Rome Hotel. I left Gay with Mother Timmermann and caught the first bus into Omaha. Somehow

Karl hadn't expected me to arrive until the next morning. He couldn't get a room at the Rome, so checked in at the Regis.

"I really didn't think he would get into Omaha until the next morning either. However, I did get a room at the Rome as I told them I was going to meet my husband there and just had to have one there or I would miss him and didn't know how else we could find each other. As it happened it was a big mix-up and we each spent the night in different hotels."

EIGHT

Welcome to West Point

T IS SHEER COINCIDENCE that the Hero of the Rhine should spend most of his life in a town with appropriately the same name as the Hudson River site of the United States Military Academy. Beyond the name, the similarity between the two towns is poles apart.

West Point, Nebraska was founded in 1857 by John D. Neligh who set up a sawmill and brickyard there. The town was named by its early settlers as the western extremity of white settlement in Pawnee Indian country. Prior to the completion of the Chicago and Northwestern spur from Omaha to West Point in 1870, it was a four-day journey from Omaha, Nebraska's largest city, by covered wagon or ox team. But those who made the trip to this county seat of Cuming County were rewarded by the rich, fertile land of the Elkhorn River Valley.

Animosity toward the Timmermann family, latent as Karl was growing up, flared up when news of his exploits hit West Point like a shock wave.

Bill Schäfer, the stern, unsmiling disciplinarian who harassed his employees for not sticking to their work, became visibly upset when Karl's mother kept bragging to her customers about Karl. On the morning after Karl led his company across the bridge, Schäfer hid the newspaper so Mrs. Timmermann could not see it. When he forbade her to listen to the radio, she sneaked out to Haeffelin Bros., the nearby hardware store, until Schäfer threatened to fire her if she didn't come back to work.

Mrs. Schäfer cautioned Mrs. Timmermann, "Don't think that your Karl did any of this. We hear other names like Engeman, Deevers and Hoge." Schäfer remonstrated: "Timmy, you talk too much about your Karl. I tell you the people in West Point are against it and it's better you keep your mouth shut. Timmy, you're making a big fool out of yourself. The people are laughing at you."

Schäfer showed his Pro-Nazi colors by pooh-poohing reports that there were any death camps in Germany. Mrs. Timmermann told me later that Schäfer had gotten angry at her for reporting that Karl had seen them with his own eyes, "Your son should be thrown out of the Army for spreading the propaganda that he personally saw concentration camps." When she showed Karl's letter to Schäfer, he really hit the ceiling.

Another incident in the Golden Rod Café stirred the anger of Karl's mother. A customer started to taunt Mrs. Timmermann, stating that Karl was a "Yellow-bellied no-account because he had married outside of his church." Mrs. Timmermann shot back: "It's his business whom he married."

The customer shouted loudly: "I'll make it my business. The trouble with you is you didn't bring him up right."

Mrs. Timmermann reacted like Harry Truman did when music critic Paul Hume panned Margaret Truman's singing. In this case, she took more direct action rather than writing an angry letter. She picked up a pitcher of water to throw in the man's face. Fortunately, Matt Schmitt was standing by and restrained Mrs. Timmermann, but not before Bill Schäfer yelled: "One more incident like this, Timmy, and I'll have to let you go."

Not long after Karl returned from combat in 1945, he and La Vera were visiting the Veterans Club. Mrs. Boelter, her son Harry, Art Decker and Jack Benne, none of whom had any use for Karl, decided to pin a buddy puppy on Karl's uniform and demand a contribution. Karl explained in measured tones that it was against Army Regulations to add a decoration to his uniform.

Mrs. Boelter and the others became offensive and yelled: "You come in here and use our club, but you're too cheap to help pay for its upkeep."

Karl raised his voice several decibels and shouted back: "I'll send you a copy of the Regulations so you'll know what I'm talking about."

Now Mrs. Boelter became even more antagonistic and shouted: "If you weren't so cheap, you wouldn't let your mother and father live in poverty without contributing to their welfare."

This was too much for Karl and a fist fight nearly broke out. Karl charged: "If I didn't have this uniform on, I'd beat the living hell out of you."

"C'mon," they taunted. "We're ready."

When La Vera started to cry, Karl broke it off quickly by saying: "Let's get out of here."

La Vera wanted to move out of West Point as soon as possible.

The source of most of the animosity actually had its roots in fellow-veterans who had risked their lives in combat and did not receive the universal credit which Karl was receiving. It is easy to understand why so much media attention was focused on Karl, rather than on other foot-slogging soldiers who had stormed some obscure hill overseas.

Here was an irresistibly newsworthy wartime development which attracted the news services, magazines, radio reporters and all manner of publicists to focus on the dramatic seizure of the first crossing of the Rhine and key figures like Timmermann who played starring roles. It was intriguing enough that the seizure of the Remagen Bridge was totally unplanned and unexpected. Add to that, the personalized story of the man who was born less than 100 miles from the bridge, and who was certainly motivated by the desire to clear the family name from the stigma of desertion.

In Washington, D.C., Congressman Karl Stefan spoke out in the U.S. House of Representatives to honor Karl's heroism.

UNITED STATES   OF AMERICA

Congressional Record

PROCEEDINGS AND DEBATES OF THE 79th CONGRESS
FIRST SESSION

HOUSE OF REPRESENTATIVES
FRIDAY, MARCH 9, 1945

Mr. STEFAN. Mr. Speaker, I know the entire membership of the House of Representatives was thrilled over the news that American troops have crossed the Rhine. This morning I was notified that the lieutenant leading the first company of infantry across that river was Lt. Carl Timmerman, of West Point, Nebr. This Nebraska hero comes from my congressional district in Nebraska, and I know that my colleagues are as thrilled as I am over this announcement. Lieutenant Timmerman and his company of American heroes represent those fine American G. I.'s who are so frequently described by Ernie Pyle. This company commander and his chiefs have been congratulated for their daring exploit by General Eisenhower. I am proud to report this news to the membership of this House.

The report reaching me indicates that in an amazing new-born D-day which surprised American Army commands as much as it did the Germans, this Infantry company commanded by this Nebraska officer, carved the first foothold on the east bank of the Rhine on Wednesday. From what I can learn Lieutenant Timmerman's company suffered no casualties from the fire of the enemy.

On behalf of all Members of the Nebraska delegation in Congress I make this brief report to the Congress, and I know that the entire membership of this House join us today in paying tribute to this fine Nebraska officer and his comrades in arms.

Ever since the news broke on March 7, 1945, Karl was honored by West Point's widely read daily newspaper, the *Omaha World-Herald*, even to the extent of raising the issue why West Point was not giving Karl his due credit.

When I was collecting material for my 1957 book, *The Bridge At Remagen*, I wrote to the editors of the hometowns of all the Distinguished Service Cross winners who crossed the Ludendorff Bridge on March 7, 1945. I received enthusiastic responses with one significant exception: The editor of *The West Point Republican*, Boyd Von Seggern, answered with a cryptic note indicating that Lt. Karl Timmermann was no longer living, and that the town never seemed to understand or appreciate his heroism.

Karl's brother Fritz told me a simple explanation: "The people of West Point vividly recalled that Karl always attended Guardian Angels School in bib overalls and dirty T-shirts, but after the war he always dressed neatly, with highly polished shoes and a car which was clean and glistened in the sunlight."

It was almost as though a black veteran returned from overseas to a segregated community, having enjoyed the freedoms of other countries, and was now acting "uppity" like a white man. Furthermore, according to his boyhood friend Gerhard Willms, Karl had on a "war face," with a maturity, which contrasted with his pre-war rowdiness.

The actual capture of the Remagen Bridge was trumpeted enthusiastically in March of 1945. When Karl and La Vera came home in October, Von Seggern ran a front-page tribute to their youngster Gay Diane:

A LETTER TO GAY DIANE

Oct. 25, 1945

Dear Little Miss:

This week was a very happy one in your very young life—your Daddy came home from across the seas to see you and your Mommy and all of the folks he holds so dear. You, being only eight months old, are too young to realize that your Daddy is a national hero; but some day you will look at him and say, "Thanks, Daddy, for helping to keep America strong and free."

Did you know that folks in West Point and Cuming county are just as proud of your Daddy, as you and your Mommy? Well, they are. In paying tribute to Lt. Karl Timmermann, they say "thanks" to all Cuming county boys who fought and died for a brave new world.

One editorial writer has said that "history walked beside the young officer that morning"—the morning your Daddy commanded the first unit that discovered the Remagen bridge and forced the first crossing of the Rhine.

We go even further—we say history walked with your grandmother, who crossed the ocean from Germany after the first World War to seek happiness in America with her American soldier husband. History has walked beside your Daddy—but it began with a young bride of foreign birth.

If your Daddy is a hero, we must add that there are some heroines in your family: Your grandmother who knew the anguish of having two sons fighting against her family in Frankfurt; your mother who lived with you, alone, waiting out the days.

It is a grateful town and county that says to you, Baby Gay Diane: "Karl Timmermann pressed to the mark. He finished his course. He kept the faith. We thank him."

Every public mention of Karl fanned the flames of skepticism among jealous veterans. Wasn't it true that a butcher boy from Toledo named Drabik was the first across the bridge? Didn't Karl follow way behind many others? Wasn't this just a foot race with Timmermann just pushed forward as part of a crowd?

Feeling began to run strong against this upstart from the wrong side of the tracks. A local patriot, Mrs. J. C. "Lillian" Elliott had arranged a colorful display in her window to honor local service-men. She displayed a red, white and blue bunting circling Karl's portrait, along with news stories of his exploit. It lasted less than 24 hours before vandals tore it down.

In 1955, I visited West Point to collect material for my book, *The Bridge At Remagen*. While talking with a local resident, I told him I was seeking material on Karl Timmermann. He immediately answered: "Well, that caused quite a stir here in town. You know, he wasn't the first to cross the Rhine."

"I always heard he was the first officer across," I said.

"No, there are several right here in West Point who crossed before Timmermann."

"Say, that's a good story," I probed. "Who were they?"

"Well my own boy, Harold Henke, carried gasoline and supplies over the Rhine long before Timmermann and he never got any credit."

So I looked up Harold Henke, and for a brief moment he basked in the glory of one-upmanship until I began to ask him the unit he was with. Suddenly, his tone became surly, as he said sharply over the phone: "If you're here to make a hero out of Karl Timmermann, you can count me out," and abruptly hung up the phone.

Army authorities later verified that Henke had served in Europe with the 7th Troop Carrier Squadron.

Shortly after the news broke in West Point of Karl's exploit, Ed Baumann, the highly respected West Point department store owner and chairman of the County chapter of "American War Dads," reported that a meeting of his committee at the city hall had voted to send a letter of congratulations to Lt. Timmermann for his heroism at Remagen. The letter eventually was sent to Karl on April 14, as follows:

West Point, Nebraska. April 14, 1945.

Dear Lieutenant Karl:

It is a privilege and great pleasure to send you congratulations on behalf of Chapter 10—Cuming County War Dads.

Your achievement in ordering your men to cross the Ludendorff bridge at Remagen—preventing the immediate destruction of the bridge and saving the lives of many Americans—was heralded over the various broadcasting networks and the press in general.

The old home town of West Point was mentioned in connection with your name and your timely feat.

The War Dads Chapter #10 of which your father is a charter member are proud of you. So are all the citizens of West Point and community.

Born in the land of the enemy you have proven yourself to be a real American. Not only did you enlist and work your way up to the rank of a commissioned officer but you have proven that the trust imposed in you was merited.

Your actions and orders at the Ludendorff bridge were timely and your remarks at interviews following were well expressed and considerate of those under your command.

Your parents, your wife and baby may well be proud of you as are we the War Dads of Cuming County and all of West Point.

May the Lord protect you so that you may return to this fair city and enjoy the companionship of your wife and baby, your parents and your friends.

Sincerely, Ed. L. Baumann, Chairman

When Karl received Ed Baumann's gracious letter, he wrote to La Vera: "I received a letter from Ed Baumann and from the American War Dads. It doesn't help me to get home sooner."

Karl's wartime correspondence with La Vera showed a negative reaction to the criticisms he was receiving in his hometown (see excerpts from the following November 1, 1944 letter): "I hate West Point too, La Vera, and I don't want to live there either. And there's nothing in the world that can compel us to stay there after this war is over. We'll go off someplace and be happy."

Despite his announced intentions, Karl and La Vera on their return decided to rent a second-floor apartment in a large house on Colfax Street.

They rented from Charles Beckenhauer, as if to defy their detractors who expected them to slink off into the Third Ward instead of taking up residence in the "better" section of West Point.

When Dwight Eisenhower was President, I arranged for all the living recipients of the Distinguished Service Cross awarded for their part in the historic seizure of the Ludendorff Bridge to get invited to the White House on March 7, 1955, to commemorate the tenth anniversary of that critical action. Since Karl had died of cancer four years earlier, President Eisenhower at my request wrote a personal letter of congratulations to his father, mother and wife La Vera.

On April 8, 1955, Leroy (Sonny) Strehle and his brother Jim, told me the following story in West Point:

"It was an unforgettable scene in Strehle's Café. Old John Timmermann came in, sporting his dirty blue pants. He reached into his pocket and drew out a crumpled letter on White House stationery, signed by President Eisenhower. He asked us to read it, since he couldn't read himself. The customers all made light of the letter, as John volubly argued unconvincingly: 'See, I told you so.'

"Only one person spoke up for John Timmermann and his son Karl: Jim Coughlin, manager of the Northwestern Bell Telephone Company. Coughlin said he had heard townspeople talking about Karl and Remagen Bridge, but thought they were all exaggerating until he saw the letter personally signed by the Supreme Commander of the Allied Expeditionary Force. Coughlin spoke up and said he was flabbergasted. He asked the customers: 'What other resident of West Point in Eisenhower's Army ever received a personal letter like this from the President of the United States? We ought to do something to honor a home-town hero!'

"One of the customers taunted: 'OK, you're a member of the American Legion, you bring it up at our next meeting!'

"Coughlin accepted the challenge. So he got up at the next Legion meeting and said: 'You people are always looking for projects. Here you have a hero right in your midst and we ought to have a celebration to honor Lt. Karl Timmermann. We ought to realize that the Legion should sponsor a big event to honor this man who has brought such glory to West Point.'

"Somebody spoke up: 'What should we do? What did you have in mind?'

"Before Coughlin could answer, Harold Henke spoke up: 'I was on the Rhine River too. I carried gasoline across the river ten days before he did.' Others spoke up, and raised all kinds of piddly little questions. Leo Bosie, a Pfc. who had won a Silver Star in the Battle of the Bulge, asked why couldn't all veterans be honored instead of singling out Karl Timmermann. Finally, a resolution was referred to a committee to be thoroughly considered and never heard from again."

When Coughlin asked around about why his resolution had received such a cold reaction, he was told by fellow business men in West Point: "You represent a public utility and people have to deal with you. Other business people have to respect public opinion in order to keep their customers."

The type of celebration which Coughlin had in mind took place in West

Point in 1953, two years after Karl's death. Between his 2nd floor office at 139 North Main Street ("The West Point Clinic") and the community hospital on the hill, moustached Dr. A. W. Anderson was an impressive figure with a reputation as a highly successful abdominal surgeon. Even more important, in a proud cow town like West Point was Dr. Anderson's Melody Grove Farm on the edge of town, where his brown Swiss cattle were the big attractions of eastern Nebraska.

On Wednesday evening, July 29, 1953, hundreds of residents of West Point and surrounding towns and farms were gathered in the West Point Auditorium to greet Dr. and Mrs. Anderson on their return from a one-month tour of Europe.

Toward evening a telephone call came in from Chicago. The Anderson plane had engine trouble between New York and Chicago, missing their connection out of Chicago to Omaha. The West Point High School band filled in the vacuum while a huge majority of the crowd patiently waited, except for a meager few with babysitting problems. One man was quoted as saying, "Dr. Anderson saved my mother's life. I ought to be able to wait a few hours for him."

Finally, although fatigued by the delays the Andersons arrived at 10:00 p.m. Tumultuous applause and cheers greeted them as Mayor W. H. Hasebroock, the proprietor of the big I.G.A. store, grasped their hands warmly and conducted them to their seats on the platform. The band played a rousing march. Everybody beamed with pride.

Mayor Hasebroock rose and presented Dr. Anderson with a scroll to which the gold seal of the City of West Point had been affixed. The inscription read:

"In recognition of many years of faithful service, this Certificate of Appreciation is presented to Dr. A. W. Anderson on the occasion of his return from a European holiday July 29, 1953 by the citizens of West Point, Nebraska and vicinity."

The auditorium burst forth with more applause and Dr. Anderson acknowledged the greeting and scroll. Then Joseph Koepping, Secretary of the Chamber of Commerce, stepped up to present Mrs. Anderson with a dozen roses. Mrs. Anderson beamed and expressed heartfelt gratitude for the warm welcome.

A cynical wag remarked afterward: "It's just unlucky for Karl Timmermann that he didn't have the foresight to raise brown Swiss cattle."

Karl's top priority when he returned to West Point was to get reacquainted with La Vera, and to get to know Gay. Karl's mother told me that when Karl first came home from Germany, "The first thing he wanted to see was his baby. She was only seven months old but of course he had never seen her. He insisted on waking her up and bringing her outside even before he got into the house. He grabbed her roughly, and she cried and cried. He handled her like a basketball."

Some of the animosity toward Karl came from religious fanatics among Catholics who resented Karl marrying a Lutheran, and Lutherans who did not like the idea of a Lutheran marrying a Catholic.

When the *West Point Republican* printed the following letter Gerhard Willms had written Mrs. Timmermann while stationed in Munster, Germany, in the Army of Occupation, it did not enhance the Timmermann reputation, and among some West Pointers it had the opposite effect:

> Munster, Germany
>
> August 6, 1946
>
> Dear Mrs. Timmermann:
>
> How are you? I hope you are fine. I received the letter and the addresses you sent me. I was in Frankfurt yesterday and I visited your father. He really was glad to see me. Your two sisters were not at home and I couldn't get to see them. I am going back to-morrow to try and see your sisters.
>
> Your brother, Walter, is dead. He died fourteen days ago. The time he spent in Dachau concentration camp was too much for him. Your father is having a very hard time and he is getting little to eat. One loaf of bread has to last him for six days. He is hoping you can help him in some way. He wants you to send him some food. He asked me all about you and I told him that every thing was fine with you. I promised him that you would send him some packages. He was in very low spirits. He thought that everyone had forgotten him.
>
> He has lost everything he had because of the Nazi party. Your two brothers were killed because they spoke against the Gestapo. Your one brother was shot and Walter was put in prison.
>
> Your father told me that Walter saw people frozen in ice, hanged, beaten and burned. Your father said that when Walter died he had been through so much that he refused to believe in heaven or hell.
>
> The home of your parents was bombed to pieces. Your father lives in a small two room house. He still has his flowers in his garden and his birds. Your sisters live about four blocks away

from him in an apartment house. I am going to take pictures the next time I visit them and I will send you them to give you an idea of how things look.

If you want to see the Dachau camp go see my mother. She has pictures of it. I visited Dachau myself and it must have been worse than hell.

Your father sends you his greetings and love. I will be very glad to do anything I can for them and for you as long as I stay in Frankfurt.

Enclosed in this letter is a picture of your father as he looks today. I want to tell you that I regret having to send you sorry news instead of happy news. Your people were killed because they believed in what was right and refused to accept Hitler and his Gestapo as leaders.

Your father wants you to say hello to Msgr. Joseph Bosheck for him. He said that Msgr. visited him a long time ago.

WEST POINT'S CHARACTER and history seemed to be oriented in different directions than to place Karl Timmermann at the top of its priorities. There follows a word picture of what West Point and Cuming County were like when Karl returned home in 1945:

The town has had a slow and steady development from the days when it was merely an outpost on the route up to the Black Hills of South Dakota and the northwest. The population had not increased rapidly in the last half century, from about 1,500 people in 1900, to 2,600 during World War II. The absence of large industries had stunted the town's growth, but also helped to stabilize its economy. West Point has had a fairly steady prosperity, and is little affected by the sharp booms and busts, which have been felt in other parts of the Middle West.

Over 30 inches of rainfall usually bless surrounding Cuming County, which has never suffered a crop failure. Cuming County is one of the three leading counties in corn production in the state of Nebraska. During many years, the county has led all counties in the state in yield per acre in oats and barley, as well as alfalfa. The greatest of all Cuming County's enterprises is the feeding of livestock. It seems hard to believe, but figures show that this county feeds 100 percent more cattle than any other county in Nebraska. The fattened cattle from the area surrounding West Point bring top prices at livestock markets, and the people and merchants of the town profit accordingly. One leading citizen of the town recently said that a typical farmer told him: "We have to make money, or else literally shove it away." Money has also become a measure of success and prestige to a greater extent than elsewhere—although this is difficult to measure.

West Point is proudly conscious of her wealth and the wealth of the surrounding countryside. The measure of a man's acumen and intelligence in the eyes of the community is the extent to which he can lay up treasures on earth. The banks in West Point testify to the general prosperity of the area by the size of their deposits, even though some people still keep their money in creamery cans in memory of the bank failures of the past. Occasionally on a Saturday night in town a few of the old pre-1934 gold notes will float around at some of the local establishments, and they are accepted by the local merchants and business men without batting an eyelash.

A person need not be ostentatious to succeed in West Point. He does not need two Cadillacs, a flashily dressed family, or an imposing mansion. Far more respected are those who can gain their reputations through having a great deal of money in reserve, while outwardly they display spacious lawns, shrubbery and flowers, a good and reasonably new car, and some exhibits at the Cuming County Fair.

The fair is a featured annual event in West Point, and Nebraska generally acknowledges it to be one of the top county fairs in the entire Cornhusker State. The first fair was held in 1872, and annually through 1897, when it was suspended for a period because it had difficulty meeting expenses. In wartime years, under the able and aggressive management of people like Ed Baumann, who manages one of the largest and best clothing stores on Main Street, the fair had profited and it constitutes a stellar attraction for people from the whole eastern part of Nebraska.

In the early 1920's, the newer and bigger country fairs in Cuming County were given a tremendous shot in the arm by some good organizing work. Joseph Koepping, head of the West Point Creamery and then President of the West Point Community Club (later the Chamber of Commerce) said at the pep meeting on September 10, 1923: "Being situated as we are, we stand in line of one of the greatest county fairs in Nebraska." Koepping and his associates made good on his word. The Cuming County Agricultural Society was formed. Ed Baumann was drafted as Secretary, and shouldered the main burden of the work. Although the success of the county fair is a cooperative venture involving all the farmers and merchants of the area, to Ed Baumann more than any single individual should go the credit for sparking the drive and imagination which helped lift the fair to the great institution which it is today.

The fair is held in the week covering the last of August and the first part of September. Hundreds of premiums are awarded annually for exhibits of horses and mules, beef cattle (shorthorn, Hereford, Aberdeen-Angus, polled shorthorn and polled Hereford), dairy cattle, swine, sheep, farm products (wheat, rye, oats, barley, clover, sorghum, beans, corn, potatoes, carrots, watermelons—to mention only a very few), flowers, home economics products, eggs, textiles (there is a special set of premiums for the "work of ladies over sixty," including aprons, afghans, spreads, potholders and many other items), paintings and other fine arts, exhibits of penmanship, maps, and other items produced by school children. There is a wide series of awards for younger people, all the way from the extensive 4-H Club awards for livestock and farm produce to the special cash awards for woodwork, arts and crafts and many other types of creative work by boys and girls.

The fair opens on Monday with a mammoth parade along Main Street, complete with bands, picturesque and ornate floats, and a rifle squad and the colors. This is easily the biggest event of the year in West Point, and the whole county turns out to participate in or view the parade.

The fair itself includes a seemingly continuous series of celebrations, entertainment, judging of prize-winners, and cheers for the victorious. Every night the fireworks display attracts a huge crowd, and each night they are treated to "73 atomic salutes, the stars and stripes with a background of spray fountains, a full-size fireworks picture of Bossy the Cow drinking from the tub" and scores of other sources of noise and blinding light.

West Point is very proud of its 75-bed Memorial Hospital, which was erected at a cost of over one million dollars. The hospital, atop the highest ground in the town, is equipped with the most modern laboratory, x-ray, orthopedic and physical therapy departments and equipment, and special sections for the care of medical, surgical, obstetrical and pediatric patients. It is owned and operated by the Franciscan Sisters of Christian Charity. The Chamber of Commerce says, "With the completion of the new hospital, West Point and surrounding territory now lacks nothing that is required to make it an ideal place in which to live and in which to rear a family. Now, not only are there ample business opportunities, good school and recreational facilities, beautiful homes and churches, wholesome and friendly neighbors, but there is now that freedom from fear of illness and accident without adequate facilities for their attention."

In Karl's time, there were five well-attended churches in West Point—two Lutheran, one Catholic, one Congregational and one Evangelical United Brethren. The strongest religions are Catholic and Lutheran, and the town was about equally divided between the total number of Catholic faith and those of the various Protestant faiths. Religious jealousies are not unknown. It is true that some controversies, which have their roots in personal or business differences may be attributed to religious differences, just as genuine religious friction between the sects may be attributed to other reasons. Whether outspoken or not, some people in West Point take their religion in such a way as to allow it to develop into a divisive force as against those of other denominations. Such feelings are never countenanced and are openly discouraged by the leaders of the churches, but of course the leaders cannot guide and control the personal feelings and prejudices of their church members. Religious prejudice does not burgeon into the open and ugly anti-Semitism which infects so many small towns, nor does it approach racial prejudice in the intensity of its feeling. But one cannot deny that a small amount of it is there, and added to other things it does furnish some explosive conflicts which occasionally surprise those who feel that all is sweetness and light in this busy little town.

The school system in West Point serves to underline the religion of its growing children. In addition to the public school, there are two other grade schools, one Catholic and one Lutheran. The West Point High School draws most of the students in the area, and it was supplemented by the smaller Guardian Angels High School sponsored by St. Mary's Catholic Church. The schools and their students do not mix, never play against each other in athletic contests, or join in any common endeavor. There was a tendency for students at West Point High School to regard those at Guardian Angels with an undefined suspicion, born of a lack of complete knowledge of what strange and secret things go on in a Catholic school, and there is likewise a tendency for those in Guardian Angels to feel, to a lesser extent, that way about the students at West Point High.

West Point has a municipal electric plant and also a municipal water plant. The Cuming County Rural Electric Cooperative has its headquarters on Main Street on the edge of town, and it does a thriving and bustling business. Ninety-nine percent of the farms in Cuming County are electrified. These stark facts have been recorded in the face of the natural conservative outlook toward socialism and government control. Some of the independent farmers objected when the REA first started running lines to their farms, occasionally digging up some ground, stringing some wires in a way which caused many feeding cattle to have to move around, and causing some inconvenience in the annual process of fattening up stock for market. Most farmers just swallowed hard and accepted their lot. They are secretly proud of rural electrification and the modern building on Main Street, which houses the County cooperative head-quarters. They think it is a fine thing, but they are generally agreed it must never happen again under a Democratic administration.

West Point and Cuming County rate high in terms of repayment of loans and mortgages, payment of taxes, and financial solvency. Cuming County ranks among the three highest credit-rated counties in the country. Property taxes are about 99.9% paid up. The county built a new court-house in West Point—a magnificent $350,000 structure which was already 100% paid for. The town and county take great pride in their lack of indebtedness—official and personal.

There are some interesting paradoxes in West Point. The town is proud of its new hospital, its schools and churches, and its fine stores and small business enterprises. This would seem to indicate that there is a good deal of community pride in the town. This trait has been fostered by the West Point Community Club, founded in the 1920's, which later developed into the West Point Chamber of Commerce and helped build the community auditorium. There are many other civic and fraternal organizations in the town, including the Lions Club, Federated Women's Club, American Legion, VFW, and other organizations of both men and women. All these organizations help to keep the community spirit alive. Yet there are occasional indications that all is not as well as it might be. As an example, shortly after World War II, a plaque was erected in front of the old Cuming County Courthouse, listing the names of the servicemen from West Point and the County who had participated in the war. The action of the elements wore down this sign until it gradually began to look shabby, then pieces started to drop off, then somebody took a large piece for a souvenir, and before long the sign became almost a mockery. Eventually it was taken down altogether and the town of West Point in the spring of 1954 had no public memorial to its war veterans.

Another small example of the paradox in the pride of West Point: The town had a small library, just off Main Street, which for a long time had a rough hand painted sign denoting its location. The rough sign slipped down between the two posts, which were holding it, and for a period of about two years until the spring of 1954, anyone looking for the Public Library was greeted by two barren and forlorn posts with no identifying sign. After two years of this, a new sign was finally placed out in front of the library. These little things may seem unimportant, but they are the things, which a stranger notices, and they may be the things, which reveal small cracks in the neat facade which West Point shows to its public.

West Point had two weekly newspapers, the *West Point Republican* and the *Cuming County Democrat*. More recently, there is only one: *The West Point News*. It formerly had a German language newspaper called the *Nebraska Volksblatt*, which suspended publication during the first World War. The *Republican* was a larger, newsier paper, which unlike the *Democrat*, carried editorials. It had a circulation which approximately equals the population of West Point, and was read by many farm families all over the county. The *Democrat* had a much smaller circulation and seemed to exist primarily for its ad and market quotations.

For example, on April 26, 1951, the *Republican* ran an editorial entitled "Peace Has Its PRICE— It Comes High, Must Be Preserved", a portion of which read as follows: "Every once in a while we hear from a subscriber who says that he's tired of war, rumors of war, explanations of warfare and prophecies as to the spread of war. In short, there are individuals who respectfully request editorials on other subjects besides war... Let us not forget that peace, like war, can be won only by the sacrifice of all of us. The race of men may yet learn that peace has its price, which all men must be willing to pay, if it is to be preserved and protected."

Boyd Von Seggern never had his head in the clouds like an impractical dreamer. He was keenly aware of how to build and strengthen West Point, and he never once lost sight of local issues. His fellow townsmen did not universally appreciate his interpretation of local issues, because most of the townspeople were more conservative than he, but he could never be classified as a radical or an impractical visionary. He had his feet on the ground, and knew how to speak the language of his readers. Sometimes they resented the fact that he had thought of an idea first, but with more frequency than not they took up his ideas and slowly acted on them. Here is an example of how Von Seggern stirred West Point to think about its post-war problems. Writing five weeks after V-E Day, in the issue of June 14, 1945, he said: "G.I. Joe will, first of all, expect a job. He'll want West Point brightly lighted. He'll want to live in a modernized home. He'll like the idea of a new post office; he'll clamor for a new courthouse. We must be prepared to meet these demands of returning veterans. We can do this only if we show faith in them; if we have faith in this community; if we have faith in ourselves."

The *Republican* and its editor harbored deep and genuine community pride. They did not merely try to curry favor with local interests or ride local hobbies. They felt a real sense of what West Point could and should mean to its citizens. "Stay Put Young Man—Prospects Are Bright at Home" the newspaper wrote.

One of the interesting aspects of Boyd Von Seggern is the way he reacts when certain forces of the town criticize him or try to get him to change his opinions. He has been subjected to all types of pressure—from the men who have covertly walked up to him on the street and palmed him with fifty-dollar bills to print or not to print a story, to the wolf-pack of outraged citizens who demanded that he retract and apologize publicly for an honest and unintentional error. A town which is benighted and self-satisfied never likes to have its conscience pricked, even ever so gently. Boyd Von Seggern stirs the conscience of West Point every now and then, not simply to start a fuss or to get a headline, but because he is calmly and lucidly reporting the news and in a soft voice calling attention to ways and means by which West Point can build a better future. When the more conservative townsfolk gang up on Von Seggern, he never fights back or angrily criticizes his detractors; he simply rolls along in his same old style, writing and saying what he thinks and refusing to alter either his outlook or opinions to conform with the prevailing trade winds or even tornadoes.

Politics meant nothing to Von Seggern, and he would just as soon take an unpopular position if he thinks it is right, regardless of whether it is Democratic or Republican. Long before the junior Senator from Wisconsin started polluting the clear reservoirs of our liberties, Von Seggern was gently writing in 1946 that we should never call a man a communist or a socialist just because we happened to disagree with his opinions. He loved to raise the sights of his readers to think about such things as the nationwide short-age of trained nurses, the need for a Missouri Valley Authority, and the issues involved in atomic control. He knew that these issues did not overly endear him to his readers, because they told him so bluntly in so many words. Nevertheless, he stuck to his last and never became flustered by criticism.

Politically, West Point and Cuming County are solidly and conserva-tively Republican. In the write-in presidential primary of April 1, 1952, Sena-tor Taft received a safe majority of the 2,356 Republicans who registered their choices. Taft rolled up 1,205 write-in votes, as against 514 for Harold Stassen, and General Eisenhower mustered only 217 ballots. It was a terrible blow to West Point when Eisenhower defeated Taft in the Republican Con-vention of 1952, and many residents had serious reservations about the "lib-eral" proposals and associates of President Eisenhower. Nevertheless, they go along with him because he is a Republican. The rabidly conservative *Omaha World-Herald* is read widely in West Point, since it is the only daily newspaper in the state that gets regularly shipped in to the town. Most towns-people spoke favorably of Wisconsin Senator Joseph McCarthy, who was the main speaker at the Dodge County convention in Fremont in April, 1954 (Dodge County is just to the south of Cuming County). This prosperous area of northeastern Nebraska never had any truck with the Populists, shunned William Jennings Bryan, and never particularly liked George Norris, whom they regarded as too radical and too independent in his thinking. Those in West Point who did support Norris did so because of his stand against our entrance into World War I; the huge German population in West Point had this much of a warm spot in their hearts for Norris.

West Point is a community founded and built by Germans and perhaps three-quarters of its population was either born in Germany or traced their ancestry back to that country. There is danger in oversimplifying a national series of characteristics, especially since there are so many different types of people in West Point. Yet one cannot resist in the temptation to relate the outlook and temperament of the townspeople to certain German traits. The people are neat and tidy in their community and personal habits, thorough and hard working in their business or professional life, dogged and determined in their convictions. One of the town's leading citizens said, in a facetious vein: "You know how Germans are: sometimes they tell themselves over and over again that something is true, and whether or not it may be a fact, if they repeat it often enough they *know* it must be true." Walter Lippmann must have been thinking of people like this when he coined the word "stereotype" to depict a mode of thinking, or a pair of colored glasses, which filters into the mind certain word-pictures, which may or may not relate to truth and objectivity. There is nothing consciously malicious about such a process, but merely evidences the extent to which people can be the captives of their upbringing and environment.

Main Street in West Point is an important backbone of the town. As with any small town, it is a magnet on weekends, drawing farmers and ranchmen from the surrounding countryside to patronize the well-stocked merchants along the white way, swap stories, refuel at one of the many bars and pubs, or stock up on some new lumber or farm machinery. The banks are open all day on Saturday, as are all the stores. There are a few stores not fortunate enough to have spots on Main Street, but almost all of them are within a block of the main thoroughfare.

Coming into West Point from the south, you confront an impressive series of fine business establishments on the outskirts of town—including a number of auto sales companies, the Rasmus Oil Co. (with a "complete line of Deep Rock petroleum products"), and off to the left of the highway is the imposing grain elevator of the Farmers Cooperative Company. To the right of the Main Street as you enter town is the trim, modern office building, and the neat, well-clipped grounds of the Cuming County Rural Public Power District. Across the street is one of the best-appearing, up-to-date small businesses in town—Hugo Plumbing and Heating—run by an energetic father and his hard-working and resourceful sons.

For about two or three blocks in the heart of town, Main Street, West Point, looks like any other town. Clothing stores, meat markets, cafés, the Rivola movie house, hardware and jewelry stores are jammed together with the two banks, the West Point Hotel, and a few professional offices. Bill Hasebroock, who in the spring of 1954 was re-elected to his fifth term as Mayor of West Point, owned and operated a general provisions I.G.A. store on Main Street, and rented frozen food lockers; the Mayor can usually be found behind the counter helping his customers. One of the oldest families in town, the Baumanns, had a bitter feud several years back, during which one young Baumann tried to shoot his uncle. Since that time, Ed Baumann and his brother have not been on speaking terms and they operate separate stores—Ed M. Baumann & Sons, and H. W. and R. L. Baumann's — both on Main Street. The Rivola Theater carried pictures like Judy Canova in "Singin' in the Corn" or "The Great Diamond Robbery." Cafés and taprooms like the Golden Rod, Camp's, the Town Pump, and several others dot Main Street. There is the usual quota of drug stores, a barbershop, shoe stores and other small shops. The Schmitt Clothing Co. and the Meier Clothing Co. are familiar shopping points along the main drag, as are the Hested stores (sort of a five-and-ten), Tony Liska's Bank Barber Shop (advertising "shower baths"), and Haeffelin Bros. (hardware). As you move to the north side of town, you find the city auditorium and a few more stores, and then Main Street melts into the residential section for a mile or so to the north.

The east side of town is the better part of West Point, with the finer homes, the fair grounds, the hospital, churches, and schools. The west side of town, west of the railroad tracks, constitutes the "Third Ward," the area down by the Elkhorn River, where the poorer families live. The western section of town also includes the Cuming County Fair Grounds and Neligh Park, a 27-acre beauty spot which includes several lakes and lagoons, cottonwood trees, a lighted baseball park adequate for night baseball, and good picnic facilities. The old John Neligh home, which gained a reputation over many years in the mid-late and nineteenth century as a center of hospitality, has been converted into the Cuming County Museum, containing relics of the Indian country and the early years of the town and county history.

Karl's terminal leave in the army ended on December 12, 1945.

Gerhard Willms, Karl's closest boyhood friend, had a big disagreement in 1940, the year Karl joined the army. During July 1940, when Karl was a full-fledged buck private at Fort Crook, he visited Gerhard every afternoon in his tent where Gerhard was enrolled in the Citizens Military Training Corps. from which Karl had graduated the year before.

Gerhard recalled: "He was very disgusted with me when I flunked the course. I was evaluated as unadaptable to military drill. Karl looked at it as a disaster. To him I was just a disfigured jerk, too tall, skinny and somewhat stupid. I stood 6' 6" at the time, at 145 lbs. [Gerhard sometimes referred to himself as "five foot, eighteen."]

"That summer I left home, hooked a freight and headed into the Dakotas for work. A florist took me in and employed me till fall, then sent me back home with $50.00. (My parents took every dime except $5.00.) Karl came home a 2nd Lieutenant, very proud and all oiled up in uniform to take his bows. I came over to visit. He gazed at me almost in apathy and taunted: 'Hello, Gerhard. When are you going to get that yellow streak out of your back and join the army?'

"We went to town, had a few beers, but he became more disillusioned when he learned I was classified as a farm worker, in 2-C."

Two years later, Gerhard was in the 10th Mountain Division. In October 1945, Karl came home from the European Theater of Operations, a hero everywhere except in his hometown—a biblical prophet without honor in his home country. Now Karl respected Gerhard.

It was mid-afternoon on a cool, sunny day when Karl said to Gerhard: "I'd like to take a walk to the place where we swam." According to Gerhard: "We walked slowly, taking in the old scenery, the trees and thickets turning to golden and brown hues. We stopped by the riverbank where we'd played cowboy games. We saw the hitching post, the imaginary saloon, the cotton-wood, and that old, rotten log out there in mid-stream. The river, in heart and folklore, had never left us. It was so receptive, almost mocking, as the large whirlpools danced and sparkled—funneling downstream. Karl looked up at the gnarled cottonwood, the one he'd climbed as a boy.

"Then he reached in his pocket and showed me his DSC. I guess he wanted me to see it, trying to make me understand, to feel that it was the second highest award a man could get. I understood. You don't get those things opening up c-rations cans and cutting yourself.

"He asked me 'What do you think of it, Gerhard?'

"I said 'You did great, Karl!' I guess it was one of the few compliments he ever had.

"We turned back in a broad loop, through the plum bush, the sandbar patch, and paused near the egress where he'd built the raft. Then, past the old slaughterhouse, now just decaying timber, and home. A year later I visited his grandfather in Frankfurt.

"I met him again at the Vet's Club in West Point in May, 1947. He was a salesman in civvies and he took pleasure in giving me a ride in his new car. 'I'll make money at this job,' he said, looking ambitious. I just nodded, not wanting to be a skeptic."

After a short period in West Point during 1945 Karl received an offer of civilian employment in 1946 with Fremont Soft Water Company. He immediately began to negotiate to buy a home in Fremont, which he moved to when he started work installing soft water systems in Nebraska homes. His new home was located at 2106 North Union Street in Fremont. In later years, Karl's youngest brother Rudy, moved to Fremont where he worked for the Hormel Company.

Karl's job included assisting in the regeneration of tanks in the Fremont plant and the servicing of the tanks in the homes. A mishap with one of the tanks injured his right foot, and he returned briefly to West Point to recuperate. He was paid $175.00 per month during the period he worked on soft water between January and August 1946.

Work with soft water service was primarily heavy, manual work, and Karl wanted to do something where he could use his head a little more. In August 1946, he took a job as a stock clerk and salesman for the S.S. Kresge Department Store in Fremont at a salary of $200.00 a month.

Karl was promised a sales managership when he started working at the Kresge store. When it became apparent by October that he would not be advanced to an administrative position, Karl began to look around for other opportunities.

From October 1946 until October 1947, Karl was employed by the Aluminum Cooking Utensil Co. whose main headquarters were in New Kensington, Pennsylvania. He started at a salary of $300.00 per month and by 1947 his salary was increased to $400.00 per month. In this position he called on prospective customers and solicited orders for wearever aluminum. He showed samples, quoted prices, and explained the durability of the aluminum products he was marketing.

According to what La Vera told me: "Karl was the happiest of all the civilian jobs he held after returning from the European Theater of Operations. Yet this took him away from home for long evenings. It began to be so much like his absences from home while he was in the Army that I didn't like it very much."

Karl had been away from the Army for two years. He really missed the Army, and finally decided to canvass the possibilities of re-enlistment to serve as a recruiter in Nebraska.

On October 28, 1947, Karl enlisted in the regular army as a Tech/Sergeant. He was promoted to Sergeant First Class in August 1948, serving until December 1948 when he was promoted to the temporary rank of 1st Lieutenant. During his enlisted service he recruited in Nebraska and Iowa. He expressed disappointment that he could not stir up any recruits in West Point.

NINE

Japan and Korea

ON THE DAY AFTER Christmas in 1948, Staff Sergeant Karl Timmermann was sworn in as a 1st Lieutenant, the rank he had held when he was discharged three years earlier. Unbeknownst to him at the time, he was headed for combat—despite the fact he thought he was just crossing the Pacific to peaceful Japan.

Karl was ordered to proceed to Fort Lawton, Washington to prepare for shipment to Yokohama. He took a train to Portland, Oregon, where he arrived at 9:30 A.M. on January 3, 1949. After eating breakfast and getting a shoe shine and getting his uniform pressed, he boarded a train for Seattle, Washington at noon. Arriving at Seattle at 4:30 P.M., he had a steak before taking a taxi to Fort Lawton where he shared a room at the officer quarters with a 1st Lieutenant from the 66th Battalion of the 2nd Armored Division who knew his brother Fritz.

Karl wrote La Vera on January 4 from Fort Lawton:

> The food is excellent. 35 cents per meal.
>
> From what I've found out so far, travel of dependents over-seas is very favorable. Everyone here says 3 to 5 months. Some are taking their cars. The next time that you're at Ft. Crook inquire at the hospital as to whether or not you and Gay can start taking your shots. It will save you much time later. I don't know as yet when I'm due to sail. I believe that it might be on the 11th if not sooner.

I'll pick up my travel pay in the morning. I'll send you a money order then.

I bought a radio this afternoon. It really looks "sharp." It is portable, color—light brown and tan. The make is RCA Victor. Cost $34.75. I really like it.

Final cholera and typhus shots were administered to Karl the week before he sailed for Yokohama and Karl reported: "Hello, My Stinkers. Boy, my right arm really hurts. I got another shot this afternoon in my right arm."

On January 6, he wrote La Vera that they would board the U.S. Army transport *David C. Shanks*. He added:

6 Jan 49

11:20 A.M.

Hello, my Sweetheart,

I just came back from the dentist. My teeth are in good shape now. They really take the time to do good work.

They picked up my foot locker and duffel bags to mark and put on the ship. Tuesday is sailing date. It will take about 14 days for the voyage.

When Karl reached Japan, he finally was able to write La Vera on January 27:

Hello, My Darling,

This is the first letter that I'm writing from Japan. I was unable to write aboard ship because I was sick during the entire trip.

I got off of the ship yesterday morning. Now I'm at the 4th Replacement Depot awaiting further assignment. Assignment to a permanent station should take place in a day or two.

La Vera, I really was sick on this trip. I bet that I've lost 20 lbs., at least. I haven't weighed yet.

Karl explained that he could get only two radio stations: a Japanese station and WVTR (the Armed Forces Network Station in Tokyo, with no commercials). He added that there was a 9-hour difference in time between Tokyo and West Point. If it is 9:00 P.M. Saturday in Japan, it is 6:00 A.M. Friday in Nebraska.

Awaiting assignment on January 28, Karl wrote: "Nothing happened today except that I got my first haircut from a Jap. He did a good job too."

On January 30, Karl informed La Vera: "The most interesting thing that I done since my arrival in Japan is I played three games of pool this morning. I played 500 rummy this afternoon with a chaplain."

Then on January 31 came this news:

> Well, I got my assignment today. I am assigned to the 7th Infantry Division which is stationed in the northern part of Japan. They just came from Korea and are replacing the 11th Airborne Division which is going to the States. I would have rather gone to southern Japan because the weather is more pleasant there. Northern Japan gets fairly cold in the winter when the icy wind blow across from Siberia. Other than the weather, one place is as good as another as far as duty and quarters for dependents are concerned. In the 7th Division, there are three Infantry regiments, the 17th, 31st and 32nd Infantry. I don't know as yet to which one I'll be assigned. I was in the 17th at Ft. Crook and Ft. Ord as a private in 1940.

Karl left by an Army pullman train from Yokohama at 10:00 on the evening of February 1st, and arrived in Sendai, Japan at 6:05 A.M. the next day, on the northern part of Honshu, Japan's main island. At Sendai, he could tune in to radio station WLKE of the Far East Network. There he discovered that he would be sent to Sapporo, a 6-hour boat trip to the northernmost Japanese island of Hokkaido.

He informed La Vera: "Remember General Piburn at Camp Polk—I reported to him this morning and acted very happy to see a 9th Armored insignia again. Maybe that's why I'm going to the Recon. Troop. That's better than straight Infantry."

Karl noted that the weather on the northern island of Hokkaido was similar to Minnesota. He added a reassuring thought to his wife: "According to the radio the weather's not so 'hot' in Nebraska. La Vera, do you get cold in bed nights? Well, think of me and warm up."

At Hokkaido, Karl noted that the 7th Mechanized Troop was replacing the 11th Airborne Division, which was returning to Camp Campbell, Kentucky. In the next few months, Karl spent many letters telling La Vera how to arrange for shipment of their car and household goods to come with Gay to bring the family together in Japan.

Karl reminded La Vera to bring Gay's toys, and warned her to change all her American money on the ship to Yokohama, as there was a fine of $1,000

Karl in Japan

for anyone caught with American money forty-eight hours after arriving in Japan.

On February 8, Karl wrote: "It's quite cold here today. I wish that spring was here. I can hardly wait for the arrival of spring, because you'll come with the spring. And you and Gay are the two most beautiful flowers that will bloom this spring."

In mid-February, Karl attended Air Transport School, following which he went to Court Martial School. He was also fully occupied preparing a 13-week training schedule for new troops.

Despite the fact that in every letter Karl tried in dozens of different ways to express his endearment for La Vera and his loneliness without his wife and daughter, he received a jarring letter which was written while he was en route to Japan. In the letter La Vera termed his letters "cold and clammy—as if you wrote only as a sense of duty. Do you love me, Karl?"

The average human being, after having repeated his eternal love, probably would have responded with outraged and injured dignity. Karl merely mailed La Vera's letter back to her with the offending paragraph circled with his comment in grease pencil: "Rewrite this."

La Vera did not answer, and Karl's mild response remained in her file, never answered or acknowledged.

On Valentine's Day Karl mentioned that they were having a blizzard, with snow and a strong wind from the northwest, since Siberia was only 400 miles away. He mentioned why it was impossible to telegraph flowers on two important days in the month: February 14 and February 18 (the latter being the magic day in 1943 when he and La Vera fell in love): "I tried for the last several days to send you flowers for Valentines Day and again for February 18th. It almost impossible to send flowers from here by telegraph. I would have to phone Tokyo and the Japanese phone system stinks."

On February 20, Karl informed La Vera why he was unable to write: "I was unable to write during the last two days because I was traveling from Sapporo to Sendai. Now I am at the Matsushima Airdrome near Yamoto, on Honshu. I'll be here at the Air Transport School for five days. I think that Rudy went to Jump School here."

On March 1st, Karl explained what he was reading and then poured out his heart to La Vera, with a recognition that he was determined through love to overcome her bouts of sadness.

> I'm reading a pretty good book now, <u>Pitcairns' Island</u> written by Nordhoff and Hall. It's a historical novel and continuation of the story, <u>Mutiny on the Bounty</u>. I'm doing quite a bit reading. I have quite a collection of books.

> La Vera, I love you, I love you so very very much. You're wonderful and perfect. I know that you are lonely and blue at times, La Vera, I'm too. La Vera, you feel that way because you day dream of the happy moments we've had in the past and they make you blue. But really, my darling, they're joyous times and our future will be the same and even better.

> It's true that the present seems dismal. I don't like it either, but I day-dream of holding you in arms again. La Vera, I want to make you happy, but all I've done so far is make you sad and unhappy. Please forgive me, La Vera, I love you more than it's possible for any other man to love his wife. I'll always love you.

> So, Darling, please, forgive me for bringing misery and unhappiness to you. If you look to the future and know that I love you maybe your sadness and loneliness will leave you. La Vera, you know that I love you and that I'll love you always. I'm the luckiest man in the world to have you. I love everything about you. I love you, La Vera.

Karl revealed his secret method of getting up in the morning: "I've quite a system in getting out of bed in the morning. The alarm goes off at 0555, then I turn on the light and radio. At 0600 the radio begins to play the <u>Star Spangled Banner</u> and that's when I get up. I eat breakfast at 6:30; go to work at 7:30. One officer in the company stands reveille. When my turn comes I get up at 5:00. There are four officers in the company."

On March 2, Karl told La Vera how much superior the horses at Camp Crawford at Hokkaido were to ride as contrasted to the horses he rode back in the states: "Since today is Wednesday, I didn't work this afternoon. Instead Capt. Lybarger (troop commander) and I went horseback riding into the hills. We have about 84 horses now. They are former Japanese Cavalry horses. And they're nothing like the nags that we rode in Missouri. They also have a riding school here at Crawford."

During March, Karl had the rare opportunity to be in charge of the escort detail to meet General William F. Dean, the commanding general of the 7th Division at the train depot at Sapporo. Mrs. Dean had just arrived from the states. Karl added: "The 7th Rcn. always acts as Honor Guard for generals. General Dean is giving a formal reception at the Grand Hotel in Sapporo next Saturday nite. The Grand Hotel is the officers club. The only time that I've been there is the morning of my initial arrival in Hokkaido. I ate breakfast there."

After the North Koreans invaded South Korea across the 38th parallel on June 25, 1950, General Dean became prominent in the news when he was captured along the fluid front lines on July 18, 1950, and was not repatriated until September 1953, after which he was awarded the Army's highest decoration—the Medal of Honor.

KARL'S FAVORITE BROTHER was Fritz. He did not have as much respect for his youngest brother, Rudy, who had served time at Father Flanagan's Boys' Town in Nebraska, where he had the questionable reputation of being "the only young man whom Boys' Town could not hold."

Writing to La Vera on March 5, Karl stated: "Have you been able to keep Rudy out of your hair? If he gives you any trouble, hit him with a ball bat."

He also noted: "I sat on a Courts Martial board yesterday morning to try a character just like Rudy. He got 6 months."

On March 6, Karl informed La Vera of his desire to earn a college degree: "I'm taking a course in college English; four hours a week. The course will end in about five or six weeks. Next Monday or Tuesday I'm going to take a test, which, if I pass, will give me credit for one year college. Then through the Army's educational program I can take correspondence courses from the University of Nebraska. After you're here in Japan, you may take the courses with me. Of course, La Vera, I realize that you don't need it, but you can help educate me."

On March 14, Karl reported: "I'm going to a Troop Information and Education school this week. And as part of the course I have to give a talk on U.S. and Russian relations tomorrow morning."

On March 19, Karl took a 60-mile trip: "It's a blizzard today again. This morning I and three men with two 'jeeps' had to make a 60 miles round trip road reconnaissance to Chitose Airdrome and back. It was a blizzard all the way. It was quite cold and we got stuck with both jeeps twice. The trip took about five hours."

On March 23, Karl related to La Vera the nature of his job at Camp Crawford and his general schedule: "La Vera, you've asked what my job is and how many hours a day I work and what time I get up in the morning. Well, I get up at six and go to work at seven-thirty. Quit at the end of the day at 4:30. Wednesday and Saturday afternoon are off. My job is Platoon Leader of 1st Platoon and in addition to that I make the training schedule for the entire company. La Vera, you'll learn more about the Army after you arrive here."

He added the next day: "You asked how I like my assignment. I believe that it's one of the best in the 7th Inf. Division."

The majority of the correspondence between Karl and La Vera, aside from the mutual and heartfelt expressions of endearment and fond references to Gay, concerned preparations which La Vera was making for her transoceanic trip to Japan.

Karl reported: "Pregnant women have priority, if you were pregnant, you'd be here already. Maybe we shouldn't have worried so much about it."

Projecting into the future as to how long they would be in the Far East, Karl speculated: "We will be scheduled to leave for the States in June 1951. So therefore you can plan to be here in the Orient for about two years. Gay will be 6½ years old when she gets back to the U.S. It's really hard to believe that Gay is four years old already and you're 27 and I'm only 18."

More high-ranking officers were due at Camp Crawford according to Karl: "We might have two honor guards this week. Both the Commanding Generals of the 8th Army and IX Corps are going to visit Crawford. I hope that I won't have to command both of them."

As March drew to a close, Karl teased La Vera about the slow mail delivery:

29th March 1949, 9:00 P.M.

Hello, my Darling,

No mail to day—I guess I should get angry and start saying you don't love me, that you're forgetting me etc. Well, La Vera, that's what you do when you don't receive any mail from me. But, La Vera, I know that you love me (of course your love for me is only half as much as I love you). As a matter of fact, I think that I love you at least a billion times more than you love me.

In one of his typical letters to Gay, Karl wrote on April 8:

8th April 1949

Hello, my little "Big Girl"

I received your letter. I'll save it and you can read it to me when you arrive here.

Are you being a good girl, Gay? I hope so because only real good girls can come to Japan. I know that you'll be real good, won't you? And be sure to hold on to Mommy's hand when you're on the ship so that she doesn't fall in the ocean. Gay, you have to take good care of Mommy on the trip. And tell her that I love her very, very much and I love you too, you "old stink bomb."

Karl reported on April 8 on his physical exam: "I took a physical examination this afternoon. I'm in excellent physical condition. My blood pressure was only 112 which is very low. I've lost ten pounds in weight since my last physical exam. The excess weight was around the waist (as you know). I weigh 179.

"This morning at 10:00 I went to the Quartermaster Bakery here on the post to have coffee and rolls. I received the invitation from the Bakery Officer, Lt. Rubottom, whom I met at Ft. Lawton. If I would remain here a week I'd get fat."

Speculating on an addition to the family, Karl wrote on April 13: "Yes, La Vera, I guess we should plan for another child in the near future. As it is, Gay will be at least five years older than our next baby. What do you think, Sweetheart?"

On May 7, the 7th Division held a parade for its commander, General William F. Dean.

On May 8, the 4th anniversary of the end of the war in Europe, Karl tried to reassure La Vera about Communist-controlled China: "La Vera, don't be too alarmed over the China situation. The Chinese have been fighting either with the Japs or among themselves since the early 1930s."

On the morning of May 10, Karl commanded the escort guard for General Dean, who left his post as commander of the 7th Division and his place was taken by General David Barr.

On May 12, the official orders finally came through to authorize La Vera and Gay to come to join Karl in Japan early in July. Karl bought a new pair of brown leather boots for Gay. He wondered if they would fit and offered an alternative: "Did you tell Gay about her new boots? What did she say? I hope they'll fit her. If not, we'll have to save them for our next child."

On June 8, Karl reported he had gotten sick from a shot "for Japanese sleeping sickness." He also told La Vera how much fun he was having horseback riding: "I try to get the same horse each time. I ride a horse named Cap. A very spirited animal who hates to walk and stand still."

On June 10, Karl reported: "I received a letter from the Department of the Army yesterday. It permanently changed my branch of service from Infantry to Armored Cavalry."

IN CONTRAST TO EARLY 1949, when La Vera had some very low moments as Karl was shipped to Japan, she and Gay were overjoyed with their accommodations at Camp Crawford, Hokkaido, Japan when they arrived at the end of July.

La Vera wrote to her mother from Camp Crawford on September 19, 1949:

"I just gave Gay a bath and put her to bed.

"We moved into Camp Crawford two weeks ago tomorrow. We have an end apartment of a 4-apartment building. Downstairs we have a living room, dining room and kitchen. Upstairs we have two bedrooms and a bath. The house is comfortably furnished with nearly everything you want. Even the dishes are real nice. About the only thing it lacked was a can opener and a bread board and now they've supplied us with them. I will be glad when our household goods get here though so I can use wearever again. Then Gay will have her toys, too. The trunks should come any day now.

"Karl is out in the field with problems again this week. He was all of last week. This should be for the end of it this year, though. I won't see him until Saturday noon now. Otherwise, he is home for lunch every day and at five every evening. On Wednesday and Saturday they get off at noon.

"Last week we went to a reception for Mrs. MacArthur and General Walker and his wife. We were introduced and shook hands with all of them. There was a party for all the officers and families afterward.

"We like it here real well. We have two house girls now. I keep busy, though. There is so much social life. I've been on a merry-go-round ever since I arrived. There are so many things to go to. We recently saw the opera 'Madame Butterfly'.

"It really takes clothes over here. The ladies really dress for the receptions."

LA VERA TOLD ME HOW MUCH she reveled in the spacious 4-room apartment to which the family was assigned. She especially appreciated the Japanese house-

Karl bought Gay a new bicycle in Japan.

maids assigned to take care of every chore, and how friendly the other officer wives were. Four-year-old Gay loved the open spaces available for her to play and also playmates near her age. The well-stocked Post Exchange (P.X.) seemed to carry more reasonable and varied items than were obtainable in Omaha, including dolls and other toys to intrigue Gay.

Now that the family was all together, of course there were no detailed letters to reveal the highlights of Karl's training and leadership during the last half of 1949.

The appraisals of Karl's military performance in Japan differed sharply from the low regard which Col. Seeley registered in Europe. I talked at length with Major Kenneth Farnham, who reported to me:

Acrobatic Gay in Japan.

"I was G-2 (intelligence) of the 7th Division, and as such gave combat tests to Timmermann's platoon in the Reconnaissance Company. It was a good combat outfit and always tested at or near the top. The men had a lot of respect for Timmermann as an officer. He was an aggressive and outspoken officer who was a good combat leader. He did a particularly effective job as a leader in the aggressor force in the March 1950

maneuvers. He was serious and conscientious about his work.

"It was a long time after he had been with the 7th Division that I realized he had had anything to do with the Remagen Bridge. Even then, he did not mention it himself, but another officer told me about it. Timmermann was not the kind of a man who would talk about something that he had accomplished and brag about it."

Captain Robert Lybarger, Company Commander of the 7th Reconnaissance Company, made this appraisal of Platoon Leader Timmermann for the latter's 201 file:

"This officer is very energetic, in good physical condition, has a high degree of initiative, a good mental outlook, and lives by a high moral code."

La Vera, Gay and Karl in Japan

Three weeks before the North Korean forces streaked across the 38th parallel in an attempt to conquer South Korea, Karl wrote to his mother:

3 June 1950

Dear Ma,

Gay had the measles. She's alright now; she was outside today.

I just returned from a 3 days trip to the southern part of Hokkaido with my platoon.

Next year at this time we'll be heading back to the United States. The time over here really goes fast.

I hope that everything is OK with you. What is Rudy doing?

So long for now,

Your Son,

Karl

IT BECAME OBVIOUS after the outset of the Korean war on June 25, 1950, that sooner or later Karl's 7th Recon Company would be drawn into combat.

Meanwhile, Karl had a chance to see his brother, Fritz, as he wrote his mother from Camp Crawford on July 30, 1950:

> 30 July 1950
> Hokkaido, Japan
>
> Dear Ma,
>
> I had two telephone calls from Fritz since his arrival in Japan. One call came on the day his plane landed, which was the day before yesterday. The second call came this morning about 10:00 o'clock. His address is 87th Maintenance Company, Tokyo Ordinance Center. He doesn't know whether or not he'll go to Korea.
>
> The world is certainly getting smaller. It only took him thirty hours to get here.
>
> How are things with you. How are Rudy and Pa getting along?
>
> We've been having quite warm weather here recently. I wish that it would rain.
>
> La Vera and Gay are the same as ever. Gay is growing like a weed.
>
> So long for now, Your Son, Karl

On August 6, 1950, Karl's Recon Company left Camp Crawford for combat maneuvers and he wrote La Vera on August 13: "I received mail to-day. It is enclosed herein. I wish that I would have received a letter from you. We've been apart a week and it seemed like a month. La Vera, I love you, love you more and more each day.

"My platoon is leaving for a problem tonite at 8:30 this evening. We should return some time after mid-nite."

The next day when Karl wrote that he was leaving for "you know where" around the first week in September, of course he meant he was heading for combat in Korea:

> Hello Sweetheart,
>
> I just returned from an Officers' School at Division Headquarters. It seemed a waste of my time. I got in from the problem at 4:00 this morning. We (the 2nd Platoon) succeeded in capturing the General.
>
> We'll leave for "you know where" around the 1st week of September. I hope that it comes to an end before then.

On August 19 Karl informed La Vera: "Tomorrow, my platoon goes into the field for one week to fight against the 32nd Infantry. I look forward to a miserable week."

On August 22, Karl explained the reason why he was so miserable during field operations: "I came back to camp with my platoon this morning. We're going out into the field for two more days on Thursday morning. These last two days were miserable because it rained constantly. I took my writing paper with me in order to write to you. The rain ruined my papers and stamps."

By September 3, Karl could report that his trip to the combat zone in Korea was imminent:

3rd Sept. 1950
9:00 P.M.

My Darling La Vera,

Tomorrow we leave here to get on the ship. So I don't know yet when I'll write my next letter to you.

We got back to Camp at 3:00 this morning. It was a really tiring ride.

On September 6, Karl mentioned the composition of his platoon: "I have 11 Koreans assigned to my platoon. One of them is an Officer and one speaks English."

In his next letter Karl could mention the invasion ship he had boarded but not its destination. He was headed for the bold venture to land behind the North Korean lines at the port of Inchon in one of the most dramatically successful operations of the Korean War:

7th Sept 50
7:45 P.M.

My Darling,

I'm aboard the U.S.N.S. Ainsworth in Yokohama. They are now removing the gangplank and preparing for sailing. I wish that you I and Gay were sailing to the States together.

On the same day that Karl wrote, La Vera also wrote her mother in West Point. She wanted to move south to be closer to Karl, but Karl advised her that it would be safer for her to remain at Camp Crawford with Gay. La Vera expressed to her mother her puzzlement as to what to do as well as her apprehension for Karl's safety:

Camp Crawford, Japan

September 7, 1950

Dear Mother:

Karl called me today from Yokohama. He was leaving for Korea. I was hoping it would be over by now, but it doesn't look anywhere near finished.

Gay and I spent five days in Tokyo with Karl last week. We had a wonderful time. We were lucky that we were able to have that much time together again.

Most of the dependents have gone back to the states. I could be back there too, but I wanted to see Karl as much as possible. There are about fifty families here yet. There are Japanese troops in here now.

I really don't know if I'm coming home or not. If they move us further south near Tokyo, I may stay. I think Karl would like me to remain in Japan near him and yet we both can't decide what I should do. I guess it would be wise to return to the states. If I do, I should before the winter.

We took the train to Tokyo to see Karl and Gay had a big time with the soldiers on the train. They really think she's quite the gal. Gay slept in the upper berth on the train and she thinks that's big stuff.

In an attempt to ease La Vera's mind about the Inchon invasion, on September 9 Karl wrote to La Vera about what he had been reading aboard ship: "I just finished reading a book, 'Clattering Hoofs.' It was a good western. I'm going to start another entitled 'Trail's End' by the same author, Wm. MacLeod Raine."

On September 26, 1950, Karl brought La Vera up to date on the combat activities of his outfit in North Korea:

26 Sept 50, 4:00 P.M.

My Darling La Vera,

Today is the first day of rest since the company landed in Inchon. We are now located at Anyang-ni. My platoon was the first troops in that town on the 20th. The next day the 7th Rcn. took Suwon. That nite we had a tank battle there. Enemy losses— 3 tanks, ours none. Col. Hampton was killed that nite. Lt. Miller was taken prisoner, but escaped.

Yesterday we covered the 32nd Inf. right flank as it crossed the river to take Seoul.

In the 2nd platoon, there has been only two minor wounds. I hope I can maintain that record. The platoon has operated just as I trained them, and I believe I gave them the right training.

Finally, on October 1, 1950, Karl wrote about his success at Inchon, noting "We took the town of Inchon this morning—no opposition from the enemy." Karl then elaborated:

The 7th Rcn Co was in combat almost a week before the rest of the division even got ashore. We took the town of Suwon but the 31st Inf. got credit for it. They came to Suwon about three days after we. La Vera, don't believe everything you read or hear.

So far this war I've had only two men wounded in a minor sense. One of my jeeps in my platoon was run over by an enemy tank the night we took Suwon. All the men escaped injury.

On October 2, Karl reported to La Vera from Inchon: "This morning I sent 2 squads from my platoon on a patrol to the northeast. They returned completing their mission and did not encounter any enemy."

He then added this gruesome news: "I talked to an officer from the 31st Infantry. He informed me that Lt. Engh and Lt. Fuss were killed. Major Olson lost one of his arms. The 32nd Infantry had 57% loss when they fought to take Seoul. The 17th Infantry saw very little combat."

La Vera brought Karl's mother up-to-date in a lengthy letter written October 5, 1950, from Camp Crawford:

If you've been following the 7th Div. you know approximately where Karl is. They were in on the Inchon invasion and since Karl left Yokohama I've had one letter from him written Sept 26th. That's all so far. That was his first day of rest since they landed. It was written from near Suwon. They had seen heavy fighting, but his platoon had no dead, only 2 slightly wounded.

However, I keep hearing about the different ones in the 7th Div. that are killed and it's difficult when you know so many of them and I know their wives and there's nothing I can do for them. It's a bad situation. I only hope it's over soon. Maybe Karl will be back here by Christmas. I only hope and pray that he stays safe.

I have an opportunity to move to Sendai next week and just don't know what to do. It is farther south nearer Tokyo.

I've been teaching the Kindergarten this week. They want me for the permanent teacher, but I just don't know if I should stay with it. There are 17 pupils and some of the boys are so mean. It's only mornings but it's very strenuous work and I'm so tired and nervous when I get home. I may keep it until they find another teacher.

Back at Pusan in southern Korea, Karl wrote to La Vera: "The latest rumor is that we are going to get aboard ship here on the 15th of the month for the invasion of North Korea. I wish that this darn war was over."

On October 12, Karl wrote his mother from Pusan, repeating the scary rumor but also expressing pardonable pride in the combat performance of his platoon:

Dear Ma,

As you probably know by now the 7th Division took part in the Inchon Invasion. At present we are waiting here to embark again for another invasion. This time, as the rumors go, it will be near the Manchurian Border. I think that the whole world is crazy.

In the 2nd Platoon there has been only two minor wounds. I hope that I can maintain that record. The platoon has operated just as I trained them and I believe I gave them the right training.

TEN

The Final Year

ON OCTOBER 12, 1950, Karl had a pain and a lump in his groin that caused him to report to the medics where he was ordered to report to the 8054th Evacuation Hospital.

From Pusan, Korea, Karl wrote his mother on October 14:

> Dear Ma:
>
> At the present time I'm at the 8054th Evacuation Hospital waiting transportation back to Japan. The doctors here think that I have a tumor.
>
> The 7th Division is in the process of loading aboard ship for the invasion of North Korea. This war should be over in about two weeks after the invasion.

La Vera and Karl thought his return to the states was a "good break" at first. She added: "The doctors did not let us in on the seriousness of the illness."

When La Vera and Gay arrived in San Francisco after her mid-October flight from Tokyo, she contacted a Red Cross worker who told her that Karl had been sent to Fitzsimons General Hospital in Denver.

On November 20, 1950, La Vera wrote to Karl's mother:

"Karl started taking his X-ray treatments today. He has to lie under the X-ray several minutes each day for a month or longer. He's feeling stronger every day, but still has a hard time getting around. He's lost weight, but I guess that's common after an operation."

On March 10, 1951, La Vera wrote Karl's mother about their trip to Denver:

> We got here O.K. We stayed the first night in McCook. Karl was sick and I drove from Hooper the rest of the way. We got here the next day about 3:00 o'clock. We moved into a motel apartment about a mile from the hospital. It's small, but modern and clean. It costs $25 a week, so we plan to move into something more reasonable later on.
>
> Yesterday we found out that Karl's X-rays showed that he has the same thing in his left lung. They will give him 4 weeks of x-ray therapy in the chest starting on Monday. If the condition doesn't change they will operate to remove the lung. We will be here a long time yet, so I guess I'll start Gay in school Monday.
>
> Karl has been here with me nearly all week and has been feeling fine. Starting Monday I guess he'll be spending most of the time at the hospital.
>
> We're going to a movie tomorrow and maybe take some pictures. The weather has been so nice all week, but is snowing.

One day while Gay was playing outside the motel where they were staying near the hospital, she found a wristwatch. With great enthusiasm she showed it to her father. Karl immediately told her: "We must place this with the motel manager to see if he can locate the rightful owner. Then, if the manager is unable to locate the owner after a week, only then can you keep it."

It was a good lesson in honesty.

On March 30, 1951, La Vera wrote to Karl's mother:

"Karl is home most of the time. He gets passes at noon on Tuesday, Friday, Saturday and all day Sunday. He always is back at the hospital at 8 in the morning for x-ray therapy. Karl looks well and feels much better than he did during x-ray. He's gained about 7 lbs. too.

"The tumors (cancer) on his lung have gotten smaller since the treatment and we hope they disappear completely, and don't spread anywhere else."

On April 16, 1951, she reported:

"We still don't know whether or not he'll need another operation. The one tumor has disappeared, but the larger one is still there, but smaller. It may disappear, too, as the x-ray isn't through working.

"Karl feels quite well most of the time, except for being tired most of the

Photos of Karl while undergoing treatment at Fitzsimons General Hospital in Denver.

time. The x-ray treatments do that. He usually naps in the mornings and afternoons awhile.

"Gay weighs 50, does dishes, empties garbage, going to the store. Quite the helper around the house."

On April 23, 1951, Karl penned the following letter to his favorite brother Fritz, once again indicating that his youngest brother Rudy, a real "sad sack," had angered most of the family:

23rd April 1951

Hello Fritz,

Your letter came this morning. It only took four days to get here.

I haven't any idea as to when I'll be released from the hospital. And then after I get out I don't know whether I'll go back to duty. They might retire me. If they retire me I'll get about $240.00 per month.

I guess Rudy is a "Bed Pan Jockey." I got a letter from him last week. I think that he thinks we should feel sorry for him because he is in Korea. I would like to have had him in my platoon, I would have broken his bull head.

Well, Fritz, take it easy.

I'll be seeing you, Karl

On May 7, 1951, La Vera wrote:

"This is Monday night and Karl's at the hospital, so I'll write a few lines before going to bed. We were up at the hospital this evening and all went over to the club awhile. Karl and I shoot pool, and Gay watches 3 rooms, storage room and bath.

"Karl's tumors have disappeared, and since then they have discovered no new ones. I only hope he is cured. Time will tell. The x-ray treatments should be over the first part of June. We plan to come down to West Point the middle of June as he'll get another leave."

On May 30, 1951, Karl traveled to Hugo, Colorado with La Vera and Gay, where Karl delivered what onlookers described as a "brief but inspiring" Memorial Day address. An enthusiastic crowd greeted the Hero of the Rhine and warmly applauded his patriotic remarks.

The newspaper in Hugo started its coverage with this sentence: "One of the best Memorial Day programs ever held in Hugo was given Wednesday." The news reporter commented that Lt. Timmermann's address was "brief but impressive." Karl packed a good deal of substance into a tightly organized and well-planned delivery, which was typed out on note sheets, as follows:

> In the last half century our nation has fought two wars and is now fighting the third. Our sole purpose in these conflicts, as in all the wars in which we have been engaged since 1776, was and still is the preservation of peace, liberty and the rights and dignity of man. Every year at this time we gather to pay homage to our war dead. We try to re-assure ourselves and their loved ones that their heroic deeds were not needless—that their supreme sacrifices were not in vain. These brave men, who died in such places as Bunker Hill, Gettysburg, San Juan Hill, France in 1918, the vast areas of the earth in World War II and now in Korea, will have died without a cause IF— if we fail to carry on their fight. Yes, they will have died in vain if the things for which they fought vanish from the grasp of mankind.
>
> Annually, on Memorial Day, we who have survived the horrors of war re-dedicate ourselves to the preservation of the principles set forth in the Declaration of Independence and the Bill of Rights. We pledge ourselves to the causes of peace and freedom. We must pool our efforts. We must be determined in our goal—to truly keep this great nation of ours the land of the free and the home of the brave.

At Hugo, as photos reveal, Karl certainly did not appear to be his former, vigorous self, and he privately complained that his shoulders had to be slightly stooped so he could not stand as straight and razor-sharp as he would have liked. La Vera said he was in much pain during the ceremony.

Karl at Hugo, Colorado, May 30, 1951 (Memorial Day)

On July 5, La Vera reported to Karl's mother what was perhaps an over-optimistic report from one of the Fitzsimons' nurses.

July 5th, 11:45 P.M.

Dear Mother,

This won't be long as I'm really tired tonight. It's a job running back & forth to the hospital and trying to keep up on the house work.

I know you are worried about Karl as I am. At first I thought he had late-stages of cancer in the chest, but I talked to the nurse last night and she said he did have a form of pneumonia as a result of the x-ray therapy and a slight cold.

However, I plan to talk to the doctor tomorrow and find out just what the score is.

Karl feels some better today and doesn't cough as much. He's coughed up so much blood and slime. His temperature is still around 102 and he gets hypos, penicillin and all kinds of pills. He's still in bed and is too weak to even bathe himself. I really think he's getting better tho.

I take Gay up to the hospital afternoons and usually leave her in the nursery at night when I go up again.

If this should be more serious I'll call you and maybe you'll want to come. But as it is, I think the worst is over and he'll just be weak for a very long time.

On August 19, La Vera wrote to Karl's mother:

Sunday, Aug. 19,

Dear Mother,

We received your letter and were glad to hear that you got home O.K. Hope your headaches have left you and that you're feeling better.

Karl is about the same. Some days he feels better than others. He still doesn't go out, only to the hospital on Tuesdays.

Gay has been a real good girl again (no spankings, either). She plays out right by the basement windows, so we can watch her. The landlady's girl plays with her again and we chase "Pesty" away.

I went uptown one day to get Karl 6 operettas, "The Student Prince," "The Firefly," "Rose Marie," "The Chocolate Soldier," "Naughty Marietta" and "Roberta."

I really keep busy now. Say "hello" to the Roberts and <u>der lieber mann</u>. Ha!

Love,
La Vera, Karl & Gay

On August 28, La Vera wrote:
"Karl stayed in the car, as he can't walk much because of his breathing.
"Karl had a letter from Monsignor Bosheck today. He enjoyed getting it."
I think by September 13, La Vera began to realize that Karl's illness was incurable. On that date she wrote to Karl's mother:
"Karl hasn't been feeling well at all. He coughs up so much blood and slime. I bought a nice, gray easy chair with ottoman to match. It cost $71, so

it's really nice. The other chair was so hard and he sits all day, so he may as well be as comfortable as possible.

"Karl's last X-rays showed tumors in his other lung, not the one that is inflamed from X-ray, but the other. The doctor told him it was there. They can't give him any more treatment unless the other lung clears up soon.

"Karl has 14 operettas now."

Karl made many friends among the doctors, patients, nurses and other associates with whom he came in contact at Fitzsimons. One of his new friendships was cemented with Col. Lester K. Olsen, who had to leave for the Command and General Staff College at Fort

Karl with his wife, mother and daughter during the last months

Leavenworth, Kansas shortly before Karl's death. Col. Olsen took time to write a lengthy personal letter of encouragement to Karl in September. One day when he had been visiting Karl in Denver at the hospital, as La Vera told me later:

"Col. Olsen made me cry at the hospital one day when he came to my car to tell me what a fine person Karl was and how sorry he was that Karl had to go.

"I pressed his hand, walked away and burst into tears. I tried to dry them, but Karl saw.

"'What are you crying about?' he asked.

"'Oh, Col. Olsen is so nice,' I answered."

In his spare time at Fitzsimons, Karl sketched some of his thoughts and ideas. Quite striking was one sketch in which he portrayed "cancer" as a hydra-headed dragon which consumed the human body and could not be repulsed. La Vera added that in the final days "Karl feared the great unknown which confronted him: death. He compared it to venturing out into strange territory during combat, except that in combat you had your friends, companions and buddies around, where there was nobody else around when you sought help in the unknown territory as you approached death."

La Vera's last letter was written about three weeks before Karl's death:

Sunday, Sept. 30, 1951

Dear Mother,

I'm up at the hospital with Karl. He isn't feeling well at all. He's been getting hypos a lot these past few days. Because his throat hurts so much, he barely talks at all.

I really think I should spend more time up here with him, but with Gay going to school it's difficult to be up here much. I have to leave here at 8 at night to get her to bed in time so she can get up in the morning.

If your health permits and you want to, maybe you should come out again. Karl is getting worse every day and I should stay with him as the service isn't too good in the hospital.

When you get this letter call me at the hospital between 6 and 8 P.M. and I'll let you know how things stand. I hope he improves before then.

Thanks for Gay's nightie and the other things. She really likes them.

She lost a front tooth, so looks like a Grandma now.

You telephone me here then between 6–8 and I'll let you know if things are better.

Love, La Vera, Karl & Gay

THE HERO OF THE RHINE died on Sunday evening, October 21, 1951. La Vera very much wanted to have Karl buried in Arlington National Cemetery, but that would have prevented friends of the family from attending the services.

Karl was buried with full military honors at Fort Logan National Cemetery in Denver on Thursday, October 25, 1951. He said that he would not rest if he were buried in West Point, Nebraska.

Karl is interred in Section H, Grave 195 at the Fort Logan National Cemetery, 3698 South Sheridan Boulevard in Denver.

ELEVEN

Recognition

ASIDE FROM THE CONTEMPORANEOUS news accounts of the capture of the Ludendorff Bridge on March 7, 1945, little or no attention was directed at Lt. Timmermann's exploit until 1955. At that time there were several articles commemorating the tenth anniversary of the first crossing of the Rhine, plus the reunion of the living recipients of the Distinguished Service Cross hosted at the White House by President Dwight D. Eisenhower, the Supreme Commander under whose command the operation had occurred.

President Eisenhower also created the "Society of the Remagen Bridge" and at the 10th anniversary White House meeting of the Living DSC winners, the President presented each man with a certificate to make them charter members of the Society. I then asked President Eisenhower to send a posthumous certificate to Karl's mother, which he did.

Publication of *The Bridge at Remagen* in 1957 which mentioned the failure of the city of West Point to honor Timmermann stimulated a number of letters throughout the country, expressing sympathy for Timmermann and also sensitizing some people in West Point to correct the record.

West Point's mayor, W. H. Hasebroock, told me: "Well, I suppose we could have had some type of ceremony for Lt. Timmermann, but most people were tired of the war, also there were many deserving veterans who came home from World War II."

Ed Baumann, the highly respected local department store owner, who had run for Governor of Nebraska in 1929, and also as head of the local "War Dads" who had sent a letter of congratulations to Karl in 1945, told me:

March 3, 1955

Dear Mrs. Timmermann:

One of the most dramatic events of World
War II was the crossing of the Remagen
Bridge, the tenth anniversary of which occurs
on March 7.   Your husband Karl was the first
officer to cross that bridge, at a time when the
enemy troops were trying to blow it up.   I
would like to give renewed assurance that you
have reason to be proud of what he did for his
country.

My best wishes to you.

Sincerely,

Dwight D. Eisenhower

Mrs. La Vera Timmermann
1680 Rosemary Street
Denver, Colorado

"Karl was a real gentleman and a true blue soldier. He was a hero. But the town belittled him. The old man 'wind-jammed' around town bragging about Karl, but he hurt Karl. The Catholics resented his marrying a Lutheran. I tried to help, but they would have none of it."

In 1959, Fort Dix, New Jersey, opened a new theater and ran a contest among the soldiers to choose a name for it. One of the soldiers who had read my book won the contest by submitting the name "Timmermann Theater." Some years later I brought Karl's sister Mary to view the building named after her brother.

In the spring of 1960, John F. Magill, Jr., a World War II paratrooper in Europe and supervising Principal of Blain Union School District near Harrisburg, read about Karl and was shocked to learn that West Point did nothing to honor him. Magill told the Blain High School students about this unsung war hero, inspiring them to come forward with a two-pronged plan: First, a student-run commemorative program honoring Lt. Timmermann, and second, a presentation of a suitable memorial to Karl's mother and family in West Point later that summer.

Society of the Remagen Bridge

First crossing of the Rhine by
Allied Forces in the Campaign of 1944–1945
March 7, 1945
9th U.S. Armored Division
of the III U.S. Corps of the First U.S. Army

To Karl H. Timmermann

Tenth Anniversary
March 7, 1955

Dwight D. Eisenhower
President of the United States
1945 Supreme Commander
Allied Expeditionary Force

Presented posthumously —
in honor of a gallant soldier

For Mrs. Mary Timmermann,
mother of three American
soldier sons and a soldier daughter,
with great respect.

Dwight Eisenhower

In 2001, the Timmermann Theater at Fort Dix, N.J., was renamed the "Timmermann Center."

The Freshman Class supervised the research on Karl's exploit, even to the extent of corresponding with Dr. I. L. Thompson, the Timmermann family doctor, and other residents of West Point, plus the War Department to verify the official record. The Junior Class raised the expense money to create a Bas-Relief memorial for presentation to the Timmermann family.

The Blain School Band, veterans and town officials assembled on the athletic field where Principal Magill delivered an address entitled "The Life And Contributions of Karl Timmermann." After the address, the students marched back to the school where they placed a huge wreath under the copper Bas-Relief memorial, depicting 1945 wartime scenes from Germany in 1945. Included in the memorial were large photos of Lt. Timmermann, his tombstone in Fort Logan National Cemetery, and a reproduction of the color painting of the battle for the Ludendorff Bridge supplied by the War Department.

The plaque which Magill's school crafted reads as follows:

"Dedicated to Lieutenant Karl Timmermann, United States Army. Whose courage was too soon forgotten . . . No stranger to prejudice, his compassion knew no boundary; this was a leader loved by his enlisted men. Be proud if you knew him, whose courage and leadership at the Remagen bridge enabled five thousand American boys to return alive to their homes and saved suffering to ten thousand more . . . March 7, 1945.

"He served once more at Inchon in Korea . . . 1950. His untimely death in 1951 was perhaps hastened by the ravages of war and burden of responsibility.

"In grateful appreciation: The Blain Union School, Blain, Pennsylvania."

John Magill also wrote an article about Karl Timmermann which was printed in the March-April, 1995 issue of *The Purple Heart Magazine*, in the course of which Magill stated:

"From the day of his conception, Karl Timmermann would be destined to suffer many cruel blows—most of them not of his doing. All of his short life, he was driven by the desire to win back his family name which was rightfully theirs to begin with, in a democratic society. Most of all, he wanted from his hometown—not recognition, mind you, just acceptance.

"Yes, this young man, who at 22 years of age led his men across the demolition-laden bridge at Remagen, never received that which most of us take for granted. May his life serve as a warning to us, in this land of freedom, that a man should not be labeled or judged except on his own merits or shortcomings! May his example serve to awaken a sometimes complacent America to the fact that liberty and freedom have exacted a heavy toll. This man, I think, paid more than his fair share."

It is interesting that an obscure little Pennsylvania town hundreds of miles east of Nebraska should single out a combat veteran whom they never met for a hero's celebration, in contrast to the town where the hero grew up which brought out the band for an area-wide welcome to greet a surgeon and cattle-owner on his return from a non-combat European vacation.

As time went on, the conscience of West Point surfaced. In 1965, 20 years after Karl and his men seized the Ludendorff Bridge, West Point decided to name the Little League Baseball Field, where Karl used to raid the watermelon patch, after the bad boy of the "Bloody Third Ward." Timmerman Memorial Field was dedicated on May 31, 1965 (mis-spelling his name).

Karl's father had died in 1955, and his mother in 1963, so it was unfortunate they could not personally share in the first glimmer of glory to come from West Point to honor their son. Gathered on the grassy centerfield of the ball park were members of the late Lieutenant's family, including his wife, married in 1955 to telephone company executive Jack Hansen of Denver; Karl's daughter, Mrs. Frank Estey of Peoria, Illinois, Karl's favorite brother, Fritz of Leavenworth, Kansas, and his sister Mary Roberts of Omaha.

Former Mayor W. H. Hasebroock who ten years earlier had explained why West Point did not immediately honor Karl, as a State Senator praised Karl's bravery: "It is entirely proper that the athletic field should be dedicated to his memory. This is the neighborhood in which Lt. Timmermann spent his boyhood.

"He should be an inspiration to all who participate in games on this field as well as spectators and all those that hear the name, Lt. Timmermann, as

Color Guard for 1965 dedication

From left to right: Karl's sister Mary; wife, La Vera; daughter, Gaye; brother, Fritz

the first officer to cross the Remagen Bridge on March 7, 1945, for which he received the Distinguished Service Cross."

Senator Hasebroock concluded his remarks by citing Timmermann as "A young man of determination and courage, a hero in every sense of the word."

In 1965, West Point Mayor John Soll stated: "We started to get blamed for not doing anything to honor Karl. It was picked up by the news media. We had the space for the field and thought 'Why not name it after him?'

"You can't blame the youngsters for what was said about the Timmermann name. You know how rumors get so out of hand."

Edward C. Nitz, who was in charge of presentation and retirement of the colors in the 1965 ceremony, stated at the time that he remembered that the taunts continued after Karl returned from the war.

"I don't know why children have to carry the sins of their parents," Nitz said. "In small towns you get a bunch of people in a beer joint . . . There were those who did resent his father. In this day and age we would call them a bigot."

Cuming County Sheriff Harold "Deke" Welding said at the time: "I used to run around with Karl when we were kids. Some people held it against the rest of the family because of the father's actions." As for the lack of a home-coming for the war hero, Welding said this: "A lot of servicemen deserved to be greeted as a hero. But people here didn't seem to go out of their way for things like that. It was possible his name made a difference."

Charles E. Moulton (whose father had been murdered), the VFW Commander who gave the dedicatory address in 1965, was a Third Ward neighbor of Karl when he was a child. Moulton commented: "When the Park was being planned, a lot of people said we should do something to honor Karl. Some people didn't think much of the idea."

There was only one small problem with the 1965 dedication: The giant scoreboard misspelled Timmermann's name!

Not long before Karl's mother's death in 1963, she received the following poignant letter from William Mann of Denver:

"I interviewed Karl on his arrival at Fitzsimons Army Hospital, and we became very good friends. I was civilian Assistant Public Information Officer at the time and was at Fitzsimons throughout the Korean War.

"Karl typified everything that I have always admired and respected in an army officer: absolute integrity and the highest ideals, as well as professional excellence and competence. He had all three in abundance and I think he sensed a kinship with me, for the day before he passed away, he asked one of the fine Army doctors who attended him to send me up to see

him. When I came into his room, he was experiencing a paroxysmal cough-
ing spell, but he recognized me at once and extended his hand. That was all,
but I'll never forget it, not only for my high regard for the man, but also for
the affection I felt for him.

"I am one who believes most firmly in the survival of the human personality after the change we call death, so be assured you will again behold him
in time. No man achieves the stature he did without having had the guiding
hand of a fine mother, so I salute you." Sincerely, William Mann, Formerly
Captain of Infantry, USAR (Presently Lt. Col., Colorado National Guard).

In 1985, Ross Rasmussen of Blair, Nebraska, brought still another honor
to Karl. Ross, a war-time buddy of Karl, joined members of the 87th Division, of which Karl was a member prior to attending Infantry Officer Candidate School, in a nostalgic 40th anniversary tour of European battlefields in
October, 1985. A proposal by Rasmussen to honor Timmermann was adopted
by the 40 & 8 of the 1018 voitures at their July 1985 meeting.

The 87th Division held a ceremony commemorating Timmermann's exploit at the Ludendorff Bridge on October 8. A copy of the resolution honoring Karl was placed in a water-proof tube and thrown into the Rhine by
Rasmussen. Copies of the documents were given to Remagen's Burgermeister,
Hans Peter Kürten.

In 1994, the late historian Stephen E. Ambrose suggested to me that we
get together about 50 Remagen battle veterans and interested World War II
historians to tour European battlefields and join the mammoth 50th anniversary celebration at the remains of the Remagen Bridge on March 7, 1995.
We were fortunate to be joined by La Vera and Jack Hansen, who had enjoyed 40 years of happily married life, including many cruises and trips to
other countries.

In mid-1994, there was a vacancy caused by a retirement in the leadership
of the Cuming County Veterans Service Office. Robert L. Wostoupal of
Beemer, a town six miles northwest of West Point, won the competition for
the job. A 1960 graduate of West Point High School, Wostoupal had served
for 21 years in the U.S. Army in such diverse posts as Vietnam, Alaska,
Augsburg (Germany), Fort Bliss, Texas, and St. Louis. He had risen to the
rank of Master Sergeant, participated in eleven campaigns, and collected
numerous Army Commendation Medals. From the start, he was a bundle of
energy, initiative and enthusiasm.

While he was in the Army and stationed in St. Louis, Wostoupal wrote a
very prescient letter to the editor of the *West Point News* taking him to task
for failing to call attention to the 40th anniversary of Lt. Timmermann's

leadership in seizing the bridge at Remagen on March 7, 1945. Wostoupal wrote:

"Lt. Timmermann's actions and great devotion to duty didn't even rate so much as a two-liner on the back page. It is difficult for me to imagine how the 40th anniversary of such a historic event could go unnoticed in your paper. The *Omaha World Herald* gave full credit to Lt. Timmermann, something his home town failed to do.

"Unfortunately, how soon we forget or don't want to remember the sacrifices performed by those who personally knew the horrors and agony of war. It is fine people like Lt. Karl Timmermann who helped make it possible for us to enjoy the many freedoms we all too often take for granted, now, many years later.

"I am disappointed, to say the least, in your failure to give honor to Lt. Timmermann, now, forty years later."

The *West Point News*, in bold type following Wostoupal's letter, rather lamely admitted having overlooked the 40th anniversary and then protested that they had "Printed several accounts of Lt. Timmermann's heroism, most recently three years ago when the new sign at Timmermann (sic) Park was installed. Neither the newspaper nor the community has forgotten."

That was not enough for Bob Wostoupal, determined to bring honor not only to Lt. Timmermann, but to West Point itself through an appropriate ceremony.

Wostoupal first broached the idea at a meeting of the Veterans Of Foreign Wars, of which he was a member. Someone in the back grumbled: "But his father was a bootlegger." Bob shot back: "So, what? So was John F. Kennedy's father." The idea met no further opposition.

In October of 1994, Wostoupal received the blessing of Karl's widow La Vera, with whom he kept in frequent contact to insure that every detail met her approval. Instead of setting up a committee to plan the affair, he decided to avoid wrangling by making the decisions himself quickly and crisply. It was a fortunate choice.

Wostoupal then started planning for the celebration to take place on March 7, 1995, the 50th Anniversary of Lt. Timmermann's heroic exploit. He made several trips to the Nebraska State Capitol in Lincoln to enlist the support of the Legislature and Nebraska's Governor E. Benjamin Nelson, to declare March 7, 1995, "Karl Timmermann Appreciation Day."

At 9:30 a.m. on February 23, 1995, Governor Nelson staged a public signing of the proclamation which Wostoupal had drafted:

Proclamation

WHEREAS,   LT Karl H. Timmermann, 01311343, Infantry, US Army, was Commander of Company A, 27th Armored Infantry Battalion, during World War II; and

WHEREAS,   On March 7, 1945, in Remagen, Germany, upon reaching the Ludendorff Railroad Bridge across the Rhine River, aware that the bridge was prepared for demolition, and in the face of heavy machine gun, small arms and direct 20mm gun fire, LT Timmermann began a hazardous trip across the bridge; and

WHEREAS,   Upon reaching the bridge towers on the far side, LT Timmermann cleared them of snipers and demolition crews and, still braving the intense machine gun and shell fire, reached the eastern side of the river where he eliminated hostile snipers and gun crews from along the bank and on the face of the bluff overlooking the river; and

WHEREAS,   By his outstanding heroism and unflinching valor, LT Timmermann materially contributed to the establishment of the first bridgehead across the Rhine River; and

WHEREAS,   General Eisenhower declared "the ten minutes between 1550 and 1600 on March 7, 1945, the most momentous in combat history"; and

WHEREAS,   Acclaimed over the nation as the "Hero of the Rhine," LT Timmermann, a West Point, Nebraska native, was awarded the Distinguished Service Cross for extraordinary heroism in action against the enemy by illustrating the high degree of initiative, leadership and gallantry toward which all soldiers strive.

NOW, THEREFORE,   I, E. Benjamin Nelson, Governor of the State of Nebraska, DO HEREBY PROCLAIM the 7th day of March, 1995 as

LIEUTENANT KARL H. TIMMERMANN
APPRECIATION DAY

throughout the State of Nebraska and urge all citizens to take due note of the observance.

IN WITNESS WHEREOF, I have hereunto set my hand, and cause the Great Seal of the State of Nebraska to be affixed this 23rd day of February, in the year of our Lord one thousand nine hundred and ninety-five.

Attest:

Secretary of State   Governor

Then State Senator C. N. "Bud" Robinson of Blair brought up the following resolution which passed the Nebraska Legislature unanimously on March 7, 1995, and was signed by Governor Nelson:

NINETY-FOURTH LEGISLATURE
FIRST SESSION
LEGISLATIVE RESOLUTION 62

Introduced by Robinson, 16

"WHEREAS, what many regard as the "greatest feat in World War II" occurred between 3:50 p.m. and 4:00 p.m. March 7, 1945, when the 9th Armored Division of Company A, 1st Battalion, 27th Armored Infantry Regiment of the United States Army crossed the Rhine River at Ludendorff Bridge near Remagen, Germany; and

"WHEREAS, this crossing gave the Allied Forces in Europe control of a key strategic position in their drive to conquer Nazi forces; and

"WHEREAS, General Dwight D. Eisenhower later described the ten minutes between 3:50 and 4:00 p.m. on March 7, 1945, "the most momentous in combat history"; and

"WHEREAS, this crossing took place in the face of Nazi forces' attempts to destroy the bridge with explosives, thereby posing great danger to the 9th Armored Division; and

"WHEREAS, Lt. Karl Timmermann of West Point, Nebraska, led the American forces which seized Ludendorff Bridge at Remagen March 7, 1945; and

"WHEREAS, in the twenty-four hours after Lt. Timmermann and his forces secured Ludendorff Bridge, nearly eight thousand troops were able to cross to the eastern bank of the Rhine, thereby expanding the bridgehead; and

"WHEREAS, prior to this action at Remagen, Lt. Timmermann fought at the Battle of the Bulge in 1944, where he was wounded; and

"WHEREAS, for his leadership, courage, and service to his country, Lt. Timmermann was awarded the Distinguished Service Cross; and

"WHEREAS, March 7, 1995, marks the fiftieth anniversary of the 9th Armored Division's and Lt. Timmermann's heroic action; and

"WHEREAS, churches in West Point, Nebraska, will ring their bells between 3:50 and 4:00 p.m. on March 7, 1995, in recognition of Lt. Timmermann's role in the decisive feat at Remagen; and

"WHEREAS, Governor Ben Nelson has declared March 7, 1995, Lt. Karl H. Timmermann Day in Nebraska.

"NOW, THEREFORE, BE IT RESOLVED BY THE MEMBERS OF THE NINETY-FOURTH LEGISLATURE OF NEBRASKA, FIRST SESSION:

"1. That the Legislature recognizes Karl Timmermann for his heroic action in World War II.

"2. That a copy of this resolution be sent to the Mayor of the City of West Point, Nebraska, and to the Editor of *The West Point News*.

Meanwhile, over in nearby Snyder, where Karl had spent his first few years of his life in this country, not to be outdone, they issued a proclamation and three certificates honoring Karl, La Vera and Karl's sister Mary.

Wostoupal then arranged with the U.S. Postal Service and West Point's Postmistress, Mrs. Jean Roemer to have a special pictorial postal cancellation on March 7, 1995. The cancellation is a drawing of the bridge at Remagen, performed on the first floor of the Cuming County Courthouse, designated as "Lt. Karl H. Timmermann Station, U.S. Post Office, 127 E. Bridge St., West Point, NE 68788."

Church bells throughout West Point and Snyder rang between 3:50 and 4:00 p.m. on March 7, during the period fifty years earlier when Lt. Timmermann had led his Armored Infantry across the Ludendorff Bridge.

As if this weren't enough, Wostoupal produced a 50-minute video featuring battle scenes from Remagen and highlighting Lt. Timmermann's heroism. The video was aired on local television and copies were made available to collectors.

Because of the attendance of La Vera and Jack Hansen at the Remagen events in March, Bob Wostoupal with his usual genius decided to make both March 7 and Karl's June 19 birthday a double-edged celebration. He used his strongly determined persuasive powers to commit Governor Nelson to a personal address at West Point and also to declare both June 18th and 19th as additional "Karl Timmermann Appreciation Days." June 18 being a Sunday, the choice of that date insured a larger crowd.

Wostoupal's efforts also extended to a letter to the Editor of the *West Point News* urging readers to lobby Governor Nelson to declare "Karl Timmermann Appreciation Day." As the big event approached for the June 18 ceremony at St. Mary's Church, Wostoupal confessed, "I am overwhelmed with cooperation." In fact, the cooperation was so enthusiastic that scores of individuals and groups tried to get time to appear on the program. Wostoupal privately told friends that if he had granted every request, it would take days to complete the program. So he resorted to a tough-man paring down of the agenda to bare essentials.

His efforts won front-page features in the *Fremont Tribune* and an accolade in the *Omaha World-Herald*.

On June 18, Governor Nelson's helicopter landed 20 minutes early for the 4:00 p.m. celebration at St. Mary's Catholic Church. The Governor's early arrival was taken in stride by Trooper Folkers of the Nebraska State Patrol, who quietly informed Bob Wostoupal. Bob in turn arranged for the Governor to greet the members of the Timmermann family who were special guests:

A Hero of Remagen

BRAVERY UNDER FIRE: Robert Wostoupal of West Point holds photograph of Lt. Karl Timmermann. In the background is a park named for the World War II hero.

Town Now Honors Man It Snubbed

BY JASON GERTZEN
WORLD-HERALD STAFF WRITER

There were no parades for Karl Timmermann when he came home from the war.

Timmermann was credited by no less than Gen. Dwight Eisenhower with extreme bravery under fire for participating in actions on March 7, 1945, that shortened World War II in Europe by months.

But many people back home in West Point, Neb., could not overlook Timmermann's birth in Germany. Nor could they forget that he was the son of a U.S. soldier who had deserted his unit during World War I to marry a German woman.

THE WORLD-HERALD

"I will admit he did not get the praise or glory he deserved," said Robert L. Wostoupal of West Point, the Cuming County veterans service officer. "He was a single lieutenant with a handful of infantry who had done what every general had dreamed about."

Timmermann, then a 22-year-old lieutenant, was the first American officer to cross the Rhine when he spearheaded the capture of the Ludendorff railroad bridge at Remagen, Germany. That action provided the Allied army with a path to pierce the heart of the German defenses and finally bring the war to a close.

Karl's widow, La Vera Timmermann Hansen and her husband, Jack Hansen; Karl's daughter, Gaye Estey; Karl's sister, Mary Timmermann Ellis; and Karl's sister-in-law, brother Fritz's widow, Mary Ann Timmermann who had made the journey from her home in Fort Leavenworth, Kansas.

Other special guests included four loyal veterans of Karl's Company A of the 27th Armored Infantry Battalion, who had participated in Karl's capture of the Remagen Bridge: Elmer Lindsey of Weston, Mo; Ralph Shackelford of Platte City, Mo.; Almon Parson of Hunter, Kan.; and Alexander Giles of Macksville, Kan. Karl's classmates in the Guardian Angels High School Class of 1940 who attended the ceremony included Harold Cyrier of Bullhead City, Arizona, and West Point residents Matt Hugo, Bud Mahlberg, Joe Knobbe, Mrs. Ruth Lueckenhoff Reimann, Mrs. Fred Gelster and Hank Stalp.

Over 750 men, women and children packed the St. Mary's Catholic Church to attend the program.

Excerpts from the ceremony follow:

Robert L. Wostoupal: "Governor Nelson, honored guests, ladies and gentlemen: Good afternoon. Welcome to Remagen Remembered, commemorating the 50th anniversary of the crossing of the Rhine River, on 7 March 1945.

"General George Smith Patton said, 'Wars may be fought with weapons but they are won by men. It is the spirit of the men who follow and of the man who leads that gains the victory.'

"We are greatly privileged to pay tribute to one of such men, West Point's most famous son, Karl H. Timmermann, known around the world as the 'Hero of the Rhine.' On March 7th, Governor Nelson proclaimed 'Lt. Karl H. Timmermann Appreciation Day' statewide. Because of our tribute today and Karl's birthday tomorrow, the Governor has again proclaimed both June 18th and 19th 'Lt. Karl H. Timmermann Appreciation Days' throughout the state of Nebraska. The Governor has been joined in his tributes by members of the 94th Legislative Session who recognized Karl Timmermann for his heroic action.

"To further explain, the unit commanded by Lt. Timmermann, Company A, 27th Armored Infantry Battalion was part of the historically famous 9th Armored Division awarded the Presidential Unit Citation. This honor recognized exceptionally outstanding heroism or meritorious conduct in the performance of outstanding services.

"The tributes to Lt. Timmermann are numerous. From the *Omaha World-Herald* on 7 March 1995, the headlines read, 'State Honors World War II Hero Posthumously.' From the President of the United States, Bill Clinton:

THE WHITE HOUSE

WASHINGTON

As you gather in West Point, Nebraska, to mark
the fiftieth anniversary of the capture of Ludendorf
Bridge at Remagen, Germany, I am proud to join you
in honoring the veterans whose courage and sacrifice
made victory possible.

On this solemn occasion, we recall a time when
America and its allies were engaged in a bitter
struggle against forces that threatened the freedom
of nations everywhere. In March 1945, U.S. forces
recognized that the success of the European campaign
depended upon control of the strategically vital
Rhine River. With extraordinary tenacity and skill,
Second Lieutenant Karl Timmermann led the charge
across the Ludendorf Bridge, carrying the world
significantly closer to securing the liberation of
Europe. The peace and freedom we enjoy today is a
result in large part to the valiant sacrifices of
those brave men.

On behalf of a grateful nation, I salute each
of you for your exemplary service. Best wishes for
a memorable and enjoyable reunion.

Bill Clinton

"Lt. Timmermann has reached out and inspired the youth of the community. Kelly Steffen, an 8th grader at Guardian Angels pre-high school in West Point, will deliver the following tribute which she has composed:

Lt. Timmermann

So bold, so true,
While our flag flew;

A solder at the sight,
Gazing in the morning light;

Looking upon the enemy line;
Looking across the dreadful Rhine.

No time to spare
For courage in the air,

Cross to destiny;
Looking for early victory.

Soon will war come to end.
We found a hero in our friend.

Full of heart I see a man;
I hear them call him Lt. Timmermann.

by: *Kelly Steffen*

The public is cordially invited to attend

"Remagen Remembered,"

honoring the memory and accomplishments of

Lt. Karl H. Timmermann,

on Sunday, June 18, 1995 in West Point.

SCHEDULE OF EVENTS

11:30 A.M.   The West Point Veterans' Club, 246 So. Main, will open to the public, with menu specials available.

1:30-3:30 P.M.   Ken Hechler, author of the book, **The Bridge at Remagen**, will be on hand to autograph his book. Copies of the book will also be available for purchase, as will commemorative postcards, some with special cancellations. Refreshments will be served by the Legion and VFW auxiliaries.

4:00 P.M.   A special service, **"Remagen Remembered,"** will be held at St. Mary's Catholic Church, 343 N. Monitor, West Point. Robert L. Wostoupal, Cuming County Veteran Service Officer, will serve as master of ceremonies, and Father Gary Ostrander, pastor of St. Mary's, will give the invocation and Scripture reading. Tributes to the Timmermann family will be presented by Robert Wostoupal. Musical selections will be provided by **Kay Kile**. Members of the 5049th U.S. Army Reserve Forces School will participate.

Speakers at the service will include **Nebraska Governor Ben Nelson** and Col. Charles J. Barr, Commander of the 5049th U.S. Army Reserve Forces. The keynote address will be delivered by **the Honorable Ken Hechler**, Secretary of State of West Virginia and author of the book, **The Bridge at Remagen**.

Following the service, the unveiling and dedication of a monument honoring Lt. Timmermann's memory and accomplishments will be held at **Timmermann Park in West Point.**

Then. . .   After the dedication at Timmermann Park, a social evening, including a brief ceremony, will take place at the West Point Veterans' Club.

The public is invited and encouraged to attend these events.

"On this day of gratitude special tribute should be paid to other Timmermann family members. Let's begin with Karl's mother, Mary Timmermann. This extraordinary German girl left behind her own country shortly after World War I to come to America. Though the clouds of darkness were descending on her homeland, Mrs. Mary Timmermann followed the light of freedom to West Point. Locals still recall her talent and her years of cooking delights at the Golden Rod Café. She established herself as an industrious citizen and a one hundred percent American.

"It is my special privilege to introduce our most distinguished first speaker, a man who has graciously taken time out of his overwhelming schedule to be with us today. Ladies and gentlemen, Governor Ben Nelson."

Governor Nelson: "Good afternoon. Honored guests, the Timmermann Family, friends and fellow Nebraskans and a special welcome back to Nebraska, Secretary of State Ken Hechler from West Virginia. We're delighted that you're here to join us.

"This is a special day in many ways. It's a special day because it represents a time in history that is vivid in the minds of so many. Not simply for the grotesque nature of war but for the honor of victory and for the recognition of the power over tyranny as accomplished by the acts of brave individuals. It's a special day because it's Father's Day; Lt. Timmermann's daughter is with us. He was a son, father, a husband, brother, friend, a hero and a creation of God. This world is perhaps today as much as at any time sorely in need of heroes. And although we do not want to encourage our children to turn to war as a solution to the problems of the future, we can look to the men and women of our armed forces as true heroes for their commitment for what they have done to advance the cause of peace.

"Lt. Karl Timmermann was a hero's hero. He had the courage to follow orders. He had the courage to give orders and he had the courage to place his foot on the end of the bridge at Remagen and begin the journey of his life. Over the years, perhaps the story of Remagen and Lt. Timmermann has become larger than life. But the point of the story is one of courage, one of hope; that's why it is larger than life. The young people of West Point and of Nebraska can look to the event and this man as a guide for the times in their lives that they will need that courage, that commitment, that ability to step forward and say, 'I stand for something and I put my life at risk for it.'

"However, it's also important to see that the man we honor today and cause that he advanced, freedom, that he was like us, a person. Like all of us, he wasn't immortal. In fact, he suffered from illness and died at an early age. I understand from some sources that he could even be ornery and that's encouraging for all of us. He was a prankster.

"Well, that's the story of a man. That's the story of a human being, one who rose above himself to advance the cause of freedom and put his life at risk. That same courage of Lt. Timmermann came from a human spirit, that same spirit that dwells within all of us. A spirit that we often view as imperfect but to think that at such a perfect moment as the taking of the bridge came out of an imperfect spirit gives us all hope that we might be able to do similar things under similar conditions. It underscores our need to thank those men and women who have given so much for the military efforts that today we can enjoy a continuing freedom. One that as we go about our daily business we should never forget its price. A struggle that perhaps is taking place in Bosnia or Cuba or in other parts of the world where we recognize that strife is in our midst. We hope that there will be other Lt. Timmermanns who will rise above their own humanity and do those things that are brave, that will stand for something in their own time.

"I think it was Theodore Roosevelt who said, 'A man who is good enough to shed his blood for his country is good enough to be given a square deal afterward. More than that, no man is entitled to and less than that, no man shall have.' And while today we remember Lt. Timmermann, let us also remember the veterans in Norfolk, those who are in homes across the country, those who share in their own lives that commitment to service. And while we today recognize him, we know that if he were here we could pin a medal on him but the recognition that we do and that we have before us today, I think in many respects is far more symbolic and important than a medal. Because it is an honoring of a life, an honoring of a family that has paid that ultimate price for sacrifice that means so much to the advancement of the cause of freedom. Since he is no longer walking in our midst but is within our memory, let us content ourselves with the remembrance so that the lesson that he gave us, that lesson of courage, may in fact live on for others to enjoy as well."

Mr. Wostoupal: "Thank you, Governor Nelson. Ladies and gentlemen, it is again my pleasure to introduce our second guest, a military man of tremendous accomplishment, Col. Charles J. Barr, Commander of the 5049th U.S. Army Reserve Forces School in Omaha."

Col. Charles J. Barr: "Good afternoon Governor Nelson, distinguished guests, fellow veterans, family and friends of Lt. Timmermann. This is a wonderful day here in West Point, Nebraska, and for the soldiers of the 5049th Reserve School to represent the United States Army at this memorial service. The capture of the Ludendorff Bridge at Remagen by Lt. Timmermann's infantry company is one of those great World War II stories which I first read about in Ken Hechler's book when I was back in high school, the book *The Bridge at Remagen*. Because my dad and the fathers of many of my classmates in school were — are World War II veterans. I grew up hearing a lot about the war.

"Look at your programs. Look at the picture of Lt. Timmermann in your program or in the front of the church. Lt. Timmermann's photograph, ladies and gentlemen, is a picture of a grimy, weary, combat-toughened soldier with that thousand-yard stare. He's looked into the eye of the tiger. He's seen the elephant. Those of you who have been there know what those phrases mean.

"In 1977, while I was assigned to the 2nd Armored Cavalry Regiment in Germany, I made a point to go to Remagen Bridge or what was left of the Remagen Bridge. I visited Bastogne, St. Vith and the Siegfried Line, which is still there today; dragon teeth, barbed wire and pill boxes. And I visited, as I said, Remagen . . .

"I climbed the huge towers at the west end of the bridge and I looked to the east side. I recalled the book Ken Hechler wrote. I thought about the assault that crossed the bridge led by Lt. Timmermann and the courage it must have required of him and his men to step out onto that bridge after it had already been rocked by an explosion to drop it into the river. And I saw the movie about the event. Some say Lt. Timmermann doesn't deserve all the credit he received for the events at Remagen on 7 March 1945. Some say he was doing his duty as was expected, nothing more. Some say he really didn't lead the assault across the bridge. To those people I say, you are wrong.

"Ken Hechler was there. Some of you were there. Lt. Timmermann was there leading, cajoling and encouraging the movement of his platoon leaders and soldiers across the massive steel monster in addition to coordinating Company A's supporting weapons fire during that 10 minute attack. All this while the enemy is bearing down on them with machine guns, mortar fire, etc. etc.

"History has written that it was Lt. Timmermann who led the men onto the bridge and across the other side. Because he did, his trickle of men across the Rhine became a flood of soldiers and equipment to cross that valued barrier into the heart of Germany which shortened the war by months. It is pure folly to say that Lt. Timmermann is not a hero.

"Our nation has a long history of men and women answering their nation's call to arms in times of national emergencies. During World War II, Lt. Timmermann and over 12 million other citizens answered our nation's call to redeem the promise of freedom and dignity for all Americans and much of the free world. Lt. Timmermann and his sacrifices rendered the promise that IS America which President Roosevelt insisted be stamped on the reverse side of the World War II victory medal. Those inscriptions read, 'Freedom from fear and want. Freedom of speech and religion.' That's what you were fighting for. From Lexington and Concord to Desert Storm and Haiti, the citizen soldiers of America have risen to the occasion. All gave some, some gave all. Were it not for you veterans and the Lt. Timmermanns throughout our nation's history, we would not be here in uniform today. The price they paid, the prices you paid are what allow us to serve today in a free nation.

"Today there are four members of Company A here among us and at this time I would like Ralph Shackelford, Alex Giles, Elmer Lindsey and Almon Parson to please stand and be recognized. Gentlemen . . . please remain standing, gentlemen, please remain standing because for myself and on behalf of all active national guard and reserve soldiers, I simply thank you and salute you, Lt. Timmermann and all veterans here today."

Following the ceremony at the church, the audience reconvened at Timmermann Park for the dedication of the monument to Lt. Timmermann.

The attractive monument is a diamond shaped black granite stone with the inscription in gray letters. The monument itself is flanked by two huge cement eagles, with black interlocking bricks forming a path to the monument. The words of the poem which Karl carried in his wallet are inscribed on the monument.

The outstanding success of the monument was due to the masterful work of Rick Wimer, whose imaginative committee worked closely with Earl Boston of the West Point Monument Co. Wimer's committee included West Point residents Bud Mahlberg, MacDee Stoltzman, Harold Schmader and Linda and Michael Mizikar. The $7,000 memorial was funded with donations.

Rick Wimer expressed these sentiments in a letter to the *West Point News:*

"Sunday was a day for West Point to remember and stand proud. Some say it should have happened years ago, but I say better late than never. I can't express my gratitude enough for Bob Wostoupal, who started working on this event one year ago. His hard work paid off, as the entire day went very smoothly."

Mr. Wostoupal at the park ceremony: "On Memorial Day, 1965, a ceremony was held on this site dedicating Timmermann Field. We gather once again 30 years later to dedicate a monument to a West Point, Nebraska native, Lt. Karl H. Timmermann, the 'Hero of the Rhine.' This is a proud and long overdue occasion, a most impressive tribute to Karl Timmermann. This memorial acknowledges and recognizes his service and sacrifice, a dream has come true."

Col. Charles J. Barr: "Thank you for taking the time to attend this memorial unveiling ceremony. Mr. Wostoupal asked if I would assist him in this part of the tribute to Lt. Timmermann. I would like to say a few words about some of Lt. Timmermann's values and these are character, commitment and courage, some of which were talked about within the last couple of hours.

"Dr. Martin Luther King had a dream that his children would some day live in a land where they would be judged not by the color of their skin but by the content of their character. A variation of that theme would be to judge a person not by his forefathers' actions but by their own actions. Karl Timmermann grew up being taunted over his father's army desertion and the fact that he was born in Germany. But Karl's mother, no doubt also on the receiving end of some well targeted ill-will, was a strong influence on Karl. She instilled quality character traits in Karl.

"Lt. Timmermann had commitment. Right after high school Karl enlisted in the U.S. Army. He didn't wait to be drafted. The draft had started in 1940, when President Roosevelt realized that war would come eventually to America, which it did. I think he was committed to removing some of the tarnish of the Timmermann name brought on by his father's actions when he deserted the army. He wanted to serve in the institution from which his father had left dishonorably. Karl liked the army. He proved to be a leader and he was accepted to Officer Candidate School at Fort Benning and was commissioned a 2nd Lt.

"He trained long and hard for many months with his armored infantry platoon in the 9th Armored Division at Fort Riley, Kansas and they were shipped overseas. He was committed to his men and they were committed to him. This was demonstrated time and time again, both in training and in combat in Europe. And of course he committed himself on 6 March 1945 when he was tapped on the shoulder, and said 'You're it, Bud. You're the new Company Commander, the new Company Commander of Company A, 27th Armored Infantry Battalion, Combat Command B, 9th Armored Division.' The next day, on March 7, 1945, he committed himself to stepping out in the assault across the Ludendorff Bridge.

"When the Korean War broke out, Lt. Timmermann again committed himself to selfless service and volunteered for combat in a second war. He landed at Inchon with the 7th Infantry Division in September 1950, part of General MacArthur's task force.

"Here's a man who served over five years in the United States Army and throughout the entire involvement of the United States in World War II. He won many combat decorations including the Distinguished Service Cross, Bronze Star, Purple Heart, campaign medals, combat infantry badge and other awards. That's enough hardware and proof for me that I don't need to say any more about courage. When he returned home to his wife and daughter and some civilian work, five years later, he was at it again in Korea.

"How could anyone question Lt. Timmermann's commitment, courage and character? As I listened to the ceremony today and I watched the tape that Mr. Wostoupal sent me of the 7 March ceremony, I could not help but notice the hint of Karl's destiny being mentioned with Mr. Wostoupal's description of his high school graduation program and what Father Boschek said. Yesterday, Mr. Wostoupal phoned and gave me Karl's class motto which was 'Either I shall find a way or make one.' Lt. Karl Timmermann had commitment, courage and character and at Remagen, Germany; he made a way across the bridge.

"Admiral James Forrestal, one of our highest ranking admirals during World War II who later became Secretary of the Navy said, 'Always conduct yourself so you will be welcome to return to your home town.' Karl Timmermann conducted himself with honor and we should all be proud of him.

"Those conclude my remarks and before we unveil the memorial, I would ask that you look at the program because Mr. Wostoupal has printed in the program the words on the stone if you can't see the stone. But I was told that these words, this short poem, was something that Lt. Timmermann carried throughout his army career in his wallet and basically it says that during war time we really appreciate our service men and women but when we're not at war we tend to forget about them."

Mr. Wostoupal: "Thank you, Sir. The moment we have long waited for is now at hand, the unveiling of the monument. La Vera, Jack, Gaye, Mr. Hechler, Mary, Mary Ann . . .

"This memorial is a beautiful gift from many people. For your contributions, we are most grateful. To everyone who contributed their time, money, effort, and above all their love to this project we say thank you. What was once a dream has now become a reality."

Inscribed on the monument:

> God and the soldier — we adore
> In times of danger — not before
> Time has passed — things have righted
> God is forgotten — the soldier slighted

Col. (Now Brig. Gen.) Barr expressed his reaction to the ceremonies in the following letter he penned to La Vera:

19 July 1995

Dear La Vera,

Thank you for the nice note of thanks you sent a couple weeks ago. It was an honor for the 5049th USARF School soldiers and myself to be able to participate in the Memorial service for Lt. Karl Timmermann on 18 June 95 in West Point. Yes, Mr. Bob Wostoupal had everything very well organized and left no stone unturned.

I really enjoyed meeting you, Jack, your daughter, and other family members. It was nice to meet Mr. Ken Hechler also. He has kept the memory of Lt. Timmermann alive in print with his extensive writings. And meeting four of Karl's Company A soldiers was also special. It was an honor for me to be able to speak at the Memorial service and dedication at Timmermann Park.

Several of my soldiers said they were honored to be able to carry the battle tested colors of honor of the 9th Armored Division and 27th Armored Infantry Battalion. It was a poignant and proud day for all of us. To me, the day was special also because I was able to connect with real heroes of WWII. The sacrifice of Lt. Timmermann and your entire generation during that war were great. We must never forget.

A forgotten Timmermann cousin, Emory Timmermann of California (a former iron worker) showed up at the monument ceremonies donating a large steel eagle, which Wostoupal placed atop the flagpole in the park.

La Vera brought with her a number of Karl's military and other keepsakes, which Wostoupal arranged to place in a permanent display case at the club headquarters of the Veterans of Foreign Wars. The following year La Vera and Jack visited the display and expressed their enthusiastic support.

As described in the following news article, Wostoupal's further mission to Nebraska's state capitol again resulted in resounding success:

Karl Timmermann Memorial Bridge signs are in place

The third week of May, signs went up on each side of the Highway 32 bridge over the Elkhorn River. The bridge had been named the Karl Timmermann Memorial Bridge.

Bob Wostoupal, Cuming County

Signs have been erected to commemorate the bridge over the Elkhorn River as the Karl Timmermann Memorial Bridge.

Veteran's Service Officer, thought the name would be appropriate considering where it was located.

"Karl swam in the river, fished there and ice skated on the river," Wostoupal said. "It's adjacent to Timmermann Park, close to where his home was, and is located next to the memorial along Highway 32."

Wostoupal started the quest for naming the bridge long before the new bridge was built.

"The first confirmation of my letter requesting the naming of the bridge went to Norfolk in July of 1995," Wostoupal said.

The request was filtered through the system and finally in April of last year Wostoupal was asked to appear before the State Highway Commission for the Department of Roads at a public hearing in Lincoln. There he gave a presentation on requesting the naming of the bridge. After a unanimous vote of approval from the State Highway Commission, the resolution was sent to Gov. Nelson for his signature.

There was no ribbon cutting or dedication of the bridge, due to a safety factor, Wostoupal said.

"I didn't feel it was feasible to close the bridge for a dedication due to the traffic," he said. "Besides, the simplicity of the sign speaks for itself."

The late famous World War II historian Stephen E. Ambrose, recalling La Vera's trip to Remagen he had organized on the 50th anniversary of Karl's heroism at Remagen, penned this personal note to her in 1996:

12/16/96

Dear Mrs. Hansen,

Of course I remember you and that wonderful trip together. It was good of you to write—I much appreciate it.

Happy Trails,

Stephen E. Ambrose

P.S. I taught a WWII course this fall in Madison—350 students—I told them in some detail about Karl's dash across the bridge— then called his feat the defining moment in the history of the U.S. Army in ETO.

About the Author

Ken Hechler entered the Army as a private, received his commission upon completion of Officer Candidate School in the Armored Force at Fort Knox, Ky., and was assigned as a combat historian in the European Theater of Operations early in 1944. He commanded a four-man team that covered the capture of the Remagen Bridge on March 7, 1945, after which he interviewed Lt. Karl H. Timmermann on two occasions. He is the author of *The Bridge at Remagen*, which sold over 600,000 copies and was made into a full-length motion picture. He retired as a Major and was subsequently promoted to Colonel in the Army Reserve.

Hechler is a graduate of Swarthmore College, received a Ph.D. at Columbia University and prior to World War II taught political science at Columbia and Barnard colleges. Following World War II, he taught at Princeton University and served as a White House speech-writer for President Harry Truman. He has also served as a professor of political science at Marshall University, West Virginia State University and the University of Charleston. He was elected to the U.S. House of Representatives in 1958, serving nine elected terms and specializing in coal mine health and safety and protection of the environment. He was the only Congressman to march with Dr. Martin Luther King, Jr., at Selma in 1965.

In 1984, he was elected to the first of four terms as West Virginia Secretary of State. In 2002, he received the Truman Public Service Award, "given annually to an outstanding public servant who best typifies and possesses the qualities of dedication, industry, ability, honesty and integrity that distinguished Harry S. Truman."

If you like this book, Ken Hechler's e-mail is ken@kenhechler.com or address 101B Greenbrier St., Charleston, WV 25311, telephone: 304-343-1116.